THE LEADERSHIP SCORECARD

Series Editor: Jack J. Phillips, Ph.D.

LATEST BOOKS IN THE SERIES

The Leadership Scorecard
Jack J. Phillips and Lynn Schmidt

Bottom-Line Call Center Management
David L. Butler

Bottom-Line Organization Development
Merrill Anderson

The Diversity Scorecard
Edward E. Hubbard

Handbook of Training Evaluation and Measurement Methods, 3rd Edition
Jack J. Phillips

The Human Resources Scorecard
Jack J. Phillips, Patricia Pulliam Phillips, and Ron D. Stone

Managing Employee Retention
Jack J. Phillips and Adele O. Connell

The Project Management Scorecard
Jack J. Phillips, G. Lynne Snead, and Timothy W. Bothell

Return on Investment in Training and Performance Improvement Programs, Second Edition
Jack J. Phillips

Visit **http://books.elsevier.com/humanresources** to see the full range of books available in the series.

THE LEADERSHIP SCORECARD

JACK J. PHILLIPS, Ph.D.
LYNN SCHMIDT

ELSEVIER
BUTTERWORTH
HEINEMANN

AMSTERDAM • BOSTON • HEIDELBERG • LONDON
NEW YORK • OXFORD • PARIS • SAN DIEGO
SAN FRANCISCO • SINGAPORE • SYDNEY

Elsevier Butterworth–Heinemann
200 Wheeler Road, Burlington, MA 01803, USA
Linacre House, Jordan Hill, Oxford OX2 8DP, UK

 Recognizing the importance of preserving what has been written, Elsevier prints its books on acid-free paper whenever possible.

Library of Congress Cataloging-in-Publication Data

Phillips, Jack J., 1945–
    The leadership scorecard/Jack J. Phillips, Lynn Schmidt.
        p. cm. – (Improving human performance series)
    Includes bibliographical references and index.
    ISBN 0-7506-7764-3 (alk. paper)
    1. Leadership–Evaluation.   2. Executives–Training of–Evaluation.   I. Schmidt, Lynn.
II. Title.   III. Series.

HD57.7.P494 2004
658.4′092–dc22

                                                                    2004046953

British Library Cataloguing-in-Publication Data
A catalogue record for this book is available from the British Library.

ISBN: 0-7506-7764-3

For information on all Butterworth–Heinemann publications visit our Web site at www.bh.com

04 05 06 07 08 09 10 8 7 6 5 4 3 2 1

Printed in the United States of America

Contents

Preface, xi

Acknowledgments, xvii

Part I   Leadership Scorecard Foundation, 1

1   Developing Leaders, 3
   The Leadership Development Imperative, 3
   Leadership Development Challenges, 5
   Leadership Development Methods, 7
   Feedback, 9
   Challenging Experiences, 11
   Formal Developmental Relationships, 16
   Leadership Training, 21
   Reflection, 22
   Leadership Development Accountability, 23
   Final Thoughts, 26
   References, 27

2   Creating the Leadership Scorecard, 31
   Leadership Scorecard Pre-Work, 32
   The Leadership Scorecard Foundation, 33
   An Evaluation Framework, 34
   The ROI Model, 36
   Operating Standards and Philosophy, 49
   Implementation Issues, 50
   Application and Practice, 51
   Leadership Scorecard Benefits, 51
   Final Thoughts, 52
   Introduction to Case Study, 54
   Case Study—Part A—International Car Rental, 54

Discussion Questions, 57
References, 57

Part II   Leadership Scorecard Methodology, 59

3   Measuring Indicators, Satisfaction, and Learning, 61
Measuring Indicators, 61
Measuring Satisfaction, 63
Questionnaires and Surveys, 63
Using Satisfaction Data, 69
Measuring Learning, 70
Testing, 70
Administrative Issues, 75
Final Thoughts, 76
Case Study—Part B—International Car Rental, 76
Discussion Questions, 77
References, 79

4   Measuring Application and Business Impact, 80
Questionnaires, 81
Interviews, 88
Focus Groups, 91
Observations, 92
Business Performance Monitoring, 95
Action Planning and Follow-Up Assignments, 97
Performance Contracts, 104
Selecting the Appropriate Method, 106
Data Tabulation Issues, 109
Shortcut Ways to Measure Application and Business Impact, 110
Final Thoughts, 110
Case Study—Part C—International Car Rental, 111
Discuss Questions, 111
References, 115

5   Isolating the Effects of a Leadership Development
Program, 116
Preliminary Issues, 116
Use of Control Groups, 121
Trend Line Analysis, 124
Forecasting Methods, 126
Participants' Estimate of Leadership Development Impact, 128

Management Estimate of Leadership Development's Impact, 137
Subordinate Input on Leadership Development's Impact, 139
Calculating the Impact of Other Factors, 139
Using the Techniques, 140
Final Thoughts, 141
Case Study—Part D—International Car Rental, 141
Discussion Questions, 143
References, 143

6 Converting Business Measures to Monetary Values, 145
Preliminary Issues, 145
Techniques for Converting Data to Monetary Values, 149
Converting Output Data to Contribution, 149
Calculating the Cost of Quality, 152
Converting Employee Time, 153
Using Historical Costs, 154
Using Internal and External Experts' Input, 155
Using Values from External Databases, 156
Using Estimates from Participants, 158
Using Estimates from Immediate Managers, 159
Linking with Other Measures, 159
Using Leadership Development Staff Estimates, 161
Selecting the Appropriate Measures, 161
Accuracy and Credibility of Data, 163
Final Thoughts, 166
Case Study—Part E—International Car Rental, 166
Converting Business Measures to Monetary Values, 167
Discussion Questions, 168
References, 168

7 Tabulating Leadership Development Program Costs, 169
Cost Strategies, 169
Cost Tracking Issues, 172
Major Cost Categories, 175
Cost Reporting, 180
Cost Accumulation and Estimation, 180
Final Thoughts, 184
Case Study—Part F—International Car Rental, 186
Discussion Questions, 187
References, 187

8 Calculating the Return on Investment, 189

Basic ROI Issues, 189
ROI Interpretation, 192
Final Thoughts, 203
Case Study—Part G—International Car Rental, 203
Discussion Questions, 204
References, 205

9 Identifying the Intangible Benefits, 206

Key Issues, 206
Typical Intangible Measures, 213
Final Thoughts, 222
Case Study—Part H—International Car Rental, 222
Discussion Questions, 224
References, 224

Part III Leadership Scorecard Implementation
Considerations, 225

10 Communicating Results and Overcoming Resistance, 227

The Importance of Communication, 227
Principles of Communicating Results, 229
Analyzing Communication Needs, 231
Planning the Communication, 233
Developing the Information: The Formal Evaluation Report, 236
Communicating the Information, 240
Analyzing Reactions to Communication, 243
Overcoming Resistance to a Leadership Measurement, 244
Planning the Implementation, 245
Cost-Savings Approaches, 248
Final Thoughts, 251
Case Study—Part I—International Car Rental, 252
Discussion Questions, 253
References, 253

11 Forecasting an ROI, 254

Why Forecast an ROI?, 254
The Trade-Offs of Forecasting, 256
Preprogram ROI Forecasting, 258
Forecasting with a Pilot Program, 262

Forecasting ROI with Reaction Data, 263
Forecasting ROI with Learning Data, 265
Forecasting ROI with Skills and Competencies, 268
Forecasting Guidelines, 270
Final Thoughts, 272
Case Study—Part J—International Car Rental, 273
References, 274

PART IV   Leadership Scorecard Case Studies, 275

12   Developing Leaders at Imperial National Bank, 277
Background, 277
Data Collection Plan, 279
Reaction and Learning, 285
Application, 286
Business Impact, 288
Program Costs, 293
ROI Analysis, 294
Intangible Benefits, 297
Results, 298
The Author, 300

Index, 303

About the Authors, 319

Preface

LEADERSHIP DEVELOPMENT ACCOUNTABILITY

Leadership development continues to be one of the most challenging and intriguing issues facing organizations. The interest in leadership development continues to grow year after year. The topic appears on many conference and convention agendas. Articles appear regularly in practitioner and research journals. Books continue to be developed on the topic and consulting firms continue to tackle this critical and important issue.

Along with the interest in leadership development comes the interest in accountability. Several issues are driving the increased interest in accountability. Pressure from clients and senior managers to show the return on their leadership development investment is probably the most influential driver. Competitive economic pressures are causing intense scrutiny of all expenditures, including all leadership development costs. Total quality management, re-engineering, and Six Sigma have created a renewed interest in measurement and evaluation, including measuring the effectiveness of leadership development. The general trend toward accountability with all staff support groups is causing some leadership development departments to measure their contribution. These and other factors have created an unprecedented wave of applications for a leadership scorecard.

NEEDED: A LEADERSHIP SCORECARD

What is needed is a rational, logical approach to measurement and evaluation that can be simplified and implemented within the current budget constraints and resources of the organization. This book presents a proven scorecard methodology based on almost 20 years of development and improvement. It is a process that is rich in tradition and refined to meet the demands facing leadership development departments.

The scorecard methodology described in this book meets the requirements of three very important groups. First, the practitioners who have used this model and have implemented the scorecard process in their organizations continue to report their satisfaction with the process and the success that it has achieved. This scorecard methodology is user-friendly, easy to understand, and has been proven to pay for itself time and time again. A second important group, the clients and senior managers who must approve leadership development budgets, want measurable results, preferably expressed as a return on investment. The scorecard methodology presented here has fared well with these groups. Senior managers view the process as credible, logical, practical, and easy to understand from their perspective. More importantly, it has their buy-in that is critical for their future support. The third important group is the evaluation researchers who develop, explore, and analyze new processes and techniques. When exposed to this methodology in a two-day or one-week workshop, the researchers, without exception, give this process very high marks. They often applaud the techniques for isolating the effects of training and the techniques for converting data to monetary values. Unanimously, they characterize the process as an important—and needed—contribution to the field.

WHY THIS BOOK AT THIS TIME?

Currently there is no book that offers a comprehensive, practical presentation on a leadership scorecard that uses a process that meets the demands of the three groups previously described. Most models and representations of the scorecard process ignore, or provide very little insight into, the two key elements essential to developing the scorecard: isolating the effects of the leadership development program and converting data to monetary values. Because there are many other factors that will have an influence on output results, this book provides various strategies to isolate the effects of the leadership development program, far more than any other presentation on the topic. Not enough attention has been provided to the issue of assigning monetary values to the benefits derived from quality leadership development programs. This book presents various strategies for converting data to monetary values.

Target Audience

This book should be of interest to anyone involved in leadership development including the leaders themselves. The primary audience for this book is executives, managers, and professionals involved in leadership development, coaching and mentoring programs, action learning projects, training, and performance improvement. Whether an individual is involved in needs assessment, instructional design, delivery, evaluation, or is a participant, this book will be an indispensable reference. Individuals in leadership development and in leadership positions (i.e., managers, supervisors, team leaders, directors, and vice presidents) will find it to be a helpful guide to measurement and evaluation. With its step-by-step approach and case presentations, it will also be useful as a self-study guide.

Structure of the Book

This book has two unique features that make it a very useful guide. First, it presents the scorecard model in a step-by-step process. The second unique feature is an application of the scorecard in a detailed case study that is based on an actual situation. The case is divided into ten parts. One part is included at the end of each chapter, beginning with Chapter 2. Readers can work through the case, step-by-step, exploring the issues uncovered in the chapter and learn how to apply them to their own organizations. The results of each part are presented in the next chapter where a new issue is addressed. This case presentation is a proven learning tool to understanding the scorecard process.

Chapter Descriptions

Chapter 1: Developing Leaders. This chapter reviews the current leadership development issues and challenges that organizations experience. A variety of leadership development methods are described in detail. The need for accountability is addressed.

Chapter 2: Creating the Leadership Scorecard. This chapter introduces the scorecard process and addresses the need for implementing a leadership scorecard. The evaluation framework is introduced and an overview of data collection methods is provided.

Chapter 3: Measuring Indicators, Satisfaction, and Learning. This chapter presents a variety of approaches to one of the most fundamental issues. Ranging from conducting surveys to conducting tests, the most common ways to collect indicator, satisfaction, and learning data are described in this chapter. Useful tips and techniques to help select the appropriate method for a specific situation are presented.

Chapter 4: Measuring Application and Business Impact. This chapter addresses the critical issues concerning how to measure the application of skills on the job and the resulting impact to the business. A variety of data collection techniques are covered. The action planning process is introduced along with tips and techniques for using the action planning process.

Chapter 5: Isolating the Impact of a Leadership Development Program. This chapter presents what is perhaps the most important aspect of the scorecard process. Ranging from the use of a control group arrangement to obtaining estimates directly from participants, the most useful techniques are presented for determining the amount of improvement directly linked to the leadership development program. The premise of this chapter is that there are many influences on business performance measures with leadership development being only one of them.

Chapter 6: Converting Business Measures to Monetary Values. This chapter presents an essential step for developing an economic benefit from leadership development. Ranging from determining the profit contribution of an increased output to using expert opinion to assign a value to data, the most useful techniques to convert both hard and soft data to monetary values are presented, along with many examples.

Chapter 7: Tabulating Leadership Development Program Costs. This chapter details specifically what types of costs should be included in the scorecard formula. Different categories and classifications of costs are explored in this chapter with the goal for developing a fully loaded cost profile for each return on investment calculation.

Chapter 8: Calculating the Return on Investment. This chapter describes the actual ROI calculation and presents several issues surrounding its development, calculation, use, and abuse. The most accepted ROI formulas are presented, along with examples to illustrate the calculation. Common ROI myths are dispelled.

Chapter 9: Identifying the Intangible Benefits. This chapter focuses on non-monetary benefits from the program. Because not all measures can or should be converted to monetary values, this chapter shows how the intangible benefits should be identified, monitored, and reported. Over 25 common intangible benefits are examined.

Chapter 10: Communicating Results and Overcoming Resistance. This chapter provides best-practice approaches for communicating leadership scorecard results. Information on how to plan for communications, select audiences and media, develop reports, and address typical issues that surface during communication is provided. The types of resistance that may be encountered when implementing a scorecard are identified along with tips and techniques for how to deal with the resistance.

Chapter 11: Forecasting an ROI. This chapter shows how the return on investment can be used to forecast the payoff of a program before it is implemented. The chapter underscores the range of possibilities available for calculating the ROI at different time frames, using different types of data.

Chapter 12: Developing Leaders at Imperial National Bank. This chapter provides a case application that shows the monetary impact of an executive leadership program. This case study explores the complexity of measuring the impact of leadership development using an action learning process. More importantly, this case shows how changes in a program design can significantly increase the actual return on investment.

Chapter 13: Executive Coaching: The ROI of Building Leadership One Executive at a Time. This chapter provides a case application that shows the monetary benefit of executive coaching. A comprehensive study is outlined that evaluates coaching using the measures that are a part of the leadership scorecard. The case study provides recommendations on how to increase the value of coaching for the business.

Acknowledgments

From Jack J. Phillips

No book is the work of the author alone; many other individuals provided input and support to make this effort a reality. I am particularly grateful for the clients I have had the opportunity to work with in my years of consulting. I have learned from every assignment involving leadership development and have translated that knowledge into this book. To all of my clients, I owe much appreciation for their willingness to engage our services and experiment with our approach.

Several individuals were very helpful in developing this manuscript. Many thanks go to my co-author, Lynn Schmidt, for developing much of this manuscript. She assumed this task on top of a very busy schedule and performed admirably with this huge challenge. Lynn understands leadership, development, and measurement. I would also like to thank Joyce Alff for her meticulous review, editing, and coordination.

I would like to acknowledge the continued support and assistance from my spouse and partner, Patti Phillips, who always inspires me to do my best and supports me in all my work.

Jack J. Phillips

From Lynn Schmidt

Everything I know about leadership I have learned from books, classes and life, and from the leaders I have had the fortune to interact with over the years. I have found leaders everywhere— corporations, universities, volunteer groups, non-profit organizations, social settings, and family gatherings. And in all types of roles—CEOs, assistants, teachers, clerks, friends, mothers, and brothers. These individuals, whether they were leading billion-dollar companies or dinner conversations, demonstrated a competence and strength that sparked my interest in leadership development. I appreciate the opportunity that I have had to learn from these individuals and thank them all.

Everything I know about measurement and evaluation I have learned from books, classes, and a special group of people—the ASTD ROI Network Advisory Committee. Special thanks go to the members of that committee for providing me with the opportunity for continuous learning: Jack J. Phillips, Patti Phillips, Toni Hodges, Merrill Anderson, Holly Burkett, Deb Wharff, Dan McLinden, Jim Chatt, Uichi Tsutsumi, Kyoko Watanabe, Bruce Aaron, Diederick Stoel, Ed Hubbard, and Lizette Zuniga.

I would also like to thank the behind-the-scenes support staff that made this book possible—Joyce Alff, the internal editor, and the staff at Elsevier/Butterworth–Heinemann. And a special note of appreciation to my three canine friends, Plato, Bailey, and Chipper, who spent many evenings waiting patiently for me to finish working on the manuscript and who made sure that I took breaks whether I thought I needed them or not.

Note: Limited portions of this book were taken from two other books that discuss the process. These sources are:

Phillips, Jack J. *Return on Investment in Training and Performance Improvement Programs*, 2nd Edition, Boston: Butterworth–Heinemann, 2003.

Phillips, Jack J., Ron D. Stone, and Patricia Pulliam Phillips. *The Human Resources Scorecard*. Boston: Butterworth–Heinemann, 2001.

PART I

Leadership Scorecard Foundation

CHAPTER 1

Developing Leaders

"At the end of the day, it's the top-flight leaders who make a business great." Larry Bossidy, former CEO of AlliedSignal, spent approximately 30 to 40 percent of his time hiring and developing leaders his first two years at AlliedSignal. He attributes AlliedSignal's success in large part to the commitment he made to leadership development (Bossidy, 2001). Leadership continues to be a critical developmental focus for organizations around the world. Research indicates that strong leadership has a positive impact on bottom-line results. Organizations with strong leadership bench strength economically outperform companies with weaker leadership.

A Corporate Leadership Council study reports that 82 percent of companies with strong leadership displayed above-average revenue growth over a six-month period (2001). In addition to increased sales and profitability, customer and employee satisfaction is higher for organizations with strong leadership. A study conducted by the Conference Board found that companies rating themselves as having strong leadership capacity appeared more often at the top of *Fortune's* list of "Most Admired" companies and were almost twice as likely to appear in the top quartile of the rankings (Csoka, 1998). Leading companies consider leadership development to be a business imperative and a critical component of business strategy and succession management.

THE LEADERSHIP DEVELOPMENT IMPERATIVE

Several factors are causing a multitude of changes in the world and are having a significant impact on the way work gets done. Factors such as changing workforce, rapidly changing technology, and changing board requirements are causing organizations to take proactive steps to plan for future leadership development.

Workforce demographics are changing in a number of ways. The number of retirees is expected to increase drastically while at the same time there will be fewer entrants into the workforce. As a result there will be more job openings available than candidates to fill them. This leads to increased competition for leaders with the ability to lead today's organizations. Increased competition requires additional focus on retaining leaders, thereby reducing the turnover of critical leadership talent creating an ongoing need for leadership development programs.

The changing demographics reflect greater diversity in the workplace—diversity with regard to race, gender, as well as generations. These changes lead to diverse employee needs. Young workers today are more concerned with work/life balance, less accepting of traditional hierarchy, and less trusting of organizations. Leaders need capabilities in the areas of people management, empowerment, and communication skills in order to lead a very diverse workforce. Leaders will need to be able to not only develop talent but also to recruit and retain top talent. This means that leaders will need to become more adept at designing more individualized, flexible work arrangements that are tailored to diverse needs (Barrett and Beeson, 2001).

Rapid changes in technology require that leaders be able to manage the changes brought on by technology and look for ways to apply new technology to business. While these changes do not require leaders to be technological experts, they do require a priority of analytical skills. Leaders need to be able to quickly sort through all of the data to see patterns and make good decisions (Barrett and Beeson, 2001).

At many organizations the board of directors is focusing more strongly on succession management and leadership development. Many board of directors are requiring that a talent pool of potential successors be identified and developed to eventually move into senior leadership positions. This requires that leaders become the developers of other leaders. Along with that, the board of directors is also focused on governance issues and ensuring that the organizations leaders are operating in an ethical manner. This, along with the financial expectations of stakeholders, requires that leaders become very ethically and financially astute.

Additional changes brought on by deregulation, globalization, and increased competition require that leaders become adept at strategic thinking, competitive positioning, and cultural awareness. These changes place further pressure on organizations to invest in leadership development.

LEADERSHIP DEVELOPMENT CHALLENGES

These changes in the way business gets done will have a significant impact on the quantity and quality of leadership talent. As studies have shown, strong leaders are essential to business success making leadership development a business imperative. Unfortunately, many organizations implement leadership development methods that result in a poor investment of time and money. Organizations focused on wisely investing their time and money in effective leadership development methods that address the issues raised earlier face four key challenges:

- accelerating the development of leadership talent;
- selecting effective leadership development methods;
- investing leadership development dollars wisely; and
- demonstrating the success of leadership development methods.

The lack of leadership talent in the pipeline presents a challenge for many organizations. Many organizations do not have the leadership talent necessary to sustain a competitive advantage. In a study conducted by the Conference Board, only one-third of respondents rated their company's leadership capacity to meet business challenges as excellent or good. This requires organizations to proactively build leadership bench strength for the future, as well as play catch-up and accelerate the development of their current leaders. Even more disconcerting is the fact that less than one-half of the survey respondents reported that developing future leaders is a major priority for their organizations (Barrett and Beeson, 2001). This suggests that over one-half of the organizations represented will not be focusing on leadership development until it is too late, too costly, or too time intensive to accelerate the development of their leaders.

Along with the challenge of accelerating leadership development comes the challenge of selecting effective leadership development methods. Research has shown that effective leadership development is achieved through a systems approach, by incorporating on- and off- the job experiences with mentoring, coaching, or training all closely aligned with development plans and business strategy. To accelerate the development of a leader it is critical to ensure that right development methods are used. Several sources suggest that a mix of leadership development methods is the most effective approach to developing leaders (Barrett and Beeson, 2001; Byham, Smith, and Paese, 2001; Charan, Drotter, and Noel, 2001; Corporate

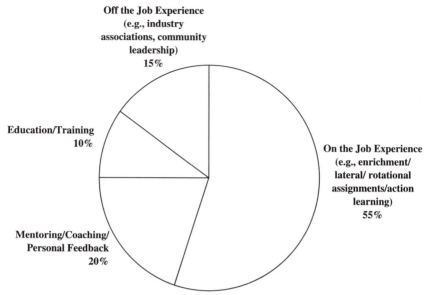

Figure 1-1. Leadership development methods.

Leadership Council, 2001, 2003; McCall, Lombardo, and Morrison, 1988; McCauley, Moxley, and Van Velsor, 1998; Zenger and Folkman, 2002). Figure 1-1 indicates that 70 percent experiences both on and off the job, 20 percent mentoring or coaching and feedback, and 10 percent education and training are an effective mix of leadership development methods.

Selecting effective leadership development methods is challenging due to "the productization of leadership development" (Ready and Conger, 2003). Many leadership development efforts are not aligned with business strategy; rather organizations are in search of a quick fix becoming focused on commercial products rather than the issues that need to be addressed. Many of these commercial products are based on a current best-selling book. The problem does not reside with the authors of these books but with the misuse of these works that takes the form of quick fix training packages implemented by organizations that have not diagnosed the business needs. As a result, organizations are unable to show a positive return on investment from the programs and a significant investment in time and money is wasted (Ready and Conger, 2003).

A division president at a Fortune 50 company was quoted as saying during a leadership development audit "We spend $120 million a year on this stuff, and if it all went away tomorrow, it wouldn't matter one bit. Leadership development in this company is nothing more than a series of disconnected programs sold by consultants to training managers who don't understand our business" (Ready and Conger, 2003). This indicates that another challenge facing organizations is investing leadership development dollars wisely. The education and development of leaders is not an inexpensive proposition. Eighty-one percent of organizations provide some form of leadership training as part of their overall training program (Corporate Leadership Council, 2003). The investment in leadership development tends to range from 5 to 25 percent of an organization's annual training budget (Delahoussaye, 2001). It was reported that the investment in executive education and leadership development approaches $16.5 billion dollars annually (Fulmer and Goldsmith, 2001). Organizations need to focus on implementing effective leadership development methods that are a wise investment of time and money. Many organizations are being challenged by their stakeholders to reduce the costs associated with leadership development and to ensure that they are getting the biggest return for their investment.

Leadership Development Methods

"Leadership seems to be the marshaling of skills possessed by a majority but used by a minority. But it's something that can be learned by anyone, taught to everyone, denied to no one" (Bennis and Nanus, 1997). As organizations begin to plan leadership development programs the first question that is often asked is "Can leaders be developed?" According to several sources the answer to that question is an emphatic "yes" (Bennis and Nanus, 1997; Byham, Smith, and Paese, 2001; Charan, Drotter, and Noel, 2001; Doh, 2003; Kouzes and Posner, 1987; McCall, 1998; McCauley, Moxley, and Van Velsor, 1998; Tichy, 2002; Zenger and Folkman, 2002).

Zenger and Folkman (2002) state, "Leaders can go from being good to being great, from being seen as adequate to being seen as extraordinary. The process for getting from good to great may differ somewhat for each person, but there is a pattern. This pattern enables leaders to discern what they need to do to deliver more value." McCall (1998) explains, ". . . leadership ability can be learned, that creating a context that supports the development of talent can become a source of competitive advantage, and that the development of leaders is itself a leadership responsibility." Based on these perspectives, leadership development is about individuals learn-ing, growing, and changing.

So then, the next question is "How best to develop leaders?" There are many leadership development methods in the market place. The challenge is to determine which of them can truly develop the leaders who can effectively lead the organizations of the future. A study conducted by the Corporate Leadership Council found that not all leadership development methods are created equal. The Corporate Leadership Council asked more than 15,000 global leaders from diverse organizations and industries to indicate the importance that they placed on 17 different development methods. Table 1-1 shows the rank order that resulted from the survey. It is important to note that the lowest-ranked programs are not un-important. The order simply means that lower-ranked programs are less important to leaders than higher-ranked programs (Corporate Leadership Council, 2001).

Table 1-1
Rank Order of Leadership Development Methods by Importance

Development program	Overall rank
Amount of decision-making authority	1
Creating leadership development plan	2
Interacting with peers	3
Meeting with an executive coach	4
Meeting with a mentor	5
Feedback	6
Turning around a struggling business	7
People-management skills course	8
Working in a new functional area	9
Working in foreign countries	10
Working in new lines of business	11
Launching new businesses	12
Number of direct reports	13
Quality of direct reports	14
Off-site seminars in business skills	15
Technical skills courses	16
Business skills courses	17

Source: Corporate Leadership Council, 2001

The most effective leadership development methods that have demonstrated bottom-line results can be grouped into the categories of feedback, challenging experiences, formal developmental relationships, and leadership training. Within these categories, several specific methods are mentioned. The methods addressed here are 360-degree feedback, job assignments, action learning, mentoring, and coaching, along with education and/or skills training. Also addressed is an element essential to all of the methods: reflection utilizing development plans, action plans, and learning journals.

Each leadership development method alone can develop leadership capabilities and be effective when well designed. Each method has greater impact when linked to other methods, and a leadership development program is especially effective when all of the methods utilized are within a carefully designed leadership development system. A leadership development system may often include specific education-based training on technical or business skills. It is also important to incorporate strategies into a leadership development program that provides support for the learners, further develops their ability to learn from experience, and encourages self-directed or self-planned learning.

Feedback

McCall (1998) states that Warren Bennis has challenged all leaders to know themselves:

"Know thyself" was the inscription over the Oracle at Delphi. And it is still the most difficult task any of us faces. But until you truly know yourself, strengths and weaknesses, know what you want to do and why you want to do it, you cannot succeed in any but the most superficial sense of the word. The leader never lies to himself, especially about himself, knows his flaws as well as his assets, and deals with them directly.

Effective leaders are self-aware. They seek out feedback, are open to criticism, and learn from mistakes. A lack of awareness, due to neglect or arrogance, can be a major contributor to derailment. This need for awareness has led to the popularity of 360-degree feedback assessments that enable the leader to find objective sources of feedback to aid in development (McCall, 1998).

Assessment is a critical component of leadership development. One tool to provide that assessment is 360-degree feedback or multirater assessments. These assessments can be useful for collecting data about performance from bosses, subordinates, peers, colleagues, and customers or suppliers. There are several advantages to 360-degree feedback. Those advantages include the fact that a large amount of feedback is consolidated into one report, the feedback includes multiple perspectives, and the feedback alone can be a powerful driving force for change and development. There are also several disadvantages, including the expense, the fact that the feedback may not be too useful if generic competencies are rated, and the large quantity of data analysis that is required when a large number of people are all taking the assessments at the same time (Rothwell, 2001).

Through their research of 43 global organizations, Rogers, Rogers, and Metlay, (2002), found six best practices that organizations use to get the most from the 360-degree process:

- Use 360-degree feedback primarily for individual development.
- Link the process and align participants with strategic imperatives.
- Exert high administrative control over every aspect of the 360-degree feedback process.
- Use senior management as role models.
- Use highly trained internal coaches to leverage your investment.
- Evaluate the return on investment or effectiveness of the process as you would any business endeavor.

The competencies that are evaluated in 360-degree feedback define clusters of behavior, knowledge, and motivations related to job success or failure and under which data on behavior, knowledge, and motivations can be reliably classified. Competencies generally fall into four categories: interpersonal skills, leadership skills, business or management skills, and personal attributes. Typically, competencies need to be behaviorally defined and the definitions must be tested for accuracy and reliability of understanding. Ten to 18 competencies will adequately describe the target group. It is often useful to develop a customized competency model for an organization. A competency model should reflect the organization's vision, business strategy, goals, and values, as well as job requirements for the target level (Byham *et al.*, 2001).

Research indicates that great leaders possess multiple strengths. Three hundred sixty-degree feedback enables leaders to identify and focus on their strengths, magnify them, or create strengths out of positive characteristics that are not fully developed. This type of feedback is also a good tool to validate if a leader has "fatal flaws" that can lead to derailment. It's recommended that a leader receive a 360-degree assessment, create a development plan to address the "fatal flaw," and then nine months later conduct a follow-up round of 360-degree feedback to determine if the "fatal flaw" has been corrected (Zenger and Folkman, 2002).

It is best to use 360-degree assessments for developmental purposes rather than administrative purposes. A developmental purpose is defined as using the feedback to put a plan in place to increase individual effectiveness. An administrative purpose is defined as using the feedback for decisions about hiring, promoting, or compensating individuals. In assessment for development, the individuals own the data. In assessment for administration, data are owned by the organization. Sufficient evidence shows that rater responses change (become more lenient) when they know the resulting data will be used for administrative purposes or made public (McCauley et al., 1998).

If 360-degree assessments are to be effective, it is critical that development plans be created and implemented. It is important that leaders are motivated by their development plans and that the development plans are linked to both individual and organizational goals. It is also suggested that activities on the developmental plan be those types of events that are more transformational, such as job assignments, ongoing feedback, and working with role models and coaches. Training and reading can be included, but should only consume a small part of the development plan (McCauley et al., 1998).

Challenging Experiences

The concept that individuals learn best from life experiences is not new. John Dewey (1938) in *Experience and Education* commented on the connections between life experiences and learning, stating that genuine education comes about through experience but that not all experience educates and some experiences can miseducate (Merriam and Caffarella, 1999). Since that time, many experts in the area of adult education have reached a similar conclusion.

In *The Lessons of Experience* (McCall, Lombardo, and Morrison, 1988) when successful executives were asked to tell about the events that changed them the majority described challenging experiences. The research documented that effective executives primarily learn through life experiences. McCall (1998) states:

Experiences that create lasting change are rarely the product of routine daily fare or of minor turns in an otherwise straight road. The experiences that changed executives were hairpin curves or stomach-turning drops that forced them to look at themselves and their context through a different lens. Transformational experiences almost always force people to face something different from what they had faced before. In a real sense, the challenge lay in what they weren't already good at, not in what they had already mastered.

Job Assignments

Job assignments are one challenging experience that can effectively develop leaders. There are a variety of types of job assignments, including task force memberships, job transitions (making a lateral move or a job rotation), expanded current assignments, new jobs, creating change such as turn around or start up assignments, overcoming obstacles in a new position, moving to a role that involves a higher level of responsibility, or managing without authority as with matrix relationships.

Job assignments are one of the oldest and most useful forms of leadership development. Leaders are able to learn by doing and working on real problems. Up until the 1980s, most leadership development activities focused on formal training programs (McCauley *et al.*, 1998)

In order to effectively use job assignments as a leadership development method, it is important to ask several key questions (Byham *et al.*, 2001):

- Will the assignment provide one or more challenges that the individual needs to master to function effectively at the executive job level?
- Will the assignment develop one or more key competencies needed by the individual?
- Will the assignment provide insights into specific personality traits that might derail the individual's climb to an executive position or provide an opportunity to practice new behaviors that will keep the individual on track?
- Will the assignment provide experience in different organizational areas?
- Will the assignment provide a realistic preview of executive life?

- Will the assignment provide exposure to potential long-term mentors, organizational leaders, or other talented professionals who have unique skills or knowledge to share?
- Will the assignment give senior executives a chance to observe the individual?
- Does the assignment fit the individual's personal and family needs?

It is important that individuals remain in job assignments long enough to accomplish their developmental objectives, but not too long. If an assignment is too short, the individual might miss out on the learning insights that come from making mistakes and correcting them. If assignments are too short, individuals move on before they see the results of their actions. If assignments are too long, the individual might miss out on other developmental experiences, as well as lead to the individual's dissatisfaction. Assignments may range from several months to two years. It is important to remember that some jobs are too critical to use as developmental assignments. The continued success of the organization may be at risk by placing individuals into critical jobs if they are not able to handle them.

As with assessments and 360-degree feedback, it is important to maximize the learning taking place from the assignments. It can be useful to provide individuals with a checklist for learning. The checklist would include questions about strengths and limitations that an individual brings to an assignment, what aspect of the job might be especially challenging, and what learning outcomes the individual expects to achieve (McCauley et al., 1998). In addition, setting developmental goals, providing access to coaches, and scheduling review meetings on developmental progress are other ways organizations can assist individuals in maximizing the learning taking place.

Learning from experience involves being able to recognize when new behaviors, skills, or attitudes are called for, engage in a variety of development experiences to learn new skills, try new approaches or reframe points of view, and develop and use a variety of learning tactics to acquire new skills, approaches, or attitudes. Learning from experience can be difficult, as most people think of learning as taking place in a classroom. It does not occur to individuals to spend time reflecting on their experiences and the lessons learned. Learning from experience can also be difficult due to the inertia that sometimes develops in individuals. They become complacent allowing the inertia to hold them back. Learning from experience can be risky, and there is an active tension in organizations between producing bottom-line results and developing people. Often individuals are not given developmental assignments where failure is a possibility and most organizations will put proven performers into key roles, which also reinforces the inertia. Learning from experience may also be difficult because it requires a level of support often unavailable in organizations. There needs to be support for the risk of learning, failure, feedback, and implementation of development plans and for individuals to persist in their efforts to learn and grow (McCauley *et al.*, 1998).

Action Learning

Action learning programs often combine feedback, challenging experiences, formal developmental relationships, skills development, and reflective practice. Assessments, challenging experiences, formal developmental relationships, and reflective practice have greater impact when part of a leadership development system. Yorks, O'Neil, and Marsick (1999) explain that the foundation of action learning is "working in small groups in order to take action on meaningful problems while seeking to learn from having taken that action." They define action learning as:

> An approach to working with and developing people that uses work on an actual project or problem as the way to learn. Participants work in small groups to take action to solve their problems and learn how to learn from that action. Often a learning coach works with the group in order to help the members learn how to balance their work with the learning from the work.

There are four levels of action learning that can be implemented (Yorks *et al.*, 1999). As one moves from level one to level four the learning outcomes become more complex, critical, and contextual.

- Level One: At level one the learning goals are centered on problem solving and the implementation of solutions for the task or the problem. The focus is on strategic issues and developing a strategic business perspective in high-potential leaders. This approach tends to reinforce a strong existing culture.
- Level Two: At level two the learning goals focus on tasks and place emphasis on problem framing and problem posing in addition to problem solving and implementation. It is expected that individuals will gain and apply skills in learning from their work.

- Level Three: At level three the learning goals are the same as at level two with the addition of explicit goals and outcomes related to personal development, self-knowledge, and learning styles. Learning coaches are incorporated along with explicit reflection on learning goals around both the task and personal development.
- Level Four: At level four, in addition to the learning goals around the task, goals, and outcomes added in level three, there is a focus on transformational learning for individuals and for building changes into the culture of the organization. Learning coaches are utilized along with a strong emphasis on critical reflection. Levels three and four incorporate assessment, challenging experiences, formal developmental relationships, and reflective practice and have greater potential for fostering transformational learning (Yorks *et al.*, 1999).

Several design decisions need to be addressed prior to implementing an action learning program. First, a needs assessment should be conducted to determine the gaps that should be addressed among the existing competencies of the program participants and the organizational needs. Second, the following design questions should be addressed:

- Should the problems addressed be ones that are of a familiar or unfamiliar nature?
- Should the program take place in a familiar or unfamiliar setting?
- Should the problems be group or individual projects?
- How will the participants be chosen?
- How much time are the participants and the organization willing to invest in the project?
- Will content learning be provided, if so, what and how?

The needs assessment will provide the foundation for deciding what level of program will be developed and answering these six questions will provide the information required to develop the program (Yorks *et al.*, 1999).

If action learning programs are structured and implemented effectively they can lead to a strong return on investment. Action learning participants are focused on solving work-related problems and the team recommendations often lead to a significant reduction in costs or increased revenue that far exceeds the costs of conducting the action learning programs. The Corporate Leadership Council

(2003) sites several significant returns on investment due to action learning programs:

- Aramark Corporation's growth rate increased from 2.1 to 8.3 percent within four years of implementing a CEO-sponsored action learning program for middle managers.
- Aramark Corporation also had profits increase by 350 percent between 1993 and 1997 for one action learning developed project.
- Ford Motor Company identified over $100 million in cost savings and another $100 million in incremental revenue through its action learning program.

FORMAL DEVELOPMENTAL RELATIONSHIPS

Leadership development often takes place through the relationships a leader forms. Talk with a leader about the people who have influenced his/her career and you will be provided with many examples, such as a boss, peer, direct report, family member, and teacher. Often, as a leader progresses up the job ladder into executive positions the support systems that once helped are no longer available. Fewer advisors are readily available with the needed knowledge and skill sets. For this reason many organizations establish formal developmental relationships by establishing formal mentoring and professional coaching programs.

Organizations often create formal developmental relationships for the following reasons:

- socialization of new managers
- preparing high potentials for more responsibility
- developing women and people of color
- meeting development needs of senior executives
- organizational change efforts

A study found that about 20 percent of organizations with at least 500 employees had at least one initiative that made use of a formal developmental relationship (McCauley et al., 1998).

Mentoring

Mentoring can be defined as people helping people or, more specifically, as "a helping relationship in which a more experienced person invests time and energy to assist the professional growth and development of another person" (Barton, 2001). The relationship is both helping and developmental in nature. Individuals can have mentors in many areas of their lives, not just professionally. Mentoring can also be formal or informal. Formal mentoring is described as "part of a program in which a mentor and protégé are paired." There is more structure with formal programs, training for the mentors and protégé, formal agreements, development plans, and evaluation processes.

There are 12 steps in the generic model for a facilitated mentoring program (Murray and Owen, 1991).

- Step One: The protégé is identified. The organization identifies the group of people who are eligible for the mentoring program. A protégé may volunteer or be nominated. The protégé's information is then entered into a database for tracking the results of the mentoring effort.
- Step Two: The development needs of the protégé are determined and an individual development plan is prepared. Assessment instruments can also be used to assist with determining developmental needs.
- Step Three: Mentor candidates are recruited. They may volunteer, be selected by a protégé, or be recruited by senior leaders.
- Step Four: Mentor candidates are screened to determine general ability and willingness.
- Step Five: A mentor is selected for a specific protégé after consideration of the development needs of the protégé.
- Step Six: A mentor orientation is held. Time commitments, types of activities, time and budget support, relationship with the protégé's manager, and reporting requirements are covered in the orientation.
- Step Seven: A protégé orientation is held. The topics covered are similar to those addressed in the mentor orientation. Other topics that may be addressed are assertiveness training and career planning.
- Step Eight: The agreement between the mentor and the protégé is negotiated. Components in the agreement would include a confidentiality requirement, length of the relationship, frequency of meetings, and time investment of each party.
- Step Nine: The protégé's development plan is executed. This is a critical step in the process.
- Step Ten: Periodic meetings are held between the mentor and the protégé. These meetings focus on performance planning, coaching, and feedback sessions.

- Step Eleven: Periodic reporting by the program coordinator takes place in order to track and evaluate the results of the mentoring process.
- Step Twelve: The conclusion of the agreement. This will be based on the time frame agreed upon. The relationship may also be concluded when one of the pair believes the relationship is no longer productive (Murray and Owen, 1991).

There are several benefits as well as challenges to implementing a formal mentoring program. A formal mentoring program can increase productivity, improve recruitment efforts, increase organizational communication and understanding, increase the motivation of senior leaders, enhance the services offered by the organization, and improve strategic and succession planning; formal mentoring programs tend to be more cost effective than training programs or professional coaches. All of these benefits can lead to a significant return on investment for mentoring programs that are effectively implemented. In turn, organizations need to be aware of the challenges that can be encountered when implementing a formal program. Formal mentoring programs may cause frustration if there are few opportunities to move up in the organization, there must be a strong commitment by the organization to developing and promoting people from within, the program must be positioned effectively in order to sell it to senior leaders, and the administration of the program can be complicated due to cross-functional pairing (Murray and Owen, 1991).

Professional Coaching

Another formal developmental relationship is that with a professional coach. A professional coach is a personal consultant who works with individuals to address their personal and professional development needs by helping them make changes that improve their performance. Often, the higher individuals move in the organization the less frequently they receive honest performance feedback. Professional coaches are especially useful in helping senior leaders develop particular skill areas that have been identified as needing improvement. When a need is identified, a professional coach is partnered with the senior leader for a short period, typically six months.

A research study conducted by the Corporate Leadership Council (2003) found that professional coaching is a growing trend, a preferred option by leaders, and that organizations are asking hard questions about the return on investment. Professional coaching is expensive compared to other leadership development alternatives, and despite the high costs involved, many organizations are not managing coaching investments in a consistent manner, which is leading to inconsistent returns. Five challenges that inhibit the effective management and utilization of professional coaches within organizations are:

- difficulty finding "best fit" professional coaches
- unfocused coaching engagements
- poor matching of coaching resources to executive requirements
- disconnects from the organizations
- inconsistent delivery and quality of coaching

The Corporate Leadership Council (2003) recommends that organizations implement a coaching standard that includes

- centralized coach recruitment employing standardized tools and templates.
- identification of coaching needs based on analysis of business needs and priorities.
- standard models that structure all coaching interventions toward progression to specific milestones and timelines and enable coach debrief and knowledge exchange.
- manager participation embedded at every point of the coaching process, with third-party mentoring providing advocacy to support development beyond coaching.
- an inventory of matching decisions to facilitate informed matching, enhanced coach deployment, and monitoring of effectiveness.

Professional coaching enables organizations to leverage the strengths and skills of talented senior leaders, enhancing the impact that these key leaders have on business results. Coaching programs develop current and emerging leaders who are committed to leveraging their strengths and building new skills. Professional coaching typically utilizes a thorough assessment process, and participants identify their strengths and growth opportunities and create a targeted plan focused on personal and professional leadership development. The goals of professional coaching are to

- accelerate and amplify a leader's impact on business results;
- cultivate executive maturity and accelerate growth and development;
- increase business and political savvy;
- build confidence to step out of the comfort zone; and
- increase organizational bench strength.

A professional coach may be used to act as a sounding board for new ideas, approaches, and strategies; guide a senior leader who is struggling with personal, professional, and career issues; provide assessment and development planning when a senior leader prefers the confidentiality afforded by an external resource; assist the senior leader in dealing with issues of chemistry between he/she and bosses, peers, and direct reports; and support the development of high potential managers and senior leaders transitioning into higher leadership positions.

In order to use coaching for effective leadership development it is important that the coach uses a business coaching model. The business coaching approach typically involves assessment, feedback, creating a development plan linked to business strategy, coaching sessions, and evaluation of the process along the way. The initial assessment phase may include in-depth interviews with the individual and their manager plus the individual's own battery of assessment instruments. Feedback from the assessment phase illuminates key areas for development. Leaders can see that further insight and increased skills will enhance their effectiveness in striving for and achieving targeted results. The key here is for leaders to spot for themselves a few areas for development that they value as significant in expanding their leadership repertoire. The individual coaching sessions begin to deepen understanding of their own leadership skill and practices (behaviors) in the identified key areas of development and to provide vehicles and opportunities for discovering new or expanded skills in those areas. The goal is to focus on the areas of development, provide realistic opportunities for the individual to understand their current behavior, offer exposure for the individual to a range of options, and further develop their leadership abilities in these specific areas.

The evaluation of the coaching engagement starts at the beginning when roles are clarified and results are targeted. Further evaluation continues as the areas for development are identified and leadership skills are expanded and captured. Ongoing evaluation takes place by assessing the achievement of goals and target results. Effectively implemented coaching programs have shown a significant return on investment. Coaching produced a return on investment of 788 percent for Nortel Networks (Anderson, Dauss, and Mitsch, 2002) and an average $100,000 return on investment for each participant in a study conducted by Manchester (McGovern, Lindemann, Vergara, Murphy, Barker, and Warrenfeltz, 2001).

LEADERSHIP TRAINING

Much of the literature indicates that leadership development in the more traditional sense (e.g., classroom-based training) is of lesser importance to leaders (Corporate Leadership Council, 2001). Often, training components used to build specific skills or knowledge are a necessary part of a leadership development program and it is important to deliver those components effectively. Leadership training has been shown to be more effective when there is a strong link to a leader's individual development plan and when the training is partnered with some of the other leadership development methods that have been described, such as 360-degree feedback, action learning, mentoring, or coaching.

A research study conducted by the Corporate Leadership Council (2003) outlined key tactics for organizations that do include a classroom component. The first tactic suggested is to offer a blended learning environment. In this case, a blended learning environment is described as inviting a mix of management academics, industry leaders, and senior company leaders as both guests and faculty. A second tactic that is suggested is to engage leaders as teachers. Partnerships with external institutions and speakers are fine, but an organization should rely on internal leaders for thought leadership. Engaging current leaders to teach future leaders is a tactic that several companies interviewed in the Corporate Leadership Council study highlighted as a particularly successful practice.

In a study conducted by the American Productivity and Quality Center (1999) on leadership development best practices, it was found that technology was considered to be useful for knowledge dissemination but could not replace the important act of bringing leaders together to deepen the learning experience. Best-practice organizations did not feel that they could fully achieve the benefits of networking via technology. When best-practice organizations were asked about their favored methods of delivery they indicated that a majority of leadership development programs were delivered face to face. Technology was often seen as a plug to fill gaps in the learning process. This same study found that best-practice organizations always assess the impact of their leadership development programs and processes. Return on investment studies have been conducted for many leadership training programs. A leadership development training program focused on creating an inclusive workplace had total benefits of $3,204,000 and a return on investment of 163 percent for Nextel Communications (Schmidt, 2003).

REFLECTION

A common thread that connects the development methods that have been outlined—assessment, challenging experiences, formal developmental relationships, and leadership training—is reflection. All of the developmental events that have been described—360-degree feedback, job assignments, action learning, mentoring, coaching, and education and skills training—emphasized the importance of utilizing tools such as development plans, action plans, and learning journals to facilitate reflection and increase the impact of the leadership development initiatives. Merriam and Caffarella (1999) list three major assumptions of reflection:

- Those involved in reflection are committed to both problem finding and problem solving as part of that process.
- Reflection means making judgments about what actions will be taken in a particular situation, and because these actions usually involve seeking changes in ourselves, other people, or in systems, there is an ethical dimension to reflective practice.
- Reflection results in some form of action, even if that action is a deliberate choice not to change practice; without this action phase, the reflective practice process is incomplete.

Reflection involves thinking through a situation either while it is happening or after it has happened. Some methods for implementing reflective practices are development plans, action plans, portfolio review, journal writing, and critical reflection. Reflection is a cognitive process (Merriam and Carrarella, 1999). Leaders can think about an experience and about ways to deal with the experience (problem-solving strategies), but to reflect critically, leaders must also examine the underlying beliefs and assumptions that affect how they make sense of the experience.

Several strategies can be used to engage in reflection. To assist with articulating assumptions, activities such as critical questioning, critical-incident exercises, criteria analysis, role play, critical debate, and crisis-decision simulations are used. These techniques require leaders to think about specific situations and then to examine how decisions are or would be made in those situations. This helps a leader see what assumptions underlie those decisions (Cranton, 1996).

To determine the sources and consequences of assumptions, a leader can keep a journal or write a life story or a professional autobiography. These methods not only assist with articulating assumptions, but focus attention on their sources and consequences. After a leader has articulated assumptions and determined the sources and consequences of those assumptions, then the leader needs to imagine alternatives to the current assumptions. Suggestions for imagining alternatives are brainstorming and creating preferred scenarios and discussing them with another individual (Cranton, 1996).

LEADERSHIP DEVELOPMENT ACCOUNTABILITY

If organizations want to accelerate the development of leaders, select effective leadership development methods, and invest leadership development dollars wisely they will need to be able to demonstrate the success of their leadership development methods. A study conducted by the American Productivity & Quality Center (1999) found that best-practice organizations always assess the impact of their leadership development process. Best-practice organizations represented in the study concerned themselves with the perceived value of their leadership development efforts. In turn, they found that best-practice organizations' leadership development processes are costly undertakings but are seen as worthwhile investments. Measurement and evaluation are ways to determine if the selected leadership development methods are working and if business results are being impacted. It is a way to overcome the leadership development challenges that organizations face.

There has been a persistent trend of accountability in organizations all over the globe. Every support function is attempting to show its worth by capturing the value that it adds to the organization. From the accountability perspective, the leadership development function should be no different from the other functions—it must show its contribution to the organization. The American Society for Training and Development (ASTD) concluded in its 2002 industry report that the number one global trend and issue facing human resource development practitioners is developing the return on investment in training (Van Buren, 2002). The trend was number two the year before, underscoring its continuing dominance.

This trend of accountability is found in both private and public sector organizations throughout the world. The following measurement trends have been identified in research and are slowly evolving across organizations and cultures in more than 35 countries (Phillips and Gaudet, 2004). Collectively, these 11 important trends have significant impact on the way accountability is addressed:

- Evaluation is an integral part of the design, development, delivery, and implementation of programs.
- A shift from a reactive approach to a proactive approach is developing, with evaluation addressed early in the cycle.
- Measurement and evaluation processes are systematic and methodical, often built into the delivery process.
- Technology is significantly enhancing the measurement and evaluation process, enabling large amounts of data to be collected, processed, analyzed, and integrated across programs.
- Evaluation planning is a critical part of the measurement and evaluation cycle.
- The implementation of a comprehensive measurement and evaluation process usually leads to increased emphasis on the initial needs analysis.
- Organizations without comprehensive measurement and evaluation have reduced or eliminated their program budgets.
- Organizations with comprehensive measurement and evaluation have enhanced their program budgets.
- The use of return on investment is emerging as an essential part of the measurement and evaluation mix.
- Many successful examples of comprehensive measurement and evaluation applications are available.
- A comprehensive measurement and evaluation process, including return on investment, can be implemented for about 4 or 5 percent of the direct program budget.

As the trend in accountability continues to grow, more and more human resource development organizations are being held accountable for results. The Top 100 companies selected by *Training* magazine for their best-practice people development initiatives have built solid business cases for developing people and have measurement and evaluation analyses down to a science (Galvin, 2003). They link development initiatives to lasting and important business metrics such as revenue, market share, quality, customer service, retention, turnover, production, and innovation. Ninety-two percent of the Top 100 companies measure training effectiveness through Kirkpatrick's Level IV of business results (Kirkpatrick, 1998) and 67 percent measure through Phillips' Level V (Phillips, 1995) return on investment (ROI). DPR Construction (ranked 60) best describes the importance of measurement and evaluation: "If you're not keeping score, it's just practice." (Galvin, 2003).

The Leadership Scorecard

In 1990 the Nolan Norton Institute sponsored a study "Measuring Performance in the Organization of the Future" (Kaplan and Norton, 1996). The motivator of the study was the thought that current performance measurement approaches, primarily financial accounting, were becoming obsolete. Representatives from a dozen companies met for a year to develop a new performance measurement model. The outcome of this study was the balanced scorecard. The balanced scorecard translates an organization's mission and strategy into a set of performance measures that provide a framework for a strategic measurement system. The balanced scorecard measures organizational performance across four perspectives: financial, customers, internal business processes, and learning and growth.

In the 8 years since the Kaplan and Norton study was completed, it is reported that 50 percent of organizations in North America and western Europe are using the balanced scorecard approach (Creelman, 2001). In a human resource (HR) measurement survey of senior HR leaders, just over one in three respondents indicated they were using a scorecard framework. In turn, 86 percent of the respondents believed that the use of measurement would increase in HR over the next two years (Creelman, 2001). During the last few years business leaders have begun to ask HR to demonstrate the value they bring to the organization. As HR moves toward a more strategic role, the use of HR balanced scorecards is increasing. There are now scorecards for every business process, including those in HR, and executives are expecting leadership development functions to be able to report the leadership score as well.

Several critical success factors have been found to have the most impact on the success of a leadership development initiative, and continuous evaluation was ranked number two in a study conducted by Linkage, Inc. (1999). Table 1-2 lists the success factors in the order of frequency that they were mentioned as being critical.

Table 1-2
Critical Success Factors that Had the Most Impact on
the Success of the Leadership Development Initiative

Critical success factors	Frequency (%)
Support and involvement of senior management	100
Continuous evaluation	73
Linking leadership development with strategic plan	73
Involving line management in design	20
Leveraging internal capacity	13
Thorough needs assessment	12
"Best-in-class" faculty	6
Pilot program before launch	6
Other	0

Source: Linkage, Inc., 1999

If a leadership development function is not keeping score, how will it know if it has accomplished its objectives? How will it know if leadership development has been accelerated, if the right leadership development methods were selected, and if leadership development dollars have been invested wisely? Using a leadership scorecard that incorporates proven measurement and evaluation techniques leads to increased effectiveness in leadership development methods and a bottom-line impact to the organization. By ensuring that leaders are being developed effectively, an organization is positioned for success and provided with a critical competitive advantage—strong leadership.

FINAL THOUGHTS

Developing leaders is an imperative for many organizations. Leaders will need to be in place that can take organizations further into the 21st century amid rapid change and chaos. If the answer to the question "Can leaders be developed?" is yes, then the next question to resolve is "What are the best ways to develop leaders?" The leadership development methods of feedback, challenging experiences, formal development relationships, and leadership training appear to have the ability to effectively develop leaders. Job assignments, 360-degree feedback, action learning, mentoring, and coaching, along with education and/or skills based training, have the potential to provide learning experiences that change behavior and result in a positive return on investment.

Reflection utilizing development plans, action plans, and/or learning journals is a common thread that connects all of the leadership development methods. Action learning programs at levels three and four incorporate all of the critical learning experiences. Each developmental event has greater impact when linked to other events, and a leadership development program is especially effective when all of the events utilized are within a carefully designed leadership development system.

Because it has been shown that strong leadership does have an impact on the bottom line, the business case for implementing a leadership scorecard is easy to make. The multitude of changes taking place in the world requires organizations to have strong leadership and to take proactive steps to address current and future leadership development needs. Proactively developing leadership talent will enable organizations to remain competitive. However, the fast pace of change presents several challenges to leadership development organizations. The following four challenges—(1) accelerating the development of leadership talent, (2) selecting effective leadership development methods, (3) investing leadership development dollars wisely, and (4) demonstrating the success of leadership development methods—create the need for leadership development organizations to be held accountable to show that the leadership development initiatives being used have had a positive impact on the bottom line.

This trend in accountability makes it increasingly important for organizations to be able to demonstrate the impact of their leadership development initiatives. The solution to this trend in accountability is for organizations to implement a leadership scorecard. By using a leadership scorecard that incorporates proven measurement and evaluation techniques, an organization will be able to demonstrate the effectiveness of its leadership development initiatives and the bottom-line impact to the organization.

REFERENCES

American Productivity & Quality Center International Benchmarking Clearinghouse. *Leadership Development: Building Executive Talent.* American Productivity & Quality Center, 1999.

Anderson, M., Dauss, C., and Mitsch, B. "The Return-on-Investment of Executive Coaching." *In Action: Coaching for Extraordinary*

Results. J. J. Phillips (series ed.), D. Mitsch, (ed.). Alexandria, VA: American Society for Training and Development, 2002, pp. 9–22.

Barrett, A., and Beeson, J. *Developing Business Leaders for 2010.* The Conference Board, 2001.

Barton, K. *Connecting with Success: How to Build a Mentoring Network to Fast-Forward Your Career.* Davies-Black, 2001.

Bennis, W., and Nanus, B. *Leaders: The Strategies for Taking Charge.* 2nd ed. HarperBusiness, 1997.

Bossidy, L. "The Job No CEO Should Delegate." *Harvard Business Review*, Vol. 79, Is. 3, March 2001, pp. 47–49.

Byham, W., Smith, A., and Paese, M. *Grow Your Own Leaders.* DDI Press, 2001.

Charan, R., Drotter, S., and Noel, J. *The Leadership Pipeline: How to Build the Leadership Powered Company.* San Francisco: Jossey-Bass, 2001.

Corporate Leadership Council. *Voice of the Leader.* Corporate Executive Board, 2001.

Corporate Leadership Council. *Maximizing Returns on Professional Executive Coaching.* Corporate Executive Board, 2003.

Corporate Leadership Council. *Leadership Development Programs for Executives at Fortune 500 Companies.* Corporate Executive Board, 2003.

Corporate Leadership Council. *Trends in Leadership Development Strategies.* Corporate Executive Board, 2003.

Cranton, P. *Professional Development as Transformative Learning: New Perspectives for Teachers of Adults.* San Francisco: Jossey-Bass, 1996.

Creelman, J. *Creating the HR Scorecard: Best Practice Strategies for Performance Management.* London: Business Intelligence Ltd., 2001.

Csoka, L. *Bridging the Leadership Gap.* The Conference Board, 1998.

Delahoussaye, M. "Leadership in the 21st Century." *Training.* September, 2001, pp. 60–72.

Dewey, J. *Experience and Education.* Collier Books, 1938.

Doh, J. "Can Leadership Be Taught? Perspectives from Management Educators." *Academy of Management Learning and Education*, Vol. 2, No. 1, 2003, pp. 54–67.

Fulmer, R., and Goldsmith, M. *The Leadership Investment.* New York: AMACOM, 2001.

Galvin, T. "The 2003 Training Top 100." *Training.* March 2003.

Kaplan, R., and Norton, D. *The Balanced Scorecard: Translating Strategy into Action.* Boston: Harvard Business School Press, 1996.

Kirkpatrick, D. *Evaluating Training Programs: The Four Levels.* 2ⁿᵈ ed. San Francisco: Berrett-Koehler, 1998.

Kouzes, J., and Posner, B. *The Leadership Challenge.* 3ʳᵈ ed. San Francisco: Jossey-Bass, 2002.

Linkage, Inc. *Best Practices in Leadership Development Handbook.* Linkage Press, 1999.

McCall, M., Lombardo, M., and Morrison, A. *The Lessons of Experience: How Successful Executives Develop on the Job.* Lexington Book, 1988.

McCall, M. *High Flyers: Developing the Next Generation of Leaders.* Boston: Harvard Business School Press, 1998.

McCauley, C., Moxley, R., and Van Velsor, E. *The Center for Creative Leadership: Handbook of Leadership Development.* San Francisco: Jossey-Bass, 1998.

McGovern, J., Lindemann, M., Vergara, M., Murphy, S., Barker, L., and Warrenfeltz, R. "Maximizing the Impact of Executive Coaching: Behavioral Change, Organizational Outcomes, and Return on Investment." *The Manchester Review*, Vol. 6, No. 1, 2001, pp. 3–11.

Merriam, S., and Caffarella, R. *Learning in Adulthood.* 2ⁿᵈ ed. San Francisco: Jossey-Bass, 1999.

Murray, M., and Owen, M. *Beyond the Myths and Magic of Mentoring: How to Facilitate an Effective Mentoring Program.* San Francisco: Jossey-Bass, 1991.

Phillips, J.J. Corporate Training: Does it Pay Off? William & Mary Business Review (1995, Summer) pp. 6–10.

Phillips, J.J., and Gaudet, C. *HRD Trends Worldwide: Shared Solutions to Compete in a Global Economy,* 2ⁿᵈ ed. Boston, MA: Butterworth-Heinemann, 2004.

Ready, D., and Conger, J. "Why Leadership-Development Efforts Fail." *MIT Sloan Management Review*, Spring 2003, pp. 83–88.

Rogers, E., Rogers, C., and Metlay, W. "Improving the Payoff from 360-Degree Feedback." *Human Resource Planning*, HR. 25, no. 3, 2002, pp. 44–56.

Rothwell, W. *Effective Succession Planning: Ensuring Leadership Continuity and Building Talent from Within,* 2ⁿᵈ ed. New York: AMACOM, 2001.

Schmidt, L. "Using Training Scorecards to Prove that Training Pays." *In Action: Implementing Training Scorecards.* J. J. Phillips (series ed.) and L. Schmidt (ed.). Alexandria, VA: American Society for Training and Development, 2003, pp. 41–64.

Tichy, N. with Cardwell, N. *The Cycle of Leadership: How Great Leaders Teach their Companies to Win.* New York: Harper-Business, 2002.

Van Buren, M. *State of the Industry*. Alexandria, VA: American Society for Training and Development, 2002.

Yorks, L., O'Neil, J., and Marsick, V. *Action Learning: Successful Strategies for Individual, Team, and Organizational Development*. Academy of Human Resource Development and Brett-Koehler, 1999.

Zenger, J., and Folkman, J. *The Extraordinary Leader: Turning Good Managers into Great Leaders*. New York: McGraw-Hill, 2002.

CHAPTER 2

Creating the Leadership Scorecard

Score is defined as the record of points or strokes made by competitors in a game or match; the act of making or earning a point or points; a tally (Webster's Unabridged Dictionary, 1998). The same source defines "scorecard" as a card for keeping score of a sports contest. Individuals who either watch or participate in sports rely on the scorecard to know who is winning the game, how the competitors compare, and if improvements are required. Leadership development functions need to keep score as well. The dollar investment in leadership development programs is significant and stakeholders want to know the return on that investment. The investment in leadership development tends to range from 5 to 25 percent of an organizations annual training budget (Delahoussaye, 2001). It has been reported that the investment in executive education and leadership development approaches $16.5 billion dollars annually (Fulmer and Goldsmith, 2001). Without a scorecard, how does the leadership development function know if they are winning the leadership development game, how their leadership development programs compare with other organizations, and if improvements are needed?

The leadership scorecard is a tool that ensures that the leadership development function is focused on accomplishing objectives that are linked to business strategy. The leadership scorecard provides a structure for establishing, tracking, compiling, analyzing, and communicating leadership development results. The leadership scorecard should be customized based on business needs and can contain a variety of measures based on what the business views as critical. A leadership scorecard can be created and implemented even when an HR or corporate scorecard does not exist. This is critical as it enables the leadership development function to take a proactive stance in the creation of measurement and evaluation strategies and become a valued business partner.

The leadership scorecard enables executives to understand the benefits of the leadership development programs to leaders and to the bottom line. The leadership scorecard also provides useful measures for the leadership development staff. The leadership development staff can find out how well a program is working and, based on leadership scorecard data, can improve the program or, if necessary, stop delivery of the program. A focus on using measurement and evaluation for the continuous improvement of leadership development programs can build the credibility of the leadership development function. Data from a leadership scorecard can be used to justify expenditures, build a business case for requesting additional budget dollars, and create management support (Schmidt, 2003).

LEADERSHIP SCORECARD PRE-WORK

When creating a leadership scorecard it is important to first do some pre-work to address the following questions: why, who, where, when, what, and how (Schmidt, 2003)? The answers to these questions are important in deciding the structure and components of the leadership scorecard.

1. *Why is the leadership scorecard being created?* A leadership scorecard that is created because there is a corporate scorecard or an HR scorecard should have direct linkages to those scorecards. A leadership scorecard that is created proactively with no other scorecards in place will need to have a linkage to the business strategy. Business strategy linkages can be made by reviewing a company's vision, mission, and goals for the year.

2. *Who is the target audience for the leadership scorecard?* Information that is tracked, collected, and compiled for the leadership scorecard will vary depending on who the target audience is or if there is more than one target audience. If the target audience is the leadership development function or a variety of company training organizations, the leadership scorecard may contain more data relevant to the continuous improvement of the leadership development programs. If the target audience is senior executives, then business metrics such as return on investment may need to be included. It is important to identify the target audiences for the leadership scorecard and do a needs assessment to find out what measures are important to each audience.

3. *Where will the leadership scorecard be maintained?* An owner needs to be assigned to the leadership scorecard. Someone should be assigned the responsibility of creating the structure for the scorecard and ensuring that design input is received from all involved parties. Also, someone needs to have accountability for the collection, compilation, and reporting of leadership scorecard data. It is important to ensure that there are adequate numbers of trained employees to maintain the leadership scorecard on an ongoing basis.

4. *When will leadership scorecard data be reported?* A component of the project plan for the leadership scorecard is a reporting schedule. Data can be reported at a variety of times. The reporting could be on a micro level, or program based, where data are calculated and reported based on the completion of a program and associated time frames for behavior change and business impact. The reporting could be on a macro level, or calendar based, where available data for all programs are reported on a monthly or quarterly basis.

5. *What data will the leadership scorecard contain?* The answers to why, who, what, and when will start to provide information concerning what data will be tracked, compiled, and reported by the leadership scorecard. The leadership scorecard could contain data from a variety of development organizations within the same company, or it could contain data from the leadership development function only. Participant satisfaction, learning, and behavior change data could be tracked, compiled, and reported for all programs or only a designated percentage of programs. Data demonstrating the impact to the business of leadership development programs might be collected and reported as benefit-cost ratios and a return on investment percentages.

6. *How will data be tracked, collected, compiled, analyzed, and reported?* No two leadership scorecards will necessarily look identical, but they will probably use similar measurement and evaluation methodologies. The five-level evaluation framework and ROI methodology serve as the basis of the leadership scorecard measurement and evaluation scheme (Phillips, 2003).

THE LEADERSHIP SCORECARD FOUNDATION

The leadership scorecard is built on a foundation that includes several important building blocks necessary for the development of

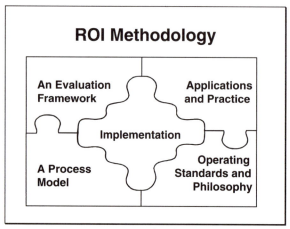

Figure 2-1. ROI methodology elements.

a comprehensive measurement and evaluation process, as shown in Figure 2-1. The remainder of this chapter focuses on each of the individual building blocks of this comprehensive process.

AN EVALUATION FRAMEWORK

The concept of different levels of evaluation is both helpful and instructive to understanding how the return on investment is calculated. Table 2-1 outlines the five levels of evaluation that serve as the framework for evaluation and the foundation for the leadership scorecard, defining the types of data collected, the sequence of collection, and the approximate timing.

- Level 1, *Reaction, Satisfaction, and Planned Action*, measures satisfaction of program participants, along with their plans to apply what they have learned. Almost all organizations evaluate at Level 1, usually with a generic, end-of-program questionnaire. While this level of evaluation is important as a customer satisfaction measure, a favorable reaction does not ensure that participants have learned new skills or knowledge (Dixon, 1990).
- Level 2, *Learning*, focuses on what participants learned during the program using tests, skill practices, role plays, simulations, group evaluations, and other assessment tools. A learning check is helpful to ensure that participants have absorbed the program material and know how to use it properly. However, a positive

Table 2-1
Five Levels of Evaluation

Level—Chain of Impact	Measurement focus	Value of information	Customer focus
1 Reaction, satisfaction, and planned action ↓	Measures participants' reaction to and satisfaction with the program and captures planned actions	Low	Consumer
2 Learning ↓	Measures changes in knowledge, skills, and attitudes		
3 Application and implementation ↓	Measures changes in on-the-job behavior and progress with planned actions		
4 Business impact ↓	Measures changes in business impact variables		
5 Return on investment	Compares program monetary benefits to the costs of the program	High	Client

Customers: Consumers = The customers who are actively involved in the training process.
Client = The customers who fund, support, and approve the training project.

measure at this level is no guarantee that what is learned will be applied on the job. The literature is laced with studies showing the failure of learning to be transferred to the job (Broad, 1997).

- At Level 3, *Application and Implementation*, a variety of follow-up methods are used to determine whether participants applied what they learned on the job. The frequency and use of skills are important measures at Level 3. While Level 3 evaluation is important to gauge the success of the application of a program, it still does not guarantee that there will be a positive business impact in the organization.
- The Level 4, *Business Impact*, measure focuses on the actual results achieved by program participants as they successfully apply what they have learned. Typical Level 4 measures include output, quality, costs, time, and customer satisfaction. Although

the program may produce a measurable business impact, there is still a concern that the program may cost too much.

- Level 5, *Return on Investment*, the ultimate level of evaluation, compares the monetary benefits from the program with the program costs. Although the ROI can be expressed in several ways, it is usually presented as a percentage or cost/benefit ratio. The evaluation chain of impact, illustrated in Table 2-1, is not complete until Level 5, ROI evaluation, is developed.

When business results and ROI are desired, it is very important to evaluate the other levels. A chain of impact should occur through the levels as the skills and knowledge learned (Level 2) are applied on the job (Level 3) to produce business impact (Level 4). If measurements are not taken at each level, it is difficult to conclude that the results achieved were actually caused by the program (Alliger and Janak, 1989). Because of this, it is recommended that evaluation be conducted at all levels when a Level 5 evaluation is planned. This is consistent with the practices of benchmarking forum members of the American Society for Training and Development (ASTD) and best-practice corporate universities as identified in a study conducted by the American Quality and Productivity Center (Phillips, 2000; Van Buren, 2002).

Also, from the perspective of the client, the value of information increases with movement through the chain of impact. ROI methodology is a client-centered process, meeting the data needs for the individuals who initiate, approve, and sponsor the program.

THE ROI MODEL

The ROI model, presented in Figure 2-2, is a step-by-step approach to develop the ROI calculation and the other measures in the ROI methodology. The ROI model is an important building block for the foundation of the leadership scorecard. Each major part of the model is described in this section, with emphasis placed on evaluation planning. The other parts of the model will be covered in more detail in the following chapters.

Evaluation Planning

Several pieces of the evaluation puzzle must be explained when developing the evaluation plan for an ROI calculation. Three

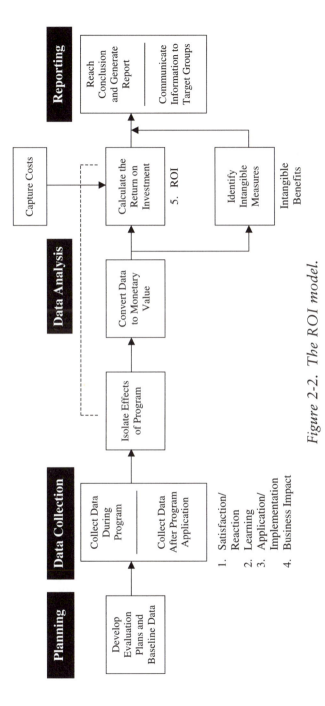

Figure 2-2. The ROI model.

specific elements are important to evaluation success and are outlined in this section.

Purpose

Although evaluation is usually undertaken to improve the leadership development process, several distinct purposes can be identified.
Evaluation is intended to

- improve the quality of learning and outcomes.
- determine whether a leadership development program is accomplishing its objectives.
- identify the strengths and weaknesses in the learning process.
- determine the cost/benefit analysis of a leadership development
  program.
- assist in marketing leadership development programs in the
  future.
- determine whether the leadership development program was
  appropriate for the target audience.
- establish a database that can assist in making decisions about
  the leadership development programs.
- establish priorities for funding.

Although there are other purposes of evaluation, these are some of
the most important ones (Russ-Eft and Preskill, 2001). Evaluation
purposes should be considered at the outset of evaluation planning.
The purposes will often determine the scope of the evaluation, the
types of instruments used, and the type of data collected. For
example, when an ROI calculation is planned, one of the purposes
would be to compare the cost and benefits of the leadership development program. This purpose has implications for the type of data
collected (hard data), type of data collection method (performance
monitoring), type of analysis (thorough), and the communication
medium for results (formal evaluation report). For most leadership
development programs, multiple evaluation purposes are pursued.

Feasibility

An important consideration in planning the leadership scorecard
is to determine the appropriate levels for evaluation. Some evaluations will stop at Level 3, where a detailed report will determine the
extent to which participants are using what they have learned.

Others will be evaluated at Level 4, impact, where the consequences of their on-the-job application are monitored. A Level 4 impact study will examine hard and soft data measures directly linked to the leadership development program. This type of study will require that the impact of the program be isolated from other influences. Finally, if the ROI calculation is needed, two additional steps are required; Level 4 impact data must be converted to monetary value and the costs of the program captured so that the ROI can be developed.

During the planning stage, the feasibility for a Level 4 or 5 impact study should be examined. Relevant questions need to be addressed:

- What specific measures have been influenced with this leadership development program?
- Are those measures readily available?
- Can the effect of the program on those measures be isolated?
- Are the costs of the program readily available?
- Will it be practical and feasible to discuss costs?
- Can the impact data be converted to monetary value?
- Is the actual ROI needed or necessary?

It is important to examine these and other questions during the planning process to ensure that the evaluation is appropriate for the leadership development program. Each issue will be examined in more detail as the ROI methodology is explained.

Objectives of Programs

Leadership development programs are evaluated at different levels as described earlier. Corresponding to the levels of evaluation are levels of objectives:

- Reaction and satisfaction objectives (level 1)
- Learning objectives (level 2)
- Application objectives (level 3)
- Impact objectives (level 4)
- ROI objectives (level 5)

Before the ROI evaluation begins, the objectives for the program must be identified or developed. The objectives form the basis for determining the depth of the evaluation, meaning that they determine what level of evaluation will take place. Historically, learning objectives are routinely developed. Application and impact objectives

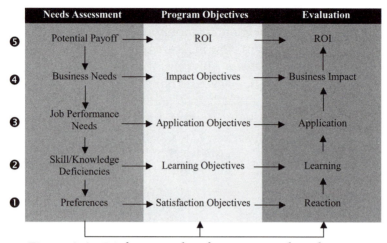

Figure 2-3. Linking needs, objectives, and evaluation.

(Adapted from: Phillips, Jack J., Ron Stone, and Patricia P. Phillips. 2001. *The Human Resources Scorecard: Measuring the Return on Investment.* Boston, MA: Butterworth-Heinemann.)

are not always in place, but are necessary for the proper focus on results.

Objectives link directly to the front-end analysis. As shown in Figure 2-3, after the business need is determined (4), the needs analysis identifies the job performance (3) necessary to meet the business need. The skills and/or knowledge (2) needed to achieve the desired performance is identified, taking into consideration the preferences (1) for the learning solution to improve skills and knowledge. In the ROI methodology, it is necessary to develop objectives at each level to ensure success and link those objectives to levels of evaluation. As Figure 2-3 illustrates, participant satisfaction objectives link to Level 1 evaluation; learning objectives link to Level 2 evaluation; application objectives link to Level 3 evaluation; impact objectives link to Level 4 evaluation; and ROI objectives link to the ROI outcome.

If the application and impact objectives are not available, they have to be developed using input from several groups such as job incumbents, program developers, facilitators, and on-the-job team leaders.

Tied very closely to setting objectives is the timing of data collection. In some cases, preprogram measurements are taken to compare with postprogram measures and, in some cases, multiple measures are taken. In other situations, preprogram measurements are not available and specific follow-ups are still taken after the program. The important issue in this part of the process is to determine the timing for the follow-up evaluation. For example, a major airline initiated data collection for an evaluation three weeks after a customer service skills training program. In another example, an Indonesian company needed five years to measure the payback for employees attending an MBA program in the United States. For most leadership development programs, a follow-up is usually conducted in the range of three to six months.

Evaluation Plans

To complete the planning process, three simple planning documents are developed: the data collection plan, the ROI analysis plan, and the project plan. These documents should be completed before the evaluation begins—ideally, this should take place before the leadership development program is designed or developed. Appropriate up-front attention will save time and frustration later when data are actually collected.

Data Collection Plan

Figure 2-4 shows a data collection planning form. This document provides a place for the major elements and issues regarding collecting data for the first four evaluation levels. Broad areas for objectives are appropriate for planning. Specific, detailed objectives are developed later, before the program is designed. The "measures" column defines the specific measure; the "method" describes the technique used to collect data; the "source" of data is identified; the "timing" indicates when data are collected; and the "responsibilities" identifies who will collect the data.

The objectives for Level 1 usually include positive reactions to the leadership development program and planned action items. If it is a new program, another category, *suggested improvements*, may be included. Reaction is typically measured on a scale, collected by questionnaires directly from participants, and administered by the facilitator.

Level 2 evaluation focuses on the measures of learning. The specific objectives include those areas where participants are expected to change knowledge, skills, or attitudes. A measure could be pass/fail if testing takes place. The timing for Level 2 evaluation is usually during or at the end of the program, and the responsibility usually rests with the facilitator.

For Level 3 evaluation, the objectives represent broad areas of program application, including significant on-the-job activities that

Program: _____ Responsibility: _____ Date: _____

Level	Broad Program Objectives	Measures	Data Collection Method and Instruments	Data Sources	Timing	Responsibilities
❶	Reaction, Satisfaction and Planned Actions					
❷	Learning					
❸	Application and Implementation					
❹	Business Impact					
❺	ROI					

Comments:

Figure 2-4. Data collection plan template.

should follow application. The evaluation method usually includes one of the postprogram methods described later and is usually conducted weeks or months after program completion. Because responsibilities are often shared among several groups, including the training and development staff, division trainers, or local managers, it is important to clarify this issue early in the process.

For Level 4 evaluation, objectives focus on business impact variables influenced by the program. The objectives may include the way in which each item is measured. If not, the measure is defined in the measures column. For example, if one of the objectives were to improve quality, a specific measure would indicate how quality is actually measured, such as defects per thousand units produced. While the preferred data collection method would be business performance monitoring, other methods such as action planning may be appropriate. The timing depends on how quickly participants can generate a sustained business impact. It is usually a matter of months after the program. The participants, supervisors, or perhaps an external evaluator may be responsible for Level 4 data collection.

The ROI objective is established, if appropriate. This value, expressed most commonly as a percent, defines the minimum acceptable rate of return for investing in the program. The program sponsor or the individual requesting the impact study usually provides the value. Twenty-five percent is an acceptable target, although often the ROI is much higher.

The data collection plan is an important part of the evaluation strategy and should be completed prior to moving forward with the leadership development program. For existing leadership development programs, the plan is completed before beginning the evaluation. The plan provides clear direction as to the type of data to be collected, how they will be collected, who will provide the data, when they will be collected, and who will actually collect them.

ROI Analysis Plan

Figure 2-5 shows the ROI analysis plan. This planning document is the continuation of the data collection plan presented in Figure 2-4 and captures information on several key items that are necessary to develop the actual ROI calculation. In the first column, significant data items are listed, usually Level 4 business impact data, but in some cases could include Level 3 items. These items will be used in the ROI analysis. The method used to isolate the effect of the program is listed next to each data item in the second column. For most cases the

Program: _____ Responsibility: _____ Date: _____

Data Items (Usually Level 4)	Methods of Isolating the Effects of the Program	Methods of Converting Data	Cost Categories	Intangible Benefits	Communication Targets	Other Influences and Issues

Figure 2-5. ROI analysis plan template.

method will be the same for each data item, but there could be variations. For example, if no historical data are available for one data item, then trend-line analysis is not possible for that item, although it may be appropriate for other items. The method of converting data to monetary values is included in the third column.

The costs categories that will be captured for the leadership development program are outlined in the fourth column. Instructions about how certain costs should be prorated would be noted here. Normally the cost categories will be consistent from one program to another. However, a specific cost that is unique to the program would also be noted. The intangible benefits expected from this program are outlined in the fifth column. This list is generated from discussions about the program with sponsors and subject-matter experts. Communication targets are outlined in the sixth column. Although there could be many groups that should receive the information, four target groups are always recommended:

1. Senior management group (sponsor)
2. Manager of participants
3. Program participants
4. Leadership development staff

All four of these groups need to know the results of the evaluation. Finally, other issues or events that might influence program implementation would be highlighted in the last column. Typical items include the capability of participants, the degree of access to data sources, and unique data analysis issues.

The ROI analysis plan, when combined with the data collection plan, provides detailed information on calculating the ROI, illustrating how the process will develop from beginning to end. Once data are collected, they will be analyzed and can be used to complete the leadership scorecard.

Project Plan

The final plan developed for this phase is a project plan. A project plan consists of a description of the program and brief detail about the program, such as duration, target audience, and number of participants. It also shows the timeline of the project, beginning with the planning of the study to the last communication of the results. This plan becomes an operational tool to keep the project on track. Sometimes, the end date drives the entire planning process. For example, a senior executive may request that data surrounding the impact study be developed and presented to the senior team at a particular time frame. With that end in mind, all the other dates are added. Any appropriate project-planning tool can be used to develop the plan.

Collectively, these three planning documents (the data collection plan, the ROI analysis plan, and the project plan) provide the direction necessary for completion of the leadership scorecard. Most of the decisions regarding the process are made as these planning tools are developed. The remainder of the project becomes a methodical, systematic process of implementing the plan. This is a crucial step in the ROI methodology, where valuable time allocated to this process will save precious time later.

Collecting Data

Data collection is central to the ROI methodology and to creating a leadership scorecard. Both hard data (representing output, quality, cost, and time) and soft data (including job satisfaction and customer satisfaction) are collected. Data are collected using a variety of methods, such as surveys, questionnaires, tests, observation, interviews, focus groups, action plans, program assignments, performance contracts, and business performance monitoring. The important challenge in data collection is to select the method or methods appropriate for the setting and the specific program, within the time and budget constraints of the organization.

Isolating the Effects of a Program

An often-overlooked issue in most evaluations is the process of isolating the effects of a program. In this step of the process, specific strategies are explored that determine the amount of output performance directly related to the program. This step is essential because many factors will influence performance data after a leadership development program is implemented. The specific strategies of this step will pinpoint the amount of improvement directly related to the leadership development program, resulting in increased accuracy and credibility of the results including the ROI calculation. Control groups, trend lines, forecasting models, participant estimations, supervisor estimations, senior management estimations, expert estimations, and customer input are techniques that have been used by organizations to address this issue.

Converting Data to Monetary Values

To calculate the return on investment, data collected in a Level 4 evaluation are converted to monetary values and compared to program costs. This requires a value to be placed on each unit of data connected with the program. A wide variety of techniques are available to convert data to monetary values. The specific techniques selected usually depend on the type of data and the situation.

This step in the ROI model is very important and absolutely necessary for determining the monetary benefits from a leadership development program. The process is challenging, particularly with soft data, but can be accomplished methodically using one or more of these strategies.

Tabulating Cost of the Program

The other part of the ROI equation is the program cost. Tabulating the costs involves monitoring or developing all of the related costs of the program targeted for the ROI calculation. Among the cost components that should be included are

- the cost to design and develop the program, possibly prorated over the expected life of the program;
- the cost of all program materials provided to each participant;
- the cost for the instructor/facilitator, including preparation time as well as delivery time;
- the cost of the facilities for the program;
- travel, lodging, and meal costs for the participants, if applicable;
- salaries, plus employee benefits of the participants who attend the program;
- administrative and overhead costs of the leadership development function, allocated in some convenient way; and
- the cost of the evaluation.

In addition, specific costs related to the needs assessment should be included, if appropriate. The conservative approach is to include all of these costs so that the total is fully loaded.

Calculating the Return on Investment

The return on investment is calculated using the monetary program benefits and costs. The benefits/cost ratio is the program benefits divided by cost. In formula form it is:

$$BCR = \frac{\text{Program benefits}}{\text{Program costs}}$$

Sometimes this ratio is stated as a cost/benefit ratio, although the formula is the same as BCR.

The return on investment uses the net program benefits divided by program costs. Net benefits are program benefits minus costs. In formula form, the ROI becomes:

$$ROI\,(\%) = \frac{\text{Net program benefits}}{\text{Program costs}} \times 100$$

This is the same basic formula used in evaluating other investments where the ROI is traditionally reported as earnings divided by investment. The ROI from some programs is large. Leadership development programs are a case in which the ROI can be quite high (frequently over 100%). The ROI value for technical and operator training on the other hand, may be much lower.

Identifying Intangible Benefits

In addition to tangible, monetary benefits, most leadership development programs will have intangible, nonmonetary benefits. The ROI calculation is based on converting both hard and soft data to monetary values. Intangible benefits are those program benefits we choose not to convert to monetary value. These include items such as

- increased job satisfaction;
- increased organizational commitment;
- improved teamwork;
- improved customer service;
- reduced complaints; and
- reduced conflicts.

During data analysis, every attempt is made to convert all data to monetary values. All hard data, such as output, quality, and time, are converted to monetary values. The conversion of soft data is attempted for each data item. However, if the process used for conversion is too subjective or inaccurate, and the resulting values lose credibility in the process, then data are listed as an intangible benefit with the appropriate explanation. For some programs, intangible,

Leadership Scorecard				
Program Title:				
Target Audience: Indicators				
Duration: Indicators				
Business Objectives:				
Results				
Satisfaction	Learning	Application	Tangible Benefits	Intangible Benefits
Level 1	Level 2	Level 3	Levels 4 & 5	
Technique to Isolate Effects of Program:				
Technique to Convert Data to Monetary Value:				
Fully-loaded Program Costs:				
Barriers to Application of Skills:				
Recommendations:				

Figure 2-6. Leadership scorecard template.

nonmonetary benefits are extremely valuable, often carrying as much influence as the hard data items.

Reporting

The final step in the ROI model is reporting leadership scorecard data. This very critical step often lacks the proper attention and planning to ensure that it is successful. This step involves developing appropriate information in impact studies and other brief reports. The heart of the step includes the different techniques used to communicate to a wide variety of target audiences. In most ROI studies, several audiences are interested in and need the information. Careful planning to match the communication method with the audience is essential to ensure that the message is understood and appropriate actions follow. The leadership scorecard is a useful tool to use for reporting. As the leadership scorecard template in Figure 2-6, demonstrates, a leadership scorecard is often developed as one-page which makes it easy to quickly communicate the results of the leadership development program (Schmidt, 2003).

OPERATING STANDARDS AND PHILOSOPHY

To ensure consistency and replication of impact studies, operating standards must be developed and applied as the process model is used to develop ROI studies. It is extremely important for the results of a study to stand alone and not vary depending on the individual

Table 2-2
Operating Standards

Guiding principles:

1. When a higher-level evaluation is conducted, data must be collected at lower levels

2. When an evaluation is planned for a higher level, the previous level of evaluation does not have to be comprehensive

3. When collecting and analyzing data, use only the most credible source

4. When analyzing data, choose the most conservative among the alternatives

5. At least one method must be used to isolate the effects of the solution

6. If no improvement data are available for a population or from a specific source, it is assumed that little or no improvement has occurred

7. Estimates of improvements should be adjusted (discounted) for the potential error of the estimate

8. Extreme data items and unsupported claims should not be used in ROI calculations

9. Only the first year of benefits (annual) should be used in the ROI analysis of short-term solutions

10. Costs of the solution should be fully loaded for ROI analysis

conducting the study. The operating standards detail how each step and issue of the process will be handled. Table 2-2 shows the ten guiding principles that form the basis for the operating standards.

The operating standards not only serve as a way to consistently address each step, but also provide a much-needed conservative approach to the analysis. A conservative approach may lower the actual ROI calculation, but it will also build credibility of the leadership scorecard with the target audience.

IMPLEMENTATION ISSUES

A variety of environmental issues and events will influence the successful implementation of the leadership scorecard and ROI processes. These issues must be addressed early. Specific topics or actions include

- a policy statement concerning results-based leadership development;
- procedures and guidelines for different elements and techniques of the evaluation process and the creation of the leadership scorecard;
- meetings and formal sessions to develop staff skills with the leadership scorecard and the ROI methodology;
- strategies to improve management commitment and support for the ROI methodology;
- mechanisms to provide technical support for questionnaire design, data analysis, and evaluation strategy;
- specific techniques to place more attention on results.

The leadership scorecard and ROI methodology can fail or succeed based on these implementation issues.

APPLICATION AND PRACTICE

It is extremely important for the leadership scorecard and ROI methodology to be utilized in organizations and develop a history of application. The ROI methodology described in this chapter and throughout the book is rich in tradition, with application in a variety of settings and over 100 published case studies. In addition, thousands of case studies will soon be deposited in a website/database for future use as a research and application tool (Phillips and Burkett, 2004). However, it is more important to obtain success with the ROI methodology within the organization and document the results as leadership development impact studies. Consequently, the leadership development staff is encouraged to develop their own impact studies to compare with others. Impact studies within the organization provide the most convincing data to senior management teams that the leadership development program is adding significant value. Case studies also provide information needed to improve processes in the different areas of the leadership development function, as part of the continuous improvement process.

LEADERSHIP SCORECARD BENEFITS

Even though there are several challenges that may be encountered when implementing a leadership scorecard, such as getting management buy-in, taking the time to do the needs assessment, and allocating resources, the benefits far outweigh the challenges. A leadership scorecard can be implemented successfully in any organization. The benefits of implementing a leadership scorecard are many. A few of the benefits that have been experienced by leadership development functions are (Schmidt, 2003)

- Management develops an understanding of the benefits of leadership development programs.
- The leadership development function is viewed as adding value to the bottom line.
- The leadership development function becomes very focused on only delivering programs linked directly to the business strategy. This results in a positive return on investment for the organization.
- The leadership scorecard data enables the leadership development function to continuously improve programs or discontinue programs that are not providing positive results.
- The leadership development function is able to assess if the program has impacted behavior change and application back on the job. This is a critical measure of success.
- Leaders are participants in programs that have impact. Leaders are able to see the value in the programs they participate in and the perception of the leadership development function is enhanced.
- The leadership development function is able to justify the annual budget. Budget cuts are not as drastic as in the past due to the leadership development functions ability to show a return on investment.
- The leadership development staff receives career enriching development in the area of measurement and evaluation.
- Communication between the leadership development function and executives becomes more frequent. The leadership development function is able to talk with executives in business terms, such as return on investment and benefit/cost ratios.

FINAL THOUGHTS

The leadership scorecard is a tool that can assist a leadership development function in contributing to the bottom line of an organization by showing its value. Figure 2-7 is a checklist used to help determine if your leadership development function is a candidate for implementing a leadership scorecard. The leadership scorecard can be used to establish, track, compile, analyze, and communicate leadership development program results. Leadership development

Read each question and check off the most appropriate level of agreement (1 = Disagree; 5 = Total Agreement). The higher the total score, the better candidate your company is for a Leadership Scorecard.

		Disagree				Agree
		1	2	3	4	5
1.	My organization is considered a large organization with a wide variety of development programs.	☐	☐	☐	☐	☐
2.	We have a large leadership development budget that reflects the interest of senior management.	☐	☐	☐	☐	☐
3.	Our organization has a culture of measurement and is focused on establishing a variety of measures.	☐	☐	☐	☐	☐
4.	My organization is undergoing significant change.	☐	☐	☐	☐	☐
5.	There is pressure from senior management to measure results of our leadership development initiatives.	☐	☐	☐	☐	☐
6.	My leadership development function currently has a very low investment in measurement and evaluation.	☐	☐	☐	☐	☐
7.	My organization has suffered more than one leadership development program disaster in the past.	☐	☐	☐	☐	☐
8.	My organization has a new director of HRD, OD or leadership development	☐	☐	☐	☐	☐
9.	My management would like to be the leader in leadership development processes.	☐	☐	☐	☐	☐
10.	The image of our leadership development function is less than satisfactory.	☐	☐	☐	☐	☐
11.	My clients are demanding that our leadership development processes show bottom-line results.	☐	☐	☐	☐	☐
12.	My leadership development function competes with other functions within our organization for resources.	☐	☐	☐	☐	☐
13.	My organization has increased its focus on linking processes to the strategic direction of the company.	☐	☐	☐	☐	☐
14.	My leadership development function is a key player in change initiatives currently taking place in my organization.	☐	☐	☐	☐	☐
15.	Our overall leadership development budget is growing and we are required to prove the bottom-line value of our processes.	☐	☐	☐	☐	☐

Total Score: _____

Figure 2-7. Is your organization a candidate for a leadership scorecard?

functions simply need to ask the questions why, who, where, when, what, and how when creating the leadership scorecard.

Foundational building blocks for the leadership scorecard include the ROI methodology and ROI process model for calculating the return on investment for a leadership development program. The step-by-step process takes the complicated issue of calculating ROI and breaks it into simple, manageable tasks and steps. When the process is planned thoroughly, taking into consideration all potential strategies and techniques, the process becomes manageable and achievable. The remaining chapters focus on the major elements of this model and ways to use it to create the leadership scorecard. The benefits of implementing a leadership scorecard far outweigh the challenges. A focus on a leadership scorecard will ensure that the leadership development function is winning the game.

INTRODUCTION TO CASE STUDY

One of the most effective ways of understanding ROI methodology and implementing a leadership scorecard is to examine an actual case study. The following is the beginning of a case that is presented in the remaining chapters of this book. Although it represents an actual situation, a few of the issues and events have been modified slightly at the request of the organization. The case reflects the issues as they are presented in each chapter. To fully understand the case and all the issues, it is recommended that each part of the case be read and the discussion questions addressed before moving to the next part of the case.

CASE STUDY—PART A INTERNATIONAL CAR RENTAL

Background

The International Car Rental (ICR) Company operates in 27 countries with 27,000 employees. The U.S. division has 13,000 employees and operates in most major cities in the United States. The learning and development (L&D) staff for ICR has developed a new program for all first-level managers in the organization. The Leadership Challenge is designed for team leaders, supervisors, and managers who are responsible for those who actually do the work (i.e., the first level of management). Program participants may be located in rental offices, service centers, call centers, regional offices, and headquarters. Most functional areas are represented, such as operations, customer service, service and support, sales, administration, finance and accounting, and IT. Essentially, this is a cross-functional program for this important job in the organization.

The Program

The Leadership Challenge involves four days of off-the-job learning with input from the immediate manager who serves as a coach for some of the learning processes. An on-line pre-work instrument and a short book must be completed before attending the program.

The program was developed from a needs assessment for all functional areas as the L&D staff determined the leadership competencies needed for first-level managers. The program focuses on typical competencies, such as problem solving, counseling, motivation, communication, goal setting, and feedback. In addition to developing skills, the L&D staff attempted to focus directly on job performance needs and business needs. Consequently, prior to attending the program, each manager was asked to identify at least two business measures in the work unit that represent an opportunity for improvement. The selected measures had to meet an additional test. Each measure had to have the potential to be influenced by team members with the manager using the competencies in the program. A description of the program was provided in advance with a list of objectives and skill sets.

The L&D staff developed the following objectives for the program:

1. Participants will rate the program as relevant to their jobs.
2. Participants will rate the program as important to their job success.
3. Participants must demonstrate acceptable performance on each major competency.
4. Participants will utilize the competencies with team members on a routine basis.
5. Participants and team members will drive improvements in at least two business measures.

A few senior executives at ICR have challenged the L&D staff to show the business impact of this program. The first two sessions of this program will be evaluated, including 36 participants total (i.e., 18 in one group and 18 in the other). Figure 2-8 shows a partially completed data collection plan for the program.

DATA COLLECTION PLAN

Program: The Leadership Challenge   **Responsibility:** Learning & Development Staff   **Date:**

Level	Objective(s)	Measures/Data	Data Collection Method	Data Sources	Timing	Responsibilities
1	**Reaction/Satisfaction** • Participants rate the program as relevant to their jobs • Participants rate the program as important to their job success	• 4 out of 5 on a 5-point rating scale	• Questionnaire	• Participants	• End of program	• Facilitator
2	**Learning** • Participants demonstrate acceptable performance on each major competency	• 4 out of 5 on a 5-point scale	• Observation of skill practices • Self assessment via questionnaire	• Facilitator • Participants	• End of program • End of program	• Facilitator • Facilitator
3	**Application/Implementation** • Participants utilize the competencies with team members on a routine basis					
4	**Business Impact** • Participants and team members drive improvements in at least two business measures					
5	**ROI** • Achieve a 20% ROI					

Comments: _____

_____

_____

Figure 2-8. The leadership challenge data collection plan.

DISCUSSION QUESTIONS

1. Discuss the adequacy of the needs assessment.
2. Can this program be evaluated to show business impact from ROI?
3. Complete the Leadership Challenge data collection plan, Figure 2-8.

REFERENCES

Alliger, G.M., and Janak, E.A. "Kirkpatrick's Levels of Training Criteria: Thirty Years Later," *Personal Psychology*, 1989, Vol. 42, pp. 331–342.

Broad, M.L. (Ed.) *In Action: Transferring Learning to the Workplace*. Alexandria, VA: American Society for Training and Development, 1997.

Broad, M.L. "Built-In Evaluation," *In Action: Measuring Return on Investment*, Vol. 1, J.J. Phillips (Ed.). Alexandria, VA: American Society for Training and Development, 1994, pp. 55–70.

Broad, M.L., and Newstrom, J.W. *Transfer of Training*. Reading, MA: Addison-Wesley, 1992.

Delahoussaye, M. "Leadership in the 21st Century." *Training*, September, 2001, pp. 60–72.

Dixon, N.M. *Evaluation: A Tool for Improving HRD Quality*. San Diego, CA: University Associates, Inc., 1990.

Ford, D. "Three R's in the Workplace," *In Action: Measuring Return on Investment*, Vol. 1, J.J. Phillips (Ed.). Alexandria, VA: American Society for Training and Development, 1994, pp. 85–104.

Fulmer, R., and Goldsmith, M. *The Leadership Investment*. New York: AMACOM, 2001.

Kirkpatrick, D.L. *Evaluating Training Programs: The Four Level*. 2nd ed. San Francisco, CA: Berrett-Koehler Publishers, 1998.

Nadler, L., and Wiggs, G.D. *Managing Human Resource Development*. San Francisco, CA: Jossey-Bass, Inc., 1986.

Phillips, J.J. *Handbook of Training Evaluation and Measurement Methods*. 3rd ed. Boston: Butterworth-Heinemann, 1997.

Phillips, J.J. *The Corporate University: Measuring the Impact of Learning*. Houston, TX: American Productivity & Quality Center, 2000.

Phillips, J.J. Return on Investment in Training and Performance Improvement Programs 2nd ed. Boston, MA: Butterworth-Heinemann, 2003.

Phillips, P.P., and Burkett, H. *The ROI Field Book*, Boston, MA: Butterworth-Heinemann, 2004.

Phillips, P.P., and Phillip, J.J. "Measuring Return on Investment in Interactive Sales Training," *In Action: Measuring Return on Investment*, Vol. 3. Alexandria, VA: American Society for Training and Development, 2001, pp. 233–249.

Russ-Eft, D., and Preskill, H. *Evaluation in Organizations*. Cambridge, MA: Perseus Publishing, 2001.

Schmidt, L. "The Value of Training Scorecards," *In Action: Implementing Training Scorecards*. Alexandria, VA: American Society for Training and Development, 2003, pp. 1–11.

Van Buren, M.E. *State of the Industry*. Alexandria, VA: American Society for Training and Development, 2002.

Webster's Unabridged Dictionary. New York: Random House, 1998.

PART II

Leadership Scorecard Methodology

Measuring Indicators, Satisfaction, and Learning

When creating the leadership development scorecard seven types of data may be reported showing the results of a leadership development program. Those seven types of data are:

1. Indicators, showing the volume and scope of leadership development.
2. Satisfaction with leadership development programs and activities.
3. Learning, the acquisition of leadership skills and knowledge.
4. Application of leadership skills and knowledge in job situations.
5. Business impact, the consequence of applying new skills and knowledge.
6. Return on investment, comparing the monetary benefits of business impact to the costs of the program.
7. Intangible benefits, the business impact measures not converted to monetary values.

Satisfaction, learning, application, business impact, ROI, and intangible benefits were outlined briefly in the previous chapter and are components of the ROI model. Measuring indicators, satisfaction, and learning will be covered in more detail in this chapter. The remaining measures will be covered in following chapters.

MEASURING INDICATORS

Although not a component of the ROI model, indicators are often necessary to include in a scorecard, but should not be confused with results. The traditional approach for measuring leadership development programs is to report indicators to the management team. While these measures are important, they usually do not reflect results, only the level of commitment, volume, efficiencies, and trends in processes. While the number of indicators is vast, it is important to include measures in the leadership development scorecard that meet the needs of top managers. Ideally, the management group should provide input on the selection of indicators and the indicators should stimulate interest with the entire management team (Phillips and Phillips, 2003). Typical indicators include:

- The number and variety of programs
- The number of employees participating in a leadership development program
- Total number of hours of learning activity per employee
- Various enrollment statistics, including demographics of participants, participation rates, completion rates, etc.
- Investment in leadership development programs reported in a variety of ways. (Total cost, cost per employee, direct cost per participant, and cost as a percent of payroll are common ways.)
- Cost recovery, if there is a charge back system.
- The types of delivery mechanisms.

Several other statistics can be reported on issues such as the use of technology, on the job training, trends, volume, and efficiencies. Any mix is appropriate to highlight and monitor an important trend (Byham, Smith and Paese, 2001). Some additional indicators specific to the leadership development process that may be tracked are:

- Percentage of employees/managers nominated to participate in a leadership development program.
- Number of people in a leadership development program compared to goals.
- Readiness of newly appointed leaders, measured on a rating scale.
- Quality of new leaders, measured on a rating scale.
- Advancement of leadership development program members (number moved upward each year).
- Percentage of times (against goal) that senior positions are filled by nonprogram participants.
- Percentage of times (against goal) that senior positions are filled from outside the organization.

- The length of time that leadership positions are opened before being filled.
- Average time in position.
- Cross-unit movement.
- Diversity of leadership development program participants (race, gender, geography, function, educational background, etc.).

Indicators usually show the degree of management's commitment to leadership development and provide a brief view of the mix of programs offered.

Measuring Satisfaction

Collecting reaction and satisfaction data during a leadership development program is the first operational phase of the ROI model. Client feedback data are powerful for making adjustments and measuring success. A variety of methods are available to capture reaction and satisfaction data during the program. The most widely used data source for reaction and satisfaction data is the program participants. Participants are frequently asked about reaction and satisfaction, extent of learning, and how skills and knowledge have been applied on the job. The challenge is to find an effective and efficient way to capture data in a consistent manner.

Questionnaires and Surveys

Probably the most common form of data collection method is the questionnaire (Alreck and Settle, 1995). Ranging from short reaction forms to detailed follow-up tools, questionnaires can be used to obtain subjective information about participants, as well as to objectively document measurable business results for an ROI analysis. With this versatility and popularity, the questionnaire is the preferred method for program data in some organizations.

Surveys represent a specific type of questionnaire with several applications for measuring training success. Surveys are used in situations where attitudes, beliefs, and opinions are captured only, whereas a questionnaire has much more flexibility and captures data ranging from attitude to specific improvement statistics. The principles of survey construction and design are similar to questionnaire design. The development of both types of instruments is covered in this section.

Types of Questions

In addition to the types of data sought, the types of questions distinguish surveys from questionnaires. Surveys can have yes or no responses when an absolute agreement or disagreement is required, or a range of responses may be used from strongly disagree to strongly agree. A five-point scale is very common.

A questionnaire may contain any or all of these types of questions (see Figure 3-1):

- An *open-ended question* has an unlimited answer. The question is followed by an ample blank space for the response.
- A *checklist provides* a list of items where a participant is asked to check those that apply in the situation.

---

1. Open-Ended Question:

   What problems will you encounter when attempting to use the new performance management process?

2. Checklist:

   From the following list, check all of the business measures that may be influenced by the application of the new performance management process.

   ☐ Resource Allocation   ☐ Cost Control
   ☐ Productivity   ☐ Response Time
   ☐ Quality   ☐ Customer Satisfaction
   ☐ Efficiency   ☐ Job Satisfaction

3. Two-Way Question:

   As a result of this program, I have a better understanding of my job in managing performance.

   YES   NO

4. Multiple Choice Question:

   Since the new program has been initiated, my team's achievement of goals has:

   a. Increased
   b. Decreased
   c. Remained the same
   d. Don't know

5. Ranking Scales:

   The following list contains six important factors that will influence the success of this program. Place a one (1) by the item that is most influential, a two (2) by the item that is second most influential, and so on. The item ranked six (6) will be the least influential item on the list.

   Rewards Systems   Training
   Supervisor Coaching   Management Support
   Communications   Resources

Figure 3-1. Sample questions.

- A *two-way question* has alternate responses, a yes/no, or other possibilities.
- A *multiple-choice question* has several choices and the participant is asked to select the one most applicable.
- A *ranking scale* requires the participant to rank a list of items.

Questionnaire Design Steps

Questionnaire design is a simple and logical process. There is nothing more confusing, frustrating, and potentially embarrassing than a poorly designed or an improperly worded questionnaire. The following steps can ensure that a valid, reliable, and effective instrument is developed (Robson, 2002).

Determine the specific information needed. As a first step in questionnaire design, the topics, skills, or attitudes presented in the program are reviewed for potential items for the questionnaire. It is sometimes helpful to develop this information in outline form so that related questions or items can be grouped. Other issues related to the application of the program are explored for inclusion in the questionnaire.

Involve management in the process. To the extent possible, management should be involved in this process as a client, sponsor, supporter, or interested party. If possible, managers most familiar with the program or process should provide information on specific issues and concerns that often frame the actual questions planned for the questionnaire. In some cases, managers want to provide input on specific issues or items. Not only is manager input helpful and useful in questionnaire design, but it also builds ownership in the measurement and evaluation process.

Select the type(s) of questions. Using the previous five types of questions, the first step in questionnaire design is to select the type(s) that will best result in the specific data needed. The planned data analysis and variety of data to be collected should be considered when deciding which questions to use.

Develop the questions. The next step is to develop the questions based on the type of questions planned and the information needed. Questions should be simple and straightforward to avoid confusion or lead the participant to a desired response. A single question should only address one issue. If multiple issues need to be addressed, separate the questions into multiple parts or simply develop a separate question for each issue. Terms or expressions unfamiliar to the participant should be avoided.

Check the reading level. To ensure that the questionnaire can be understood easily by the target audience, it is helpful to assess the reading level. Most word processing programs have features that will evaluate the reading difficulty according to grade level. This provides an important check to ensure that the perceived reading level of the target audience matches the questionnaire design.

Test the questions. Proposed questions should be tested for understanding. Ideally, the questions should be tested on a sample group of participants. If this is not feasible, the sample group of employees should be at approximately the same job level as participants. From this sample group, feedback, critiques, and suggestions are sought to improve questionnaire design.

Address the anonymity issue. Participants should feel free to respond openly to questions without fear of reprisal. The confidentiality of their responses is of utmost importance because there is usually a link between survey anonymity and accuracy. Therefore, surveys should be anonymous unless there are specific reasons why individuals have to be identified. In situations where participants must complete the questionnaire in a captive audience or submit a completed questionnaire directly to an individual, a neutral third party should collect and process data, ensuring that the identity is not revealed. In cases where identity must be known (e.g., to compare output data with previous data or to verify data), every effort should be made to protect the respondent s identity from those who may be biased in their actions.

Design for ease of tabulation and analysis. Each potential question should be considered in terms of data tabulation, data summary, and analysis. If possible, the data analysis process should be outlined and reviewed in mock-up form. This step avoids the problems of inadequate, cumbersome, and lengthy data analysis caused by improper wording or design. Figure 3-2 illustrates yes/no remarks and varying degrees of agreement and disagreement survey responses. Uniform responses make it easier for tabulation and comparisons. On a scale of strongly agree to strongly disagree, numbers are usually assigned to reflect the response. For instance, a 1 may represent a strongly disagree, and a 5, strongly agree. An average response of 2.2 on a preprogram survey followed by a postprogram average response of 4.3 shows a significant change in response. Some argue that a five-point scale merely permits the respondent to select the midpoint and not to be forced to make a choice. If this is a concern, an even-numbered scale should be used.

Develop the completed questionnaire and prepare a data summary. The questions should be integrated to develop an attractive

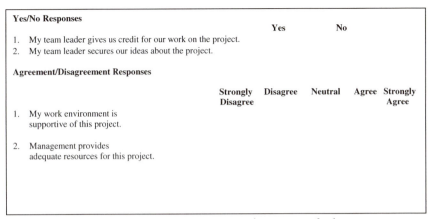

Figure 3-2. Survey responses for easy tabulation.

questionnaire with proper instructions so that it can be administered effectively. In addition, a summary sheet should be developed so that data can be tabulated quickly for analysis.

Questionnaire Content

The areas of feedback used on reaction forms depend, to a large extent, on the organization and the purpose of the evaluation. Some forms are simple, whereas others are detailed and require a considerable amount of time to complete. A feedback questionnaire should be designed to supply the information necessary to satisfy the purpose of evaluation. The following is a comprehensive listing of the most common types of feedback solicited:

- Progress with objectives. To what degree were the objectives met?
- Program content. Was the content appropriate?
- Instructional materials. Were the materials useful?
- Pre-work materials. Were the pre-work materials necessary? Helpful?
- Assignments. Were the out-of-class assignments helpful?
- Method of delivery. Was the method of delivery appropriate for the objectives?
- Instructor/facilitator. Was the facilitator effective?
- New information. How much new information was included?
- Motivation to learn. Were you motivated to learn this content?
- Relevance. Was the program relevant to your needs?

- Importance. How important is this content to the success of your job?
- Registration/logistics. Were the scheduling and registration efficient?
- Facilities. Did the facilities enhance the learning environment?
- Potential barriers. What potential barriers exist for the application of the material?
- Planned improvements/use of material. How will you apply what you have learned?
- Recommendations for target audiences. What is the appropriate audience for this program?
- Overall evaluation. What is your overall rating of the program?

Objective questions covering each of these areas will ensure thorough feedback from participants. This feedback can be extremely useful in making adjustments in a program and/or assisting in predicting performance after the program. The instructor/facilitator evaluation deserves additional comments. In some organizations, the primary evaluation centers on the facilitator (a separate form may be used for each facilitator, if there are several), covering a variety of areas such as the following:

- Preparation for sessions
- Knowledge of the subject matter, including familiarity with content and depth of understanding
- Presentation skills, including clarity of the presentation, pacing of material, and eye contact
- Communication skills, including the use of understandable language, real-life examples, and the promotion of discussion
- Assessing learner understanding and responding appropriately to learner needs and questions
- Use of appropriate technology and responding effectively to technical requirements of learners
- Encouraging application of learning through the use of real-life examples, job-related discussions, and relevant exercises

In most medium to large size organizations where there is significant training and development activity, the Level 1 instrument is usually automated for computerized scanning and reporting. Typical Level 1 questions can be developed easily for a scan sheet and programmed to present reports to help understand and use data. Some organizations use direct input into a website to develop not only detailed reports, but also to develop databases, allowing feedback data to be compared to other programs or the same program with other facilitators.

Collecting learning data using a questionnaire is very common. Most types of tests, whether formal or informal, are questionnaire based and are described in more detail in this chapter. However, several questions can be developed to use with the reaction form to gain insight into the extent to which learning took place during the program. For example, some possible areas to explore on a reaction questionnaire, all aimed at measuring the extent of learning, would be:

- skill enhancement
- knowledge gain
- ability
- capability
- competence
- awareness

In addition, other questions can focus directly on the learning issue, such as:

- difficulty of the material
- confidence in using what is learned

These questions are developed using a format similar to the reaction part of the questionnaire. They measure the extent to which learning has taken place, usually based on confidence and perception.

Using Satisfaction Data

Sometimes participant feedback is solicited, tabulated, summarized, and then disregarded. The information must be collected and used for one or more purposes of evaluation. Otherwise, the exercise is a waste of the participants' time. Some common reasons for gathering reaction and satisfaction data are:

- Monitor customer satisfaction.
- Identify strengths and weaknesses of the program.
- Develop norms and standards.
- Evaluate the leadership development staff.
- Evaluate planned improvements.

- Link with follow-up data.
- Market future programs.

Although reaction and satisfaction data should always be collected, some shortcuts can be taken. There are some essential items that must be taken care of for very short, low profile, inexpensive programs. Unfortunately, omitting Level 1 is not an option because of the critical importance of early feedback. The following three suggestions may be helpful.

- Use a simple questionnaire. A simple 10 to 15 item questionnaire using multiple choice, true/false, or even a scale rating will be sufficient for many small-scale programs.
- Collect data early and react quickly. Taking an early pulse is critical. Find out if the program is being accepted and if those involved have concerns. Then take action quickly.
- Pay attention to participants. The key stakeholders, the program participants, are critical to the process. A general rule is to always listen to this group and react to its concerns, issues, and recommendations.

MEASURING LEARNING

Learning is an important measure for any leadership development program. It measures the changes in knowledge, skills, and attitudes. It is a helpful check to ensure that program participants have acquired the targeted knowledge and skills needed to change behavior. This section focuses on simple techniques for measuring learning. Many of them have been used for years to measure learning in training programs in terms of formal testing and skill practices. Others are less formal in structure and can suffice when time is a concern or when costs need to be minimized.

TESTING

Testing is important for measuring learning in program evaluations. Pre- and postcourse comparisons using tests are very common. An improvement in test scores shows the change in skill, knowledge, or attitude attributed to the program. The principles of test development are similar to those for the design and development of questionnaires and attitude surveys. This section presents additional information on types of tests and test construction (Westgaard, 1999).

Types of Tests

Several types of tests, which can be classified in three ways, can be used. The first is based on the medium used for administering the test.

Norm-referenced test. Norm-referenced tests compare participants with each other or to other groups rather than to specific instructional objectives. They are characterized by using data to compare the participants to the "norm" or average. Although norm-referenced tests have only limited use in some leadership development program evaluations, they may be useful in programs involving large numbers of participants in which average scores and relative rankings are important. In some situations, participants who score highest on the exams are given special recognition or awards or are made eligible for other special activities.

Criterion-referenced test (CRT). The CRT is an objective test with a predetermined cut-off score. The CRT is a measure against carefully written objectives for the leadership development program. In a CRT, the interest lies in whether participants meet the desired minimum standards, not how that participant ranks with others. The primary concern is to measure, report, and analyze participant performance as it relates to the instructional objectives.

Criterion-referenced testing is a popular measurement instrument in development programs (Shrock and Coscarelli, 2000). Its use is becoming widespread and is frequently used in e-learning. It has the advantage of being objective based, precise, and relatively easy to administer. It does require programs with clearly defined objectives that can be measured by tests.

Performance testing. Performance testing allows the participant to exhibit a skill (and occasionally knowledge or attitudes) that has been learned in a leadership development program. The skill can be manual, verbal, analytical, or a combination of the three. Performance testing is used frequently in job-related training where the participants are allowed to demonstrate what they have learned. In supervisory and management training, performance testing comes in the form of skill practices or role plays. Participants are asked to demonstrate discussion or problem-solving skills they have acquired.

For a performance test to be effective, the following steps are recommended for its design and administration.

- The test should be a representative sample of the leadership development program and should allow the participant to demonstrate as many skills as possible that are taught in the program.
- Every phase of the test should be planned thoroughly, including the time, the preparation of the participant, the collection of necessary materials and tools, and the evaluation of results.
- Thorough and consistent instructions are necessary. As with other tests, the quality of the instructions can influence the outcome of a performance test. All participants should be provided the same instructions.
- Acceptable standards must be developed for a performance test so that employees know in advance what has to be accomplished to be considered satisfactory and acceptable for test completion.
- Information that may lead participants astray should not be included.

With these general guidelines, performance tests can be developed into effective tools for program evaluation. Although more costly than written tests, performance tests are essential in situations where a high degree of fidelity is required between work and test conditions.

Simulations

Another technique used to measure learning is job simulations. This method involves the construction and application of a procedure or task that simulates or models the activity for which the leadership development program is being conducted. The simulation is designed to represent, as closely as possible, the actual job situation. Simulation may be used as an integral part of the leadership development program as well as for evaluation. In evaluation, participants are provided an opportunity to try out their performance in the simulated activity and have it evaluated based on how well the task was accomplished. Simulations may be used during the program, at the end of the program, or as part of the follow-up evaluation. There are a variety of simulation techniques used to evaluate program results.

Electrical/mechanical simulation. This technique uses a combination of electronics and mechanical devices to simulate real-life situations and is used in conjunction with programs to develop operational and diagnostic skills.

Task simulation. This approach involves the performance of a simulated task as part of an evaluation.

Business games. Business games have grown in popularity in recent years. They represent simulations of part or all of a business enterprise in which participants change the variables of the business and observe the effect of those changes. The game not only reflects the real-world situation but also represents the synopsis of the leadership development program of which it is a part.

In-basket. The in-basket is particularly useful in supervisory and management training programs. Portions of a supervisor's job are simulated through a series of items that normally appear in the in-basket. These items are typically memos, notes, letters, and reports, which create realistic conditions facing the supervisor. The participant's performance in the in-basket represents an evaluation of the program.

Case study. A possibly less effective, but still popular, technique is a case study. A case study gives a detailed description of a problem and usually contains a list of several questions. The participant is asked to analyze the case and determine the best course of action.

Role playing. In role playing, sometimes referred to as skill practice, participants practice a newly learned skill as they are observed by other individuals. Participants are given their assigned role with specific instructions, which sometimes include an ultimate course of action. The participant then practices the skill with other individuals to accomplish the desired objectives.

In summary, simulations come in a wide variety. They offer an opportunity for participants to practice what is being taught in a leadership development program and have their performance observed in a simulated job condition. They can provide extremely accurate evaluations if the performance in the simulation is objective and can be measured clearly.

Informal Tests

In some situations, it is important to have an informal check of learning that provides some assurance that participants have acquired skills, knowledge, or perhaps some changes in attitudes. This approach is appropriate when other levels of evaluation are pursued. For example, if a Level 3 on-the-job application evaluation is planned, it might not be critical to have a comprehensive Level 2. An informal assessment of learning may be sufficient. After all, resources are scarce and a comprehensive evaluation at all levels becomes quite expensive. The following are some alternative approaches to measuring learning that might suffice when inexpensive, low-key, informal assessments are needed.

Exercises/Problems/Activities. Many leadership development programs contain specific activities, exercises, or problems that must be explored, developed, or solved during the program. Some of these are constructed in terms of involvement exercises, whereas others require individual problem-solving skills. When these are integrated into the program, there are several specific ways in which to measure learning.

- The results of the exercise can be submitted for review and evaluated by the facilitator.
- The results can be discussed in a group with a comparison of various approaches and solutions. The group can reach an assessment of how much each individual has learned.
- The solutions to the problem or exercises can be shared with the group and the participant and provide a self-assessment indicating the degree to which skills and/or knowledge have been obtained from the exercise.
- The facilitator can review the individual progress or success of each participant to determine the relative success.

Self-Assessment. In many applications, a self-assessment may be appropriate. Participants are provided an opportunity to assess the extent of skills and knowledge acquisition. This is particularly applicable when Level 3, 4, and 5 evaluations are planned, and it is important to know if learning has improved. A few techniques can ensure that the process is effective.

- The self-assessment should be made on an anonymous basis so that individuals feel free to express a realistic and accurate assessment of what they have learned.
- The purpose of the self-assessment should be explained, along with the plans for data. Specifically, if there are implications for course design or individual retesting this should be discussed.
- If there has been no improvement or the self-assessment is unsatisfactory, there should be some explanation as to what that

means and what the implications will be. This will help ensure that accurate and credible information is provided.

Facilitator Assessment. A final technique is for facilitators to provide an assessment of the learning that has taken place. Although this approach is very subjective, it may be appropriate when a Level 3, 4, or 5 evaluation is planned. One of the most effective ways to accomplish this is to provide a checklist of the specific skills that need to be acquired in the course. Facilitators can then check off their assessment of the skills individually. Also, if there is a particular body of knowledge that needs to be acquired, the categories could be listed with a checklist for assurance that the individual has a good understanding of those items.

ADMINISTRATIVE ISSUES

There are several administrative issues that need to be addressed for measuring learning. They are:

- *Consistency.* It is extremely important that different tests, exercises, or processes for measuring learning are administered consistently from one group to another. This includes issues such as time to respond and the actual learning conditions. These issues can be addressed in the instructions.
- *Monitoring.* In some situations it is important for participants to be monitored as they are completing the test or other measurement process. This ensures that each individual is working independently and also that someone is there to address questions.
- *Scoring.* The scoring instructions need to be developed for the measurement process so that the person evaluating the responses will be objective in the process and provide consistent scores.
- *Reporting.* In some situations, the participants are provided with the results immediately. In other situations, the actual results may not be known until later. In these situations, a mechanism for providing the scoring data should be built into the evaluation plan unless it has been predetermined that participants will not know the scores.

Although there can be several uses of learning data, the most common are to provide individual feedback to build confidence, ensure that learning has been acquired, improve programs, and evaluate leadership development staff or facilitators.

FINAL THOUGHTS

The seven measures used in the leadership scorecard are indicators, satisfaction, learning, application, business impact, ROI, and intangible benefits. This chapter covered measuring indicators, satisfaction, and learning. A variety of indicators may be important to collect and report on for a leadership development program. Measuring reaction and satisfaction is typically done for 100 percent of programs and is a critical part of the ROI model. Data can be used to make adjustments and changes to the program. Learning must be assessed to determine the extent to which the participants in a leadership development program are learning new skills, techniques, processes, tools, and procedures. Measuring learning provides an opportunity to make adjustments quickly so that changes can be made to enhance learning. A variety of options are available for measuring indicators, satisfaction, and learning, and the options can usually match any budget or situation.

CASE STUDY—PART B INTERNATIONAL CAR RENTAL

Needs Assessment

While there was some concern about the thoroughness of the needs assessment, it appeared appropriate for the situation. The needs assessment on competencies uncovered a variety of deficiencies across all the functional units and provided the information necessary for job descriptions, assignments, and key responsibility areas. Although very basic, the additional steps taken to connect the program to business impact were appropriate for a business needs analysis and a job performance needs analysis. Identifying two measures needing improvement is, in essence, a business needs analysis for the work unit. Restricting the selected measures to only those that can be influenced by the team with the leader using the skills from the program essentially defines a job performance need. (In essence, the individual leader is identifying something that is not currently being done in the work unit that could be done to enhance the business need.) Although more refinement and detail would be preferred, the results of the assessment process should suffice for this project.

ROI Appropriateness

With the business and job performance needs complete, this program is a good candidate for the ROI. (Without these two steps, it would be difficult to conduct the ROI study.) A consideration for conducting the ROI study is identifying the drivers for ROI analyses. In this case, the senior team was challenging the value of leadership development. An ROI study should provide convincing evidence about a major program. Also, this is a highly visible program that should be evaluated at this level. It was strategic and expensive. Consequently, the L&D staff pursued the ROI study and an ROI objective of 20% was established.

Figure 3-3 shows the completed data collection plan along with the types of data that will be collected for the leadership scorecard. Although several data collection methods were possible, the team decided to use a detailed follow-up questionnaire to reflect the progress made with the program. The questionnaire would be sent directly to the participant three months after program completion. At the same time, a shorter questionnaire would be sent to the participant's immediate manager. The L&D team explored the possibility of using the 360-degree feedback process to obtain input from team members, but elected to wait until the 360-degree program was fully implemented in all units in the organization. A six-month follow-up was considered instead of a three-month follow-up; however, the L&D staff thought that six months was too long to wait for results and too long for managers to make the connection between the program and the results. Focus groups, interviews, and observations were considered too expensive or inappropriate.

DISCUSSION QUESTIONS

1. What topics should be explored in the follow-up questionnaire?
2. How can a response rate of 70 percent be achieved for a five-page anonymous questionnaire to this target audience?

DATA COLLECTION PLAN

Program: ___The Leadership Challenge___   Responsibility: ___L&D Staff___   Date: _____

Level	Objective(s)	Measures/Data	Data Collection Method	Data Sources	Timing	Responsibilities
1	**Reaction/Satisfaction** • Participants rate the program as relevant to their jobs • Participants rate the program as important to their job success	• 4 out of 5 on a 5-point rating scale	• Questionnaire	• Participants	• End of Program	• Facilitator
2	**Learning** • Participants demonstrate acceptable performance on each major competency	• 4 out of 5 on a 5-point scale	• Observation of skill practices • Self Assessment via questionnaire	• Facilitator • Participants	• End of Program • End of Program	• Facilitator • Facilitator
3	**Application/Implementation** • Participants utilize the competencies with team members on a routine basis	• Various measures (ratings, open-ended items, etc.) • 4 out of 5 on a 5-point scale	• Questionnaire • Questionnaire	• Participants • Participants' Manager	• 3 months	• L&D Staff
4	**Business Impact** • Participants and team members drive improvements in at least two business measures	• Various work unit measures	• Questionnaire	• Participants	• 3 months	• L&D Staff
5	**ROI** • Achieve a 20% ROI					

Comments:

Figure 3-3. Completed leadership challenge data collection plan.

REFERENCES

Alreck, P.L., and Settle, R.B. *The Survey Research Handbook: Guidelines and Strategies for Conducting a Survey.* 2nd ed. New York: McGraw-Hill, 1995.

Byham, W., Smith, A., and Paese, M. *Grow Your Own Leaders.* Pittsburgh, PA: DDI Press, 2001.

Mondschein, M. *Measurit: Achieving Profitable Training.* Leawood, KS: Leathers Publishing, 1999.

Phillips, J.J., and Phillips, P.P. "The Corporate University Scorecard" in L.A. Berger and D.R. Berger (Eds.) *Talent Management Handbook: Creating Organizational Excellence by Identifying, Developing, and Positioning High-Potential Talent.* New York: McGraw-Hill, 2003.

Robson, C. *Real World Research: A Resource for Social Scientists and Practitioner-Researchers*, 2nd ed. Malden, MA: Blackwell Publishers, 2002.

Shrock, S., and Coscarelli, W.C.C. *Criterion-Referenced Test Development: Technical and Legal Guidelines for Corporate Training and Certification.* 2nd ed. Washington, DC: International Society for Performance Improvement, 2000.

Westgaard, O. *Tests that Work: Designing and Delivering Fair and Practical Measurement Tools in the Workplace.* San Francisco, CA: Jossey-Bass/Pfeiffer, 1999.

CHAPTER 4

Measuring Application and Business Impact

This chapter focuses on measuring application and business impact, two of the seven measures that may be used to report the results of a leadership development program in a leadership scorecard. The other measures are indicators, satisfaction, and learning, which were covered in Chapter 3, and ROI and intangible benefits, which will be covered in following chapters.

Measuring the actual application and business impact of skills and knowledge is important because these steps play a critical role in the overall success or failure of a leadership development program. If newly acquired skills and knowledge are not applied effectively, there will be no change in the performance of the individual and the corresponding business impact—and no benefit from the leadership development program. As discussed briefly earlier, the value of information increases as progress is made through the chain of impact from satisfaction (Level 1) to ROI (Level 5). Thus, information concerning application (Level 3) and business impact (Level 4) is more valuable to management than reaction/satisfaction (Level 1) and learning (Level 2). Measuring application and business impact also provides the leadership development function with the opportunity to identify the barriers and enablers to application.

Several data collection methods are available to measure application and business impact. The range of possibilities vary including the use of questionnaires, interviews, focus groups, and observation. Also included are several specific methodologies, such as action planning and performance contracting. These data collection methods are explored in this chapter.

QUESTIONNAIRES

The following items represent a comprehensive list of questionnaire content possibilities for capturing follow-up data (Harrell, 2001). Figure 4-1 presents a questionnaire used in a follow-up evaluation of a program on leadership development. The evaluation was designed to capture data for an ROI analysis, the primary method of data collection being this questionnaire. This example will be used

Leadership Development Program Impact Questionnaire

Are you currently in a supervisory or management role/capacity? Yes ❏ No ❏

1. Listed below are the objectives of the Leadership Program. After reflecting on the program, please indicate your degree of success in achieving these objectives. *Please check the appropriate response beside each item.*

Skill/Behavior	No Success	Very Little Success	Limited Success	Generally Successful	Completely Successful
A. Apply the Advantage 11-step goal-setting process	❏	❏	❏	❏	❏
B. Apply the Advantage 12-step leadership planning process	❏	❏	❏	❏	❏
C. Identify the 12 core competencies of outstanding leaders	❏	❏	❏	❏	❏
D. Identify 10 ways to create higher levels of employee loyalty and satisfaction	❏	❏	❏	❏	❏
E. Apply the concept of Deferred Judgment in five scenarios	❏	❏	❏	❏	❏
F. Apply the Advantage creative problem-solving process to an identified problem	❏	❏	❏	❏	❏
G. Identify the 7 best ways to build positive relationships	❏	❏	❏	❏	❏
H. Given a work setting situation, apply the Advantage four-step approach to deal with errors	❏	❏	❏	❏	❏
I. Practice 6 ways to improve communication effectiveness	❏	❏	❏	❏	❏

2. Did you implement on-the-job action plans as part of the Leadership Program? Yes ❏ No ❏

If yes, complete and return your Action Plans with this questionnaire. If not, please explain why you did not complete your Action Plans.

3. Have you used the written materials since you participated in the program?
   Yes ❏   No ❏

Figure 4-1. Leadership development questionnaire.

Please explain. _____

4. For the following skills, please indicate the extent of improvement during the last few months as influenced by your participation in the Leadership Program. *Check the appropriate response beside each item.*

Skill Area	No Opportunity to Apply	No Change	Some Change	Moderate Change	Significant Change	Very Significant Change
A. ORGANIZING						
1) Prioritizing daily activities	❏	❏	❏	❏	❏	❏
2) Applying creative techniques	❏	❏	❏	❏	❏	❏
3) Organizing daily activities	❏	❏	❏	❏	❏	❏
4) Raising level of performance standards in area of responsibility	❏	❏	❏	❏	❏	❏
B. WORK CLIMATE						
1) Applying coaching	❏	❏	❏	❏	❏	❏
2) Applying techniques/initiatives that influence motivational climate	❏	❏	❏	❏	❏	❏
3) Implementing actions that influenced retaining people	❏	❏	❏	❏	❏	❏
4) Implementing job enrichment opportunities for valued associates	❏	❏	❏	❏	❏	❏
5) Implementing better control and monitoring systems	❏	❏	❏	❏	❏	❏
6) Applying techniques that influenced better teamwork	❏	❏	❏	❏	❏	❏
7) Realizing improved written communications	❏	❏	❏	❏	❏	❏
8) Realizing improved oral communications	❏	❏	❏	❏	❏	❏
9) Working personal leadership plan	❏	❏	❏	❏	❏	❏

5. List the three (3) behaviors or skills from the above list that you have used most frequently as a result of the program.
   A) _____
   B) _____
   C) _____

6. What has changed about you or your work as a result of your participation in this program? (specific behavior change such as; increased delegation to employees, improved communication with employees, employee participation in decision making, improved problem solving, etc.)

_____

_____

_____

Figure 4-1. (Continued)

7. How has Cyber International benefited from your participation in the program? Please identify specific business accomplishments or improvements that you believe are linked to participation in this program. Think about how the improvements actually resulted in influencing business measures such as; increased revenue, increased overall shipments, improved customer satisfaction, improved employee satisfaction, decreased costs, saved time, etc.

_____
_____
_____
_____

8. Reflect on your specific business accomplishments/improvements as stated above and think of specific ways that you can convert your accomplishments into a monetary value. Along with the monetary value, please indicate your basis for the calculations.

Estimated monetary amount $ _____

Indicate if above amount is weekly, monthly, quarterly, or annually.

   ❑ Weekly   ❑ Monthly   ❑ Quarterly   ❑ Annually

What is your basis for your estimates? (What influenced the benefits/savings and how did you arrive at the value above)? _____
_____
_____
_____
_____
_____
_____

9. What percentage of the improvement above was actually influenced by the application of knowledge and skills from the _Leadership Program_?

  ☛ _____ % Confidence (0% = None, and 100% = All)

10. What level of confidence do you place on the above estimations?

  ☛ _____ % Confidence (0% = No Confidence, and 100% = Certainty)

11. Do you think this _Leadership Program_ represented an appropriate investment for the company?

Yes ❑   **No** ❑

Please explain. _____
_____

12. Indicate the extent to which you think your application of knowledge, skills, and behavior learned from the _Leadership Program_ had a positive influence on the following business measures in your own work or your work unit. _Please check the appropriate response beside each measure._

Figure 4-1. (Continued)

Business Measure	Not Applicable	Applies But No Influence	Some Influence	Moderate Influence	Significant Influence	Very Significant Influence
A. Work output	❑	❑	❑	❑	❑	❑
B. Quality	❑	❑	❑	❑	❑	❑
C. Cost control	❑	❑	❑	❑	❑	❑
D. Efficiency	❑	❑	❑	❑	❑	❑
E. Response time to customers	❑	❑	❑	❑	❑	❑
F. Cycle time of products	❑	❑	❑	❑	❑	❑
G. Sales	❑	❑	❑	❑	❑	❑
H. Employee turnover	❑	❑	❑	❑	❑	❑
I. Employee absenteeism	❑	❑	❑	❑	❑	❑
J. Employee satisfaction	❑	❑	❑	❑	❑	❑
K. Employee complaints	❑	❑	❑	❑	❑	❑
L. Customer satisfaction	❑	❑	❑	❑	❑	❑
M. Customer complaints	❑	❑	❑	❑	❑	❑
N. Other (please specify)	❑	❑	❑	❑	❑	❑

Please cite specific examples or provide more details: _____

_____

_____

_____

_____

13. What barriers, if any, have you encountered that have prevented you from using skills/behaviors gained in the Leadership Program? *Check all that apply.*

    ❑ I have had no opportunity to use the skills
    ❑ I have not had enough time to apply the skills
    ❑ My work environment does not support the use of these skills/behaviors
    ❑ My supervisor does not support this type of program
    ❑ This material does not apply to my job situation
    ❑ Other (please specify): _____

    If any of the above are checked, please explain if possible. _____

    _____

    _____

14. What enablers, if any, are present to help you use the skills or knowledge gained from this program? Please explain.

_____

_____

Figure 4-1. (Continued)

15. What additional support could be provided by management that would influence your ability to apply the skills and knowledge learned from the program? _____

16. What additional benefits have been derived from this program? _____

17. What additional solutions do you recommend that would help to achieve the same business results that the *Leadership Program* has influenced? _____

18. Would you recommend the Leadership Program to others?　　　　　Yes ❏　　No ❏
Please explain. If no, why not. If yes, what groups/jobs and why? _____

19. What specific suggestions do you have for improving this program? _____

20. Other Comments: _____

Figure 4-1. (Continued)

to illustrate many of the issues involving potential content items for questionnaire design with emphasis on application (Level 3) and Impact (Level 4).

Progress with objectives. Sometimes it is helpful to assess progress with the objectives in the follow-up evaluation as is illustrated in question 1 in Figure 4-1. While this issue is usually assessed during the program (because it is Level 1 data), it can be helpful to revisit the objectives after the participants have had an opportunity to apply what has been learned.

Action plan implementation. If an action plan is required in the program, the questionnaire should reference the plan and determine the extent to which it has been implemented. If the action plan requirement is very low key, perhaps only one question would be devoted to the follow-up on the action plan, as illustrated in question 2 in Figure 4-1. If the action plan is very comprehensive and contains an abundance of Level 3 and 4 data, then the questionnaire takes a secondary role and most of the data collection process will focus directly on the status of the completed action plan.

Use of program materials and handouts. If participants are provided with materials to use on the job, it may be helpful to determine the extent to which these materials are used. This is particularly helpful when operating manuals, reference books, and job aids have been distributed and explained in the program and are expected to be used on the job. Question 3 in Figure 4-1 focuses on this issue.

Application of knowledge/skills. As shown in question 4 in Figure 4-1, it is helpful to measure application by determining the level of improvement in skills linked directly to the program. A more detailed variation of this question is to list each skill and indicate the frequency of use and the effectiveness of use of these skills. For many skills, it is important to experience frequent use quickly after acquisition so that the skills become internalized. In this example, question 5 addresses the skill frequency issue.

Changes with work. Sometimes it is helpful to determine what specific activities or processes have changed about participants' work as a result of the program. As question 6 in Figure 4-1 illustrates, the participant explores how the skill applications (listed previously) have actually changed work habits, processes, and output.

Improvements/accomplishments. Question 7 in Figure 4-1 begins a series of four business impact questions that are appropriate for most follow-up questionnaires. This question seeks specific accomplishments and improvements linked directly to the program and focuses on specific measurable successes that can be identified easily by the participants. Because this question is an open-ended question, it can be helpful to provide examples that indicate the nature and range of responses requested. However, examples can also be constraining in nature and may actually limit the responses.

Monetary impact. Perhaps the most difficult question (number 8 in Figure 4-1) asks participants to provide monetary values for the improvements identified in question 7. Only the first year improvement is sought. Participants are asked to specify net improvements so that the actual monetary values will represent gains from the program. An important part of the question is the basis for the calculation, where participants specify the steps taken to develop the annual net value and the assumptions made in the analysis. It is very important for the basis to be completed with enough detail to understand the process.

Improvements linked with program. The next question in the impact series (question 9 in Figure 4-1) isolates the effects of the program. Participants indicate the percent of improvement that is related directly to the program. As an alternative, participants may be provided with the various factors that have influenced the results and are asked to allocate the percentages to each factor.

Confidence level. To adjust for the uncertainty of data provided in questions 8 and 9, participants were asked to offer a level of confidence for the estimation, expressed as a percentage with a range of 0 to 100 percent, as shown in question 10 in Figure 4-1. This input allows participants to reflect their level of uncertainty with this process.

Investment perception. The value of the program, from the viewpoint of the participant, can be useful information. As illustrated in question 11 in Figure 4-1, participants are asked if they perceive this program to represent an appropriate investment. Another option for this question is to present the actual cost of the program so that participants can respond more accurately from the investment perspective. It may be useful to express the cost as a per-participant cost. Also, the question can be divided into two parts—one reflecting the investment of funds by the company and the other an investment in the participants time in the program.

Linkage with output measures. Sometimes it is helpful to determine the degree to which the program has influenced certain output measures, as shown in question 12 in Figure 4-1. In some situations, a detailed analysis may reveal specifically which measures this program has influenced. However, when this issue is uncertain, it may be helpful to list the potential business performance measures influenced by the program and seek input from the participants. The question should be worded so that the frame of reference is for the time period after the program was conducted.

Barriers. A variety of barriers can influence the successful application of the skills and knowledge learned in the training program. Question 13 in Figure 4-1 identifies these barriers. As an alternative, the perceived barriers are listed and participants check all that apply. Still another variation is to list the barriers with a range of responses, indicating the extent to which the barrier inhibited results.

Enablers. Just as important as barriers are the enablers, those issues, events, or situations that enable the process to be applied successfully on the job. Question 14 provides an open-ended question for enablers. The same options are available with this question as in the question on barriers.

Management support. For most programs, management support is critical to the successful application of newly acquired skills. At least one question should be included on the degree of management support, such as 15. Sometimes this question is structured so that various descriptions of management support are detailed, and participants check the one that applies to their situation. This information is very beneficial to help remove or minimize barriers.

Other benefits. In most programs, additional benefits will begin to emerge, particularly in the intangible area. Participants should be asked to detail any benefits not presented elsewhere. In this example, question 16 shows the open-ended question for additional benefits.

Other solutions. The leadership development program may be only one of many potential solutions for improving performance. If the needs assessment is faulty or if there are alternative approaches to developing the desired skills or knowledge, other potential solutions could be more effective and achieve the same success. In question 17 the participant is asked to identify other solutions that could have been effective in obtaining the same or similar results.

Target audience recommendations. Sometimes it is helpful to solicit input about the most appropriate target audience for this program. In question 18, the participants are asked to indicate which groups of employees would benefit the most from attending this program.

Suggestions for improvement. As a final wrap-up question, participants are asked to provide suggestions for improving any part of the program or process. As illustrated in question 19, the open-ended structure is intended to solicit qualitative responses to be used to make improvements.

Improving the Response Rate for Questionnaires and Surveys

Content items represent a wide range of potential issues to explore in a follow-up questionnaire or survey. Obviously, asking all of the questions could cause the response rate to be reduced considerably. The challenge, therefore, is to tackle questionnaire design and administration for the maximum response rate. This is a critical issue when the questionnaire is the primary data collection method and most of the evaluation hinges on questionnaire results. The following actions shown in Figure 4-2 can be taken to increase response rate. Collectively, these items help boost response rates of follow-up questionnaires. Using all of these strategies can result in a 50 to 60 percent response rate, even with lengthy questionnaires that might take 45 minutes to complete.

INTERVIEWS

Another helpful collection method is the interview, although it is not used in evaluation as frequently as questionnaires. The

Increasing Questionnaire Response Rates

- ❑ Provide advance communication about the questionnaire.
- ❑ Clearly communicate the reason for the questionnaire.
- ❑ Indicate who will see the results of the questionnaire.
- ❑ Show how the data will be integrated with other data.
- ❑ Let participants know what actions will be taken based on data.
- ❑ Keep the questionnaire simple and as brief as possible.
- ❑ Allow for responses to be anonymous – or at least confidential.
- ❑ Make it easy to respond; include a self-addressed, stamped envelope/e-mail.
- ❑ Use the local manager to distribute the questionnaires, show support, and encourage response.
- ❑ If appropriate, let the target audience know that they are part of a carefully selected sample.
- ❑ Provide one or two follow-up reminders, using a different medium.
- ❑ Have the introduction letter signed by a top executive or administrator.
- ❑ Enclose a giveaway item with the questionnaire (pen, money, etc.).
- ❑ Provide an incentive (or chance or incentive) for quick response.
- ❑ Send a summary of results to target audience.
- ❑ Distribute questionnaire to a captive audience.
- ❑ Consider an alternative distribution channel, such as e-mail.
- ❑ Have a third party collect and analyze data.
- ❑ Communicate the time limit for submitting responses.
- ❑ Review the questionnaire at the end of the formal session.
- ❑ Allow for completion of the survey during normal work hours.
- ❑ Add emotional appeal.
- ❑ Design the questionnaire to attract attention, with a professional format.
- ❑ Provide options to respond (paper, e-mail, Web site).
- ❑ Use a local coordinator to help distribute and collect questionnaires.
- ❑ Frame questions so participants can respond appropriately and accurately.

Figure 4-2. Increasing questionnaire response rates.

leadership development staff, the participant's supervisor, or an outside third party can conduct interviews. Interviews can secure data not available in performance records or data difficult to obtain through written responses or observations (Kvale, 1996). Also, interviews can uncover success stories that can be useful in communicating evaluation results. Participants may be reluctant to describe their results in a questionnaire but will volunteer the information to a skillful interviewer who uses probing techniques. While the interview process uncovers reaction, learning, and impact, it is used primarily with application data. A major disadvantage of the interview is that it is time-consuming and requires interviewer preparation to ensure that the process is consistent.

Types of Interviews

Interviews usually fall into two basic types: structured and unstructured. A structured interview is much like a questionnaire. Specific questions are asked with little room to deviate from the desired responses. The primary advantages of the structured interview over the questionnaire are that the interview process can ensure that the questionnaire is completed and the interviewer understands the responses supplied by the participant.

The unstructured interview allows for probing for additional information. This type of interview uses a few general questions, which can lead into more detailed information as important data are uncovered. The interviewer must be skilled in the probing process.

Interview Guidelines

The design issues and steps for interviews are similar to those of the questionnaire. A few key issues need emphasis.

Develop questions to be asked. After the type of interview is determined, specific questions need to be developed. Questions should be brief, precise, and designed for easy response.

Try out the interview. The interview should be tested on a small number of participants. If possible, the interviews should be conducted as part of the trial run of the leadership development program. The responses should be analyzed and the interview revised, if necessary.

Prepare the interviewers. The interviewer should have the appropriate level of core skills, including active listening, asking probing questions, and collecting and summarizing information.

Provide clear instructions to the participant. The participant should understand the purpose of the interview and know how the information will be used. Expectations, conditions, and rules of the interview should be discussed thoroughly. For example, the participant should know if statements would be kept confidential.

Administer the interviews according to a scheduled plan. As with the other evaluation instruments, interviews need to be conducted according to a predetermined plan. The timing of the interview, the individual who conducts the interview, and the location of the interview are all issues that become relevant when developing a plan. For a large number of participants, a sampling plan may be necessary to save time and reduce the evaluation cost.

Focus Groups

An extension of the interview, focus groups are particularly helpful when in-depth feedback is needed for a Level 3 evaluation. The focus group involves a small group discussion conducted by an experienced facilitator. It is designed to solicit qualitative judgments on a planned topic or issue. Group members are all required to provide their input, as individual input builds on group input (Subramony *et al.*, 2002).

When compared with questionnaires, surveys, tests, or interviews, the focus group strategy has several advantages. The basic premise of using focus groups is that when quality judgments are subjective, several individual judgments are better than one. The group process, where participants stimulate ideas in others, is an effective method for generating qualitative data. It is inexpensive and can be planned and conducted quickly. Its flexibility makes it possible to explore a training program's unexpected outcomes or applications.

Applications for Evaluation

The focus group is particularly helpful when qualitative information is needed about the success of a leadership development program. For example, the focus group can be used in the following situations:

- evaluate the reactions to specific exercises, cases, simulations, or other components of a leadership development program
- assess the overall effectiveness of program application
- assess the impact of the program in a follow-up evaluation after the program is completed

Essentially, focus groups are helpful when evaluation information is needed but cannot be collected adequately with questionnaires, interviews, or quantitative methods.

Guidelines

While there are no set rules on how to use focus groups for evaluation, the following guidelines are helpful:

Ensure that management buys into the focus group process. Because this is a relatively new process for evaluation, it might be unknown to management. Managers need to understand focus groups and their advantages. This should raise their level of confidence in the information obtained from group sessions.

Plan topics, questions, and strategy carefully. As with any evaluation instrument, planning is critical. The specific topics, questions, and issues to be discussed must be planned and sequenced carefully. This enhances the comparison of results from one group to another and ensures that the group process is effective and stays on track.

Keep the group size small. While there is no magic group size, a range of 8 to 12 seems to be appropriate for most focus group applications. A group has to be large enough to ensure different points of view, but small enough to provide every participant a chance to freely exchange comments.

Use a representative sample of the target population. If possible, groups should be selected to represent the target population. The group should be homogeneous in experience, rank, and job level in the organization.

Facilitators must have appropriate expertise. The success of a focus group rests with the facilitator, who must be skilled in the focus group process. Facilitators must know how to control aggressive members of the group and diffuse the input from those who want to dominate the group. Also, facilitators must be able to create an environment in which participants feel comfortable in offering comments freely and openly. Because of this, some organizations use external facilitators.

In summary, the focus group is an inexpensive and quick way to determine the strengths and weaknesses of leadership development programs. However, for a complete evaluation, focus group information should be combined with data from other instruments.

Observations

Another potentially useful data collection method is observing participants and recording any changes in their behavior. The observer may be a member of the leadership development staff, the participant's supervisor, a member of a peer group, or an external party. The most common observer, and probably the most practical, is a member of the leadership development staff.

Guidelines for Effective Observation

Observation is often misused or misapplied to evaluation situations, leaving some to abandon the process. The effectiveness of observation can be improved with the following guidelines.

The observations should be systematic. The observation process must be planned so that it is executed effectively without any surprises. The persons observed should know in advance about the observation and why they are being observed unless the observation is planned to be invisible. The timing of observations should be a part of the plan. There are right times to observe a participant, and there are wrong times. If a participant is observed when times are not normal (i.e., in a crisis), data collected may be useless.

The observers should know how to interpret and report what they see. Observations involve judgment decisions. The observer must analyze which behaviors are being displayed and what actions the participants are taking. Observers should know how to summarize behavior and report results in a meaningful manner.

The observer's influence should be minimized. Except for mystery observers and electronic observations, it is impossible to completely isolate the overall effect of an observer. Participants may display the behavior they think is appropriate, and they will usually be at their best. The presence of the observer must be minimized. To the extent possible, the observer should blend into the work environment or extend the observation period.

Select observers carefully. Observers are usually independent of the participants, typically a member of the leadership development staff. The independent observer is usually more skilled at recording behavior and making interpretations of behavior. They are usually unbiased in these interpretations. Using them enables the leadership development function to avoid having to prepare observers and relieves the operating organization of that responsibility. However, the leadership development staff observer has the appearance of an outsider checking the work of others. There may be a tendency for participants to overreact and possibly resent this kind of observer. Sometimes it might be more plausible to recruit observers from outside the organization. This approach has an advantage of neutralizing the prejudicial feelings entering the decisions.

Observers must be fully prepared. Observers must fully understand what information is needed and what skills are covered in the program. They must be trained for the assignment and provided a chance to practice observation skills.

Observation Methods

Five methods of observation are utilized, depending on the circumstances surrounding the type of information needed. Each method is described briefly.

Behavior Checklist and Codes. A behavior checklist can be useful for recording the presence, absence, frequency, or duration of a participant's behavior as it occurs. A checklist will not usually provide information on the quality, intensity, or possibly the circumstances surrounding the behavior observed. The checklist is useful because an observer can identify exactly which behaviors should or should not occur. Measuring the duration of a behavior may be more difficult and requires a stopwatch and a place on the form to record the time interval. This factor is usually not as important when compared to whether a particular behavior was observed and how often. The number of behaviors listed in the checklist should be small and listed in a logical sequence, if they normally occur in a sequence. A variation of this approach involves a coding of behaviors on a form. This method is less time-consuming because the code is entered that identifies a specific behavior.

Delayed Report Method. With a delayed report method, the observer does not use any forms or written materials during the observation. The information is recorded either after the observation is completed or at particular time intervals during an observation. The observer attempts to reconstruct what has been observed during the observation period. The advantage of this approach is that the observer is not as noticeable, and there are no forms being completed or notes being taken during the observation. The observer can blend into the situation and be less distracting. An obvious disadvantage is that the information written may not be as accurate and reliable as the information collected at the time it occurred. A variation of this approach is the 360-degree feedback process in which surveys are completed on other individuals based on observations within a specific time frame.

Video Recording. A video camera records behavior in every detail, an obvious advantage. However, this intrusion may be awkward and cumbersome, and the participants may be unnecessarily nervous or self-conscious when they are being videotaped. If the camera is concealed, the privacy of the participant may be invaded. Because of this, video recording of on-the-job behavior is not frequently used.

Audio Monitoring. Monitoring conversations of participants who are using the skills taught in a program is an effective observation technique. For example, in a large communication company's telemarketing department, sales representatives are trained to sell equipment by telephone. To determine if employees are using the skills properly, telephone conversations are monitored on a selected and sometimes random basis. While this approach may stir some controversy, it is an effective way to determine if skills are being applied consistently and effectively. For it to work smoothly, it must be fully explained and the rules clearly communicated.

Computer Monitoring. For employees who work regularly with a keyboard, computer monitoring may be an effective way to "observe" participants as they perform job tasks or take specific actions. The computer monitors times, sequence of steps, and other activities to determine if the participant is performing according to what was learned in the program. As technology continues to be a significant part of jobs, computer monitoring holds more promise of monitoring actual applications on the job. This is particularly helpful for Level 3 data.

360° Feedback. Probably the most effective way to capture leader behavior change is through a 360° feedback process. This technique involves observation by several groups, collected by survey, and processed electronically. The input typically includes direct reports (followers), colleagues, immediate manager, internal (or external) customers, and self reports from the leader. This can be very powerful data to monitor changes in leader behavior.

BUSINESS PERFORMANCE MONITORING

Data are available in every organization to measure performance. Monitoring performance data enables management to measure performance in terms of output, quality, costs, and time. In determining the use of data in the evaluation, the first consideration should be existing databases and reports. In most organizations, performance data suitable for measuring the improvement resulting from a leadership development program are available (Mondschein, 1999). If not, additional record-keeping systems will have to be developed for measurement and analysis. At this point, as with many other points in the process, the question of economics enters. Is it economical to develop the record-keeping system necessary to evaluate a leadership development program? If the costs are greater than the expected return for the entire program, then it is meaningless to develop them.

Using Current Measures

The recommended approach is to use existing performance measures, if available. Specific guidelines are recommended to ensure that current measurement systems are developed easily.

Identify appropriate measures. Performance measures should be researched to identify those that are related to the proposed objectives of the program. Frequently, an organization will have several performance measures related to the same item. For example, the efficiency of a production unit can be measured in a variety of ways:

- number of units produced per hour
- number of on-schedule production units
- percent utilization of the equipment
- percent of equipment downtime
- labor cost per unit of production
- overtime required per piece of production
- total unit cost

Each of these, in its own way, measures the efficiency or effectiveness of the production unit. All related measures should be reviewed to determine those most relevant to the leadership development program.

Convert current measures to usable ones. Occasionally, existing performance measures are integrated with other data and it may be difficult to keep them isolated from unrelated data. In this situation, all existing related measures should be extracted and retabulated to be more appropriate for comparison in the evaluation. At times, conversion factors may be necessary. For example, the average number of new sales orders per month may be presented regularly in the performance measures for the sales department. In addition, the sales costs per sales representative are also presented. However, in the evaluation of a leadership development program, the average cost per new sale is needed. The two existing performance records are required to develop data necessary for comparison.

Develop a collection plan. A data collection plan defines data to be collected, the source of data, when data are collected, who will collect it, and where it will be collected. A blank copy of the plan was presented in Chapter 2, Figure 2-4. This plan should contain provisions for the evaluator to secure copies of performance reports in a timely manner so that the items can be recorded and available for analysis.

Developing New Measures

In some cases, data are not available for the information needed to measure the effectiveness of a leadership development program. The leadership development staff must work with the participating organization to develop record-keeping systems, if this is economically feasible. In one organization, a new employee orientation system was implemented on a company-wide basis. Several measures were planned, including early turnover representing the percentage of employees who left the company in the first six months of their employment. An improved employee orientation program should influence this measure. At the time of the program's inception, this measure was not available. When the program was implemented, the organization began collecting early turnover figures for comparison. Typical questions when creating new measures:

- Which department will develop the measurement system?
- Who will record and monitor data?
- Where will it be recorded?
- Will forms be used?

These questions will usually involve other departments or a management decision that extends beyond the scope of the leadership development function. Possibly the administration division, HR department, or information technology section will be instrumental in helping determine if new measures are needed and, if so, how they will be collected.

ACTION PLANNING AND FOLLOW-UP ASSIGNMENTS

In some cases, follow-up assignments can develop Level 3 and Level 4 data. In a typical follow-up assignment, the participant is instructed to meet a goal or to complete a particular task or project by the determined follow-up date. A summary of the results of these completed assignments provides further evidence of the impact of the program.

The action plan is the most common type of follow-up assignment and is fully described in this section. With this approach, participants are required to develop action plans as part of the program. Action plans contain detailed steps to accomplish specific objectives related to the program. The plan is typically prepared on a printed form such as the one shown in Figure 4-3. The action plan shows what is to be done, by whom, and the date by which the objectives should be accomplished. The action plan approach is a straightforward, easy-to-use method for determining how participants will change their behavior on the job and achieve success with training. The approach produces data from types of questions, such as:

Name: _____ Instructor Signature _____ Follow-Up Date: _____

Objective: _____ Evaluation Period _____ to_____

Improvement Measure:_____ Current Performance _____ Target Performance_____

Action Steps	Analysis
1._____	A. What is the unit of measure?_____
2._____	B. What is the value (cost) of one unit? $_____
3._____	C. How did you arrive at this value?
4._____	_____
5._____	_____
6._____	D. How much did the measure change during the evaluation period?
	(monthly value) _____
7._____	E. What percent of this change was actually caused by this
	program? _____%
Intangible Benefits:	F. What level of confidence do you place on the above
	information? (100%=Certainty and 0%=No Confidence)
	_____%

*Comments:*_____
_____
_____
_____

Figure 4-3. Action plan template.

- What steps or action items have been accomplished and when?
- What on-the-job improvements or accomplishments have been realized since the program was conducted?
- How much of the improvements are linked to the program?
- What may have prevented participants from accomplishing specific action items?
- What is the monetary value of the improvement?

With this information, leadership development professionals can decide if a program should be modified and in what ways, while managers can assess the findings to evaluate the worth of the program.

Developing the Action Plan

The development of the action plan requires two tasks: (1) determining the areas for action and (2) writing the action items. Both tasks should be completed during the program. The areas or measures for action should originate from the need for the program, the content of the program, and, at the same time, be related to on-the-job activities. Participants can independently develop a list of potential areas for action or a list may be generated in group discussions. The list may include a measure needing improvement or represent an opportunity for increased performance. Typical categories are:

- Productivity
- Sales, revenue
- Quality/process improvement
- Efficiency
- Time savings
- Cost savings
- Complaints
- Job satisfaction
- Work habits
- Customer satisfaction
- Customer service

The specific action items support the business measure and are usually more difficult to write than the identification of the action areas. The most important characteristic of an action item is that it is written so that everyone involved will know when it occurs. One way to help achieve this goal is to use specific action verbs. Some examples of action items are:

- *Learn* how to operate the new RC-105 drill press machine in the adjacent department, by *(date)*.
- *Identify* and *secure* a new customer account, by *(date)*.
- *Handle* every piece of paper only once to improve my personal time management, by *(date)*.
- *Learn* to talk with my employees directly about a problem that arises rather than avoiding a confrontation, by *(date)*.

Typical questions when developing action steps:

- How much time will this action take?
- Are the skills for accomplishing this action item available?
- Who has the authority to implement the action plan?
- Will this action have an effect on other individuals?
- Are there any organizational constraints for accomplishing this action item?

If appropriate, each action item should have a date for completion and indicate other individuals or resources required for completion. Also, planned behavior changes should be observable. It should be obvious to the participant and others when it happens. Action plans, as used in this context, do not require the prior approval or input from the participant's supervisor, although it may be helpful.

Using Action Plans Successfully

The action plan process should be an integral part of the program and not an add-on or optional activity. To gain maximum effectiveness from action plans and to collect data for ROI calculations, the following steps should be implemented.

Communicate the action plan requirement early. One of the most negative reactions to action plans is the surprise factor often inherent in the way in which the process is introduced. When program participants realize that they must develop an unexpected detailed action plan, there is often immediate, built-in resistance. Communicating to participants in advance, where the process is shown to be an integral part of the program, will often minimize resistance. When participants fully realize the benefits before they attend the first session, they take the process more seriously and usually perform the extra steps to make it more successful. In this scenario, the action plan is positioned as an application tool—not an evaluation tool.

Describe the action planning process at the beginning of the program. At the first session, action plan requirements are discussed, including an explanation of the purpose of the process, why it is necessary, and the basic requirements during and after the program. Some facilitators furnish a separate notepad for participants to collect ideas and useful techniques for their action plan. This is a productive way to focus more attention and effort on the process.

Teach the action planning process. An important prerequisite for action plan success is an understanding of how it works and how specific action plans are developed. A portion of the program's agenda is allocated to teaching participants how to develop plans. In this session, the requirements are outlined, special forms and procedures are discussed, and a completed example is distributed and reviewed. Sometimes an entire program module is allocated to this process so that participants will fully understand it and use it. Any available support tools, such as key measures, charts, graphs, suggested topics, and sample calculations should be used in this session to help facilitate the plan's development.

Allow time to develop the plan. When action plans are used to collect data for an ROI calculation, it is important to allow participants time to develop plans during the program. Sometimes it is helpful to have participants work in teams so they can share ideas as they develop specific plans. In these sessions, facilitators often monitor the progress of individuals or teams to keep the process on track and to answer questions. In some management and executive development programs, action plans are developed in an evening session, as a scheduled part of the program.

Have the facilitator approve the action plans. It is essential for the action plan to be related to program objectives and, at the same time, represent an important accomplishment for the organization when it is completed. It is easy for participants to stray from the intent and purposes of action planning and not give it the attention that it deserves. Consequently, it is helpful to have the facilitator or program director actually sign off on the action plan, ensuring that the plan reflects all of the requirements and is appropriate for the program. In some cases, a space is provided for the facilitator's signature on the action plan document.

Require participants to assign a monetary value for each improvement. Participants are asked to determine, calculate, or estimate the monetary value for each improvement outlined in the plan. When the actual improvement has occurred, participants will use these values to capture the annual monetary benefits of the plan. For this step to be effective, it may be helpful to provide examples of typical ways in which values can be assigned to the actual data (Phillips and Phillips, 2001).

Ask participants to isolate the effects of the program. Although the action plan is initiated because of the training program, the actual improvements reported on the action plan may be influenced by other factors. Thus, the action planning process should not take full credit for the improvement. For example, an action plan to reduce employee turnover in an agency could take only partial credit for an improvement because of the other variables that influenced the turnover rate (Phillips and Phillips, 2002). While there are at least nine ways to isolate the effects of a program, participant estimation is usually more appropriate in the action planning process. Consequently, the participants are asked to estimate the percent of the improvement actually related to this particular program. This question can be asked on the action plan form or on a follow-up questionnaire.

Ask participants to provide a confidence level for estimates. Because the process to convert data to monetary values may not be exact and the amount of the improvement related directly to the program may not be precise, participants are asked to indicate their level of confidence in those two values, collectively. On a scale of 0 to 100 percent, where 0 percent means no confidence and 100 percent means complete confidence, this value provides participants a mechanism to express their uneasiness with their ability to be exact with the process.

Require action plans to be presented to the group, if possible. There is no better way to secure commitment and ownership of the action planning process than to have a participant describe his or her action plan in front of fellow participants. Presenting the action plan helps ensure that the process is developed thoroughly and will be implemented on the job. Sometimes the process spurns competition among the group. If the number of participants is too large for individual presentations, perhaps one participant can be selected from the team (if the plans are developed in teams). Under these circumstances, the team will usually select the best action plan for presentation to the group, raising the bar for others.

Explain the follow-up mechanism. Participants must leave the session with a clear understanding of the timing of the action plan implementation and the planned follow-up. The method in which data will be collected, analyzed, and reported should be discussed openly. Five options are common:

1. The group is reconvened to discuss the progress on the plans.
2. Participants meet with their immediate manager and discuss the success of the plan. A copy is forwarded to the leadership development department.
3. A meeting is held with the program evaluator, the participant, and the participant's manager to discuss the plan and the information contained in it.
4. Participants send the plan to the evaluator and it is discussed in a conference call.
5. Participants send the plan directly to the evaluator with no meetings or discussions. This is the most common option.

While there are other ways to collect data, it is important to select a mechanism that fits the culture, requirements, and constraints of the organization.

Collect action plans at the predetermined follow-up time. Because it is critical to have an excellent response rate, several steps may be necessary to ensure that the action plans are completed and data are returned to the appropriate individual or group for analysis. Some organizations use follow-up reminders by mail or e-mail. Others call participants to check progress. Still others offer assistance in developing the final plan. These steps may require additional resources, which have to be weighed against the importance of having more data. When the action plan process is implemented as outlined in this chapter, the response rates will normally be very high, in the 60 to 90 percent range. Usually participants will see the importance of the process and will develop their plans in detail before leaving the program.

Summarize data and calculate the ROI. If developed properly, each action plan should have annualized monetary values associated with improvements. Also, each individual has indicated the percent of the improvement that is directly related to the program. Finally, each participant has provided a confidence percentage to reflect their uncertainty with the process and the subjective nature of some of the data that may be provided.

Because this process involves some estimates, it may not appear to be very credible. Several adjustments during the analysis make the process very credible and believable. The following adjustments are made:

Step 1: For those participants who do not provide data, it is assumed that they had no improvement to report. This is a very conservative assumption.

Step 2: Each value is checked for realism, usability, and feasibility. Extreme values are discarded and omitted from the analysis.

Step 3: Because the improvement is annualized, it is assumed the program had no improvement after the first year. Some programs should add value at years two and three.

Step 4: The improvement from step 3 is then adjusted by the confidence level, multiplying it by the confidence percent. The confidence level is actually an error suggested by the participants. For example, a participant indicating 80 percent confidence with the process is reflecting a 20 percent error possibility. In a $10,000 estimate with an 80 percent confidence factor, the participant is suggesting that the value could be in the range of $8,000 to $12,000. To be conservative, the lower number is used. Thus, the confidence factor is multiplied by the amount of improvement.

Step 5: The new values are then adjusted by the percent of the improvement related directly to the program using straight multiplication. This isolates the effects of training.

The monetary values determined in these five steps are totaled to arrive at a total program benefit. Because these values are already annualized, the total of these benefits becomes the annual benefits for the program. This value is placed in the numerator of the ROI formula to calculate the ROI.

Advantages/Disadvantages

Although there are many advantages, there are at least two concerns with action plans. The process relies on direct input from the participant, usually with no assurance of anonymity. As such, there is a possibility that the information is biased and unreliable. Also, action plans can be time-consuming for the participant and, if the participant's supervisor is not involved in the process, there may be a tendency for the participant not to complete the assignment.

As this section has illustrated, the action plan approach has many inherent advantages. Action plans are simple and easy to administer; are easily understood by participants; are used with a wide variety of programs; are appropriate for all types of data; are able to measure reaction, learning, behavior changes, and results; and may be used with or without other evaluation methods. The two disadvantages may be overcome with careful planning and implementation. Because of the tremendous flexibility and versatility of the process, and the conservative adjustments that can be made in analysis, action plans have become an important data collection tool for the ROI analysis.

PERFORMANCE CONTRACTS

The performance contract is essentially a slight variation of the action planning process with a preprogram commitment. Based on the principle of mutual goal setting, a performance contract is a written agreement between a participant and the participant's supervisor. The participant agrees to improve performance in an area of mutual concern related to the content of the leadership development program. The agreement is in the form of a project to be completed or a goal to be accomplished soon after the program is completed. The agreement spells out what is to be accomplished, at what time, and with what results.

Performance contracting is administered much the same way as the action planning process. Although the steps can vary according to the specific kind of contract and the organization, a common sequence of events is as follows:

- The employee (participant) decides to participate in a leadership development program.

- The participant and manager mutually agree on a topic for improvement with a specific measure(s).
- Specific, measurable goals are set.
- The participant is involved in the program where the contract is discussed and plans are developed to accomplish the goals.
- After the program, the participant works on the contract against a specific deadline.
- The participant reports the results to his or her immediate manager.
- The manager and participant document the results and forward a copy to the leadership development department along with appropriate comments.

The individuals mutually select the topic/measure to be improved prior to program inception. The process of selecting the area for improvement is similar to the process used in the action planning process. The topic can cover one or more of the following areas:

- *Routine performance* includes specific improvements in routine performance measures, such as production targets, efficiency, and error rates.
- *Problem solving* focuses on specific problems, such as an unexpected increase in accidents, a decrease in efficiency, or a loss of morale.
- *Innovative or creative applications* include initiating changes or improvements in work practices, methods, procedures, techniques, and processes.
- *Personal development* involves learning new information or acquiring new skills to increase individual effectiveness.

The topic selected should be stated in terms of one or more objectives. The objectives should state what is to be accomplished when the contract is complete. These objectives should be:

- written
- understandable (by all involved)
- challenging (requiring an unusual effort to achieve)
- achievable (something that can be accomplished)
- largely under the control of the participant
- measurable and dated

The details required to accomplish the contract objectives are developed following the guidelines under the action plans presented earlier. Also, the methods for analyzing data and reporting progress are essentially the same, as with the action planning process.

SELECTING THE APPROPRIATE METHOD

This chapter has presented a variety of methods to capture application and business impact data. Collectively, they offer a wide range of opportunities to collect data in a variety of situations. Several issues should be considered when deciding which method is appropriate for a situation.

Type of Data

Perhaps one of the most important issues to consider when selecting the method is the type of data to be collected. Some methods are more appropriate for Level 4, whereas others are best for Level 3. Still others are best for Levels 2 or 1. Table 4-1 shows the most appropriate type of data for a specific method. Questionnaires and surveys, observations, interviews, and focus groups are suited for all levels. Tests are appropriate for Level 2. Questionnaires and surveys are best for Level 1, although interviews and focus groups can be used, but they are often too costly. Performance monitoring, performance contracting, action planning, and questionnaires can capture Level 4 data easily.

Table 4-1
Collecting Data: The Methods

	Level 1	Level 2	Level 3	Level 4
❏ Questionnaires/Surveys	✓	✓	✓	✓
❏ Tests		✓		
❏ Interviews			✓	
❏ Focus Groups			✓	
❏ Observations		✓	✓	
❏ Action Planning			✓	✓
❏ Performance Contracting			✓	✓
❏ Performance Monitoring				✓

Participants' Time for Data Input

Another important factor in selecting the data collection method is the amount of time that participants must take with data collection. Time requirements should always be minimized, and the method should be positioned so that it is value-added activity (i.e., the participants understand that this activity is something they perceive as valuable so they will not resist). This requirement often means that sampling is used to keep the total participant time to a reasonable amount. Some methods, such as business performance monitoring, require no participant time, whereas others, such as interviews and focus groups, require a significant investment in time.

Management's Time for Data Input

The time that a participant's immediate manager must allocate to data collection is another important issue in the method selection. This time requirement should always be minimized. Some methods, such as performance contracting, may require much involvement from the manager prior to, and after, the program. Other methods, such as questionnaires administered directly to participants, may not require any manager time.

Cost of Method

Cost is always a consideration when selecting the method. Some data collection methods are more expensive than others. For example, interviews and observations are very expensive. Surveys, questionnaires, and performance monitoring are usually inexpensive.

Disruption of Normal Work Activities

Another key issue in selecting the appropriate method, and perhaps the one that generates the most concern with managers, is the amount of disruption the data collection will create. Routine work processes should be disrupted as little as possible. Some data collection techniques, such as performance monitoring, require very little time and distraction from normal activities. Questionnaires generally do not disrupt the work environment and can often be completed in only a few minutes, or even after normal work hours. On the other extreme, some items such as observations and interviews may be too disruptive for the work unit.

Accuracy of Method

The accuracy of the technique is another factor when selecting the method. Some data collection methods are more accurate than others. For example, performance monitoring is usually very accurate, whereas questionnaires can be distorted and unreliable. If actual on-the-job behavior must be captured, unobtrusive observation is clearly one of the most accurate processes.

Built-In Design Possibility

Because it is important to build in data collection for many of the evaluation plans, the relative ease at which the method can be built into the program is important; it must become an integral part of the program. Some methods, such as action plans, can be easily built into the design of the program. Other methods, such as observation, are more difficult.

For some situations, the program is redesigned to allow for a follow-up session where evaluation is addressed, along with additional modules of the program. For example, a leadership development program (a consecutive three-day program) was redesigned as a two-day workshop to build skills, followed by a one-day session three weeks later. Thus, the follow-up session provided an opportunity for additional training and evaluation. During the first part of the last day, Level 3 evaluation data were collected using a focus group process. Also, specific barriers and problems encountered in applying the skills were discussed. The second half of the day was devoted to additional skill building and refinement along with techniques to overcome the particular barriers to using the skills. Thus, in effect, the redesigned program provided a mechanism for follow-up.

Utility of an Additional Method

Because there are many different methods used to collect data, it is tempting to use too many data collection methods. Multiple data collection methods add time and costs to evaluation and may result in very little additional value. Utility refers to the added value of the use of an additional data collection method. When more than one method is used, this question should always be addressed. Does the value obtained from additional data warrant the extra time and expense of the method? If the answer is no, the additional method should not be implemented.

Cultural Bias for Data Collection Method

The culture or philosophy of the organization can dictate which data collection methods are used. For example, some organizations are accustomed to using questionnaires and prefer to use them in their culture. Other organizations will not use observation because their culture does not support the potential "invasion of privacy" associated with it.

DATA TABULATION ISSUES

Data must be collected using one or more of the methods outlined in this chapter. As data are collected, several other issues need to be addressed and clarified.

Use the Most Credible Source

This is a principle discussed earlier, but it is worth repeating. Data used in the analysis must be the most credible data available. If data are collected from more than once source, the most credible one is used, if there is clearly a difference.

Missing Data

It is rare for all the participants to provide data in a follow-up evaluation. The philosophy described in this chapter is to use only data available for the total benefits. This philosophy is based on making every attempt possible to collect data from every participant, if at all possible. In reality, the return rate of questionnaires or the participation rate of other data collection methods will probably be in the 60 to 80 percent range. Below 50 percent should be considered questionable because of the extreme negative impact it will have on the results.

Data Summary

Data should be tabulated and summarized, ready for analysis. Ideally, tabulation should be organized by particular evaluation levels and issues. Tables can be summarized, analyzed, and then reported eventually in the impact study.

Extreme Data

As data are entered, there should be some review of data for its reasonableness. Extreme data items and unsupported claims should be omitted.

These rules for initially adjusting, summarizing, and tabulating data are critical in preparing for the analysis. They take a very conservative approach and, consequently, build credibility with the target audience.

SHORTCUT WAYS TO MEASURE APPLICATION AND BUSINESS IMPACT

Although this section presented a variety of techniques to measure application and business impact, ranging from questionnaires to observation to action plans, a simplified approach for low-key, inexpensive projects is to use a simple questionnaire. The questionnaire presented in Figure 4-1 is very detailed. A much more simplified questionnaire addressing five or six key issues would be sufficient for small-scale projects. The areas that should be targeted are actual changes in:

- Work and skills applied
- Specific implementation issues
- Degree of success in implementation
- Problems encountered in implementation
- Issues that supported implementation

Another option is to combine data collected on reaction and satisfaction with data on application and business impact. These are all related issues, and a questionnaire combining the key issues may be sufficient. The important point is to collect data in the simplest way to see how well the project worked and what the impact was.

FINAL THOUGHTS

Measuring application and business impact is a critical issue for most leadership development programs. It would be hard to understand the success of a leadership development program unless there was some indication as to what program participants are doing differently—how performance has changed and, in turn, how the business was driven by the changes that participants made. These essential measures determine not only the success achieved, but areas where improvement is needed and areas where the success can be replicated in the future. In addition to performance monitoring, follow-up questionnaires and action plans, as described in this chapter, are used regularly to collect data. Other methods can be helpful to develop a complete picture of application of the leadership development program and subsequent business impact. The credibility of data will always be an issue when this level of data is collected and analyzed. Several strategies are offered to enhance the credibility of data analysis.

CASE STUDY—PART C INTERNATIONAL CAR RENTAL

Follow-Up Questionnaire

While the topics explored may vary considerably, Figure 4-4 shows the questions used with this group. Important areas to explore include application of skills, impact analysis, barriers to application, and enablers. To improve the response rates, a variety of techniques were used. Twenty of the items listed in Figure 4-2 are actually utilized in this evaluation to obtain a response rate of 81 percent. One of the most important techniques was to review the questionnaire with participants—question by question—at the end of the four-day workshop, clarifying the issues, creating expectations, and gaining commitment to provide data.

DISCUSSION QUESTIONS

1. What is the recommended method for isolating the effects of the program?
2. Complete the ROI analysis plan, Figure 4-5

Follow Up Questionnaire

Program Name   End Date of Program   Learning Provider Name

Our records indicate that you participated in the above program. Your participation in this follow-up survey is important to the continuous improvement of the program. Completion of this survey may take 45 to 60 minutes. Thank you in advance for your input.

Currency

1. This survey requires some information to be completed in monetary value. Please indicate the currency you will use to complete the questions requiring monetary value.

Currency:

PROGRAM COMPLETION

2. Did you: ○ complete ○ partially complete ○ not complete the program? If you did not complete please go to the final question.

REACTION

	Strongly Agree				Strongly Disagree	
	5	4	3	2	1	n/a
3. I did recommend the program to others.	○	○	○	○	○	○
	5	4	3	2	1	n/a
4. The program was a worthwhile investment for my organization.	○	○	○	○	○	○
	5	4	3	2	1	n/a
5. The program was a good use of my time.	○	○	○	○	○	○
	5	4	3	2	1	n/a
6. The program was a good use of taxpayer funds for public sector organizations.	○	○	○	○	○	○
	5	4	3	2	1	n/a
7. The program was relevant to my work.	○	○	○	○	○	○
	5	4	3	2	1	n/a
8. The program was important to my work.	○	○	○	○	○	○
	5	4	3	2	1	n/a
9. The program provided me with new information.	○	○	○	○	○	○

LEARNING

	Strongly Agree				Strongly Disagree	
	5	4	3	2	1	n/a
10. I learned new knowledge/skills from this program.	○	○	○	○	○	○
	5	4	3	2	1	n/a
11. I am confident in my ability to apply the knowledge/skills learned from this program.	○	○	○	○	○	○

LEARNING (continued)

12. Rate your level of improvement in skill or knowledge derived from the program content. A 0% is no improvement and a 100% is significant improvement. Check only one.
□0% □10% □20% □30% □40% □50% □60% □70% □80% □90% □100%

APPLICATION

	Major Extent				Minor Extent	
	5	4	3	2	1	n/a
13. To what extent did you apply the knowledge/skills learned during the program?	○	○	○	○	○	○
	Frequently (exceptional)				Infrequently (unacceptable)	
	5	4	3	2	1	n/a
14. How frequently did you apply the knowledge/skills learned during the program?	○	○	○	○	○	○
	High				Low	
	5	4	3	2	1	n/a
15. What is your level of effectiveness with the knowledge/skills learned during the program?	○	○	○	○	○	○

16. What percent of your total work time did you spend on tasks that require the knowledge/skills presented in this program? Check only one.
□0% □10% □20% □30% □40% □50% □60% □70% □80% □90% □100%

17. On a scale of 0% (not at all) to 100% (extremely critical), how critical is applying the content of this program to your job success? Check only one.
□0% □10% □20% □30% □40% □50% □60% □70% □80% □90% □100%

BARRIERS/ENABLERS TO APPLICATION

18. Did you perceive barriers in applying the knowledge/skills learned in this program? ○yes ○no

19. Which of the following deterred or prevented you from applying the knowledge/skills learned in the program? (check all that apply)
□ no opportunity to use the skills
□ lack of management support
□ lack of support from colleagues and peers
□ insufficient knowledge and understanding
□ lack of confidence to apply knowledge/skills
□ systems and processes within organization will not support application of knowledge/skills
□ other

Figure 4-4. Questionnaire for leadership challenge.

BARRIERS/ENABLERS TO APPLICATION (continued)

20. If you selected "other" above, please describe here.

21. Which of the following supported you in applying knowledge/skills learned in the program? (check all that apply)
    - ☐ opportunity to use the skills
    - ☐ management support
    - ☐ support from colleagues and peers
    - ☐ sufficient knowledge and understanding
    - ☐ confidence to apply knowledge/skills
    - ☐ systems and processes within organization will support application of knowledge/skills
    - ☐ other

22. If you selected "other" above, please describe here.

IMPACT

23. To what extent did this program positively influence the following measures:

	Significant Influence				No Influence	
	5	4	3	2	1	n/a
productivity	○	○	○	○	○	○
sales	○	○	○	○	○	○
quality	○	○	○	○	○	○
cost	○	○	○	○	○	○
efficiency	○	○	○	○	○	○
time	○	○	○	○	○	○
employee satisfaction	○	○	○	○	○	○
customer satisfaction	○	○	○	○	○	○
other	○	○	○	○	○	○

24. What other measure was positively influenced by this program?

25. Of the measures listed above, improvement in which **one** is most directly linked to the program? (check only one)
    - ☐ productivity
    - ☐ sales
    - ☐ quality
    - ☐ cost
    - ☐ efficiency
    - ☐ time
    - ☐ employee satisfaction
    - ☐ customer satisfaction
    - ☐ other

26. Please define the measure above and its unit for measurement. For example, if you selected "sales" your unit of measure may be "*1 closed sale.*"

IMPACT (continued)

27. For the measure listed as most directly linked to the program, what is the monetary value of improvement for one unit of this measure. For example, the value of a closed sale is sales value times the profit margin ($10,000 x 20%=$2,000). Although this step is difficult please make every effort to estimate the value of a unit. Put the value in the currency you selected, round to nearest whole value, enter numbers only. (ex. $2000.5 should be input as 2000)

28. Please state your basis for the value of the unit of improvement you indicated above. In the closed sale example, a standard value, profit margin, is used, so "standard value" is entered here.

29. For the measure listed as most directly linked to the program, how much has this measure improved in performance? If not readily available please estimate. If you selected "sales" show the actual increase in sales (e.g., 4 closed sales per month, input the number 4 here). You can input a number with up to 1 decimal point. Indicate the frequency base for the measure.

_____ ☐ daily ☐ weekly ☐ monthly ☐ quarterly

RETURN ON INVESTMENT

30. What is the annual value of improvement in the measure you selected above? Multiply the increase (Question 29) times the frequency (Question 29) times the unit of value (Question 27). For example, if you selected "sales" multiply the sales increase times the frequency to arrive at the annum value (e.g., 4 sales per month x 12 x 2000=$96,000). Although this step is difficult please make every effort to estimate the value. Put the value in the currency you selected, round to nearest whole value, enter numbers only. (ex. $96,000.5 should be input as 96,000)

31. Recognizing that other factors could have influenced this annual value of improvement, please estimate the percent of improvement that is attributable (i.e. isolated) to the program. Express as a percentage out of 100%. For example, if only 60% of the sales increase is attributable to the program, enter 60 here.

_____%

32. What confidence do you place in the estimates you have provided in the questions above? A 0% is no confidence, a 100% is certainty. Round to nearest whole value, enter a number only. (ex. 37.5% enter as 38)

_____%

Figure 4-4. (Continued)

RETURN ON INVESTMENT (continued)

33. Please estimate your direct costs of travel and lodging for your participation in this program. Put the value in the currency you selected, round to nearest whole value, enter numbers only. (ex. $10,000.49 should be input as 10,000)

_____

34. Please state your basis for the travel and lodging cost estimate above.

_____

FEEDBACK

35. How can we improve the training to make it more relevant to your job?

_____

_____

_____

Thank you for taking the time to complete this survey!

Figure 4-4. (Continued)

ROI ANALYSIS PLAN

Program:_____The Leadership Challenge_____   Responsibility:____L&D Staff_____   Date:_____

Data Items (Usually Level 4)	Methods for Isolating the Effects of the Program/ Process	Methods of Converting Data to Monetary Values	Cost Categories	Intangible Benefits	Communication Targets for Final Report	Other Influences/ Issues During Application	Comments

Figure 4-5. Blank ROI analysis plan.

REFERENCES

Harrell, K.D. "Level III Training Evaluation: Considerations for Today's Organizations," *Performance Improvement,* May/June 2001, p. 24.

Kvale, S. *InterViews: An Introduction to Qualitative Research Interviewing.* Thousand Oaks, CA: Sage Publications, 1996.

Mondschein, M. *Measurit: Achieving Profitable Training.* Leawood, KS: Leathers Publishing, 1999.

Phillips, J.J., and Phillips, P.P. "Evaluating the Impact of a Graduate Program in a Federal Agency," *In Action: Measuring ROI in the Public Sector.* Alexandria, VA: American Society for Training and Development, 2002, pp. 149–172.

Phillips, J.J., and Phillips, P.P. "Performance Measurement Training," *In Action: Measuring Return on Investment,* Vol. 3. J.J. Phillips (Ed.). Alexandria, VA: American Society for Training and Development, 2001, pp. 15–36.

Subramony, D.P., *et al.* "Using Focus Group Interviews," *Performance Improvement.* International Society for Performance Improvement, September 2002.

CHAPTER 5

Isolating the Effects of a Leadership Development Program

The following situation is repeated often. A significant increase in performance in a business measure is noted after a major leadership development program was conducted and the two events appear to be linked. A key executive asks, "How much of this improvement was caused by the leadership development program?" When this potentially challenging question is asked, it is rarely answered with any degree of accuracy and credibility. While the change in performance may be linked to the program, other factors usually have contributed to the improvement. This chapter explores the proven techniques used to isolate the effects of a leadership development program. These strategies are utilized in some of the best organizations as they attempt to measure the return on investment in leadership development.

The cause-and-effect relationship between a leadership development program and performance can be very confusing and difficult to prove, but can be accomplished with an acceptable degree of accuracy. The challenge is to develop one or more specific strategies to isolate the effects of a leadership development program early in the process, usually as part of an evaluation plan. Upfront attention ensures that appropriate strategies will be used with minimum costs and time commitments.

PRELIMINARY ISSUES

While isolating the effects of a leadership development program seems to be a logical, practical, and necessary issue, it is still much debated. Some professionals argue that to isolate the effects of a program goes against everything taught in systems thinking and team performance improvement (Brinkerhoff and Dressler, 2002). Others argue that the only way to link leadership development to actual business results is to isolate its effect on those business measures (Russ-Eft and Preskill, 2001). Much of the debate centers around misunderstandings and the challenge of isolating the effects of the process. The first point in the debate is the issue of complementary processes. It is true that leadership development is often implemented as part of a total performance improvement initiative. Other influences must work in harmony with leadership development programs to improve business results. It is often not an issue of whether leadership development is part of the mix, but how much leadership development is needed, what specific content is needed, and the most appropriate delivery needed to drive leadership development's share of performance improvement.

The issue of isolating the effects of leadership development is not meant to suggest that leadership development should stand alone as a single influencing variable to driving significant business performance. The isolation issue comes into play, however, when different owners of the processes influencing business results must have more information about the relative contribution of the different processes. In many situations, this question has to be addressed: How much of the improvement was caused by leadership development? Without an answer, or a specific method to address the issue, tremendous credibility is lost, particularly with the senior management team.

The other point in the debate is the difficulty of achieving the isolation. The classic approach is to use control group arrangements where one group is involved leadership development and another in is not. This is one of the techniques described in this chapter and is the most credible. However, the control group may not be appropriate in the majority of studies. Consequently, other methods must be used. Researchers sometimes use time-series analysis, also discussed in this chapter as trend line analysis. Beyond that, many researchers either give up and suggest that it cannot be addressed with credibility or they choose to ignore the issue, hoping that it will not be noticed by the sponsor. Neither of these responses is acceptable to the senior management team who is attempting to understand the linkage between leadership development and business success. A credible estimation adjusted for error will often satisfy their requirements. The important point is to *always* address this issue, even if an expert estimation is used with an error adjustment. In this way, the issue of isolating the effects of leadership development becomes an essential step in the analysis.

Chain of Impact: the Initial Evidence

Before presenting the techniques, it is helpful to examine the chain of impact implied in the different levels of evaluation. As illustrated in Figure 5-1, the chain of impact must be in place for the program to drive business results.

Measurable business impact achieved from a leadership development program should be derived from the application of skills/knowledge on the job over a specified period of time after a program has been conducted. This on-the-job application of a leadership development program is referred to as Level 3 in the five evaluation levels (Phillips, 1997; Kirkpatrick, 1998). Continuing with this logic, successful application of program material on the job should stem from participants learning new skills or acquiring new knowledge in the leadership development program, which is measured as a Level 2 evaluation. Therefore, for a business results improvement (Level 4 evaluation), this chain of impact implies that measurable on-the-job applications are realized (Level 3 evaluation) and new knowledge and skills are learned (Level 2 evaluation). Without the preliminary evidence of the chain of impact, it is difficult to isolate the effects of a leadership development program. If there is no learning or application of the material on the job, it is virtually impossible to conclude that the leadership development program caused any performance improvements. This chain of

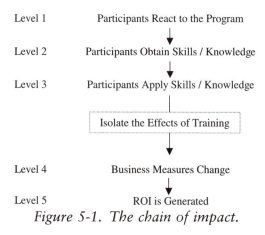

Figure 5-1. The chain of impact.

impact requirement with the different levels of evaluation is supported in the literature (Alliger and Janak, 1989). From a practical standpoint, this issue requires data collection at four levels for an ROI calculation. If data are collected on business results, it should also be collected for other levels of evaluation to ensure that the leadership development program helped produce the business results.

This approach is consistent with the approach practiced by leading organizations who participated in ASTD's benchmarking project. It was reported that most organizations collecting Level 4 data on business results also collected data at the previous three levels (Bassi and Lewis, 1999). The chain of impact does not prove that there was a direct connection to the leadership development program; the isolation is necessary to make this connection and pinpoint the amount of improvement caused by leadership development. Many research efforts have attempted to develop correlations among the different levels. This research basically states that if a significant correlation exists, the chain of impact is in place. If a significant correlation does not exist, there were many barriers that caused the process to break down. This is logical when the chain of impact is considered.

Most research in this area adds very little to the understanding of evaluation. Correlations between two levels show the connection (or disconnect) between the two. It does not mean that the concept of levels is flawed. Instead, it implies that some factor prevented the learning process from adding value. For example, most of the breakdowns occur between Levels 2 and 3. Research has shown that as much as 90 percent of what was learned is not used on the job (Kauffman, 2002).

A variety of barriers impede the transfer of the learning to the job, inhibiting the success of leadership development. This does not mean that the next level of evaluation (Level 3) is inappropriate, it just indicates that some factor is preventing the skills and knowledge from transferring to the job.

Identifying Other Factors: A First Step

As a first step in isolating leadership development's impact on performance, all of the key factors that may have contributed to the performance improvement should be identified. This step reveals other factors that may have influenced the results, underscoring that the leadership development program is not the sole source of improvement. Consequently, the credit for improvement is shared with several possible variables and sources, an approach that is likely to gain the respect of management.

Several potential sources identify major influencing variables. The sponsors may be able to identify factors that should influence the output measure if they have requested the program. The client will usually be aware of other initiatives or programs that may impact the output. Even if the program is operational, the client may have much insight into the other influences that may have driven the performance improvement.

Program participants are often aware of other influences that may have caused performance improvement. After all, it is the impact of their collective efforts that is being monitored and measured. In many situations, they witness previous movements in the performance measures and can pinpoint the reasons for changes. They are normally the experts in this issue.

Analysts and program developers are another source for identifying variables that have an impact on results. The needs analysis will routinely uncover these influencing variables. Program designers typically analyze these variables while addressing the leadership development transfer issue. In some situations, participants' supervisors may be able to identify variables that influence the performance improvement.

Finally, middle and top management may be able to identify other influences based on their experience and knowledge of the situation. Perhaps they have monitored, examined, and analyzed the other influences. The authority positions of these individuals often increase the credibility and acceptance of data.

Taking time to focus attention on variables that may have influenced performance brings additional accuracy and credibility to the process. It moves beyond the scenario where results are presented with no mention of other influences, a situation that often destroys the credibility of a leadership development impact report. It also provides a foundation for some of the techniques described in this book by identifying the variables that must be isolated to show the effects of leadership development. A word of caution is appropriate here. Halting the process after this step would leave many unknowns about actual leadership development impact and might leave a negative impression with the client or senior management, since it may have identified variables that management did not previously consider. Therefore, it is recommended that the leadership development staff go beyond this initial step and use one or more of the techniques that isolate the impact of leadership development, which is the focus of this chapter.

USE OF CONTROL GROUPS

The most accurate approach to isolate the impact of leadership development is the use of control groups in an experimental design process (Wang, 2002). This approach involves the use of an experimental group that participates in leadership development and a control group that does not. The composition of both groups should be as similar as possible and, if feasible, the selection of participants for each group should be on a random basis. When this is possible and both groups are subjected to the same environmental influences, the difference in the performance of the two groups can be attributed to the leadership development program.

As illustrated in Figure 5-2, the control group and experimental group do not necessarily have preprogram measurements. Measurements are taken after the program is implemented. The difference in the performance of the two groups shows the amount of improvement that is directly related to the leadership development program.

Control group arrangements appear in many settings, including both private and public sectors. For example, a turnover reduction program for communication specialists in a government agency used both a control group and an experimental group (Phillips and Phillips, 2002). The experimental group was compiled of individuals in a special program designed to allow participants to achieve a master's degree in information science on agency time and at agency expense. The control group was carefully selected to match up with the experimental group in terms of job title, tenure with the agency, and the college degree obtained. The control/experimental group differences were very dramatic, showing the impact of the retention solution program.

One caution—the use of control groups may create an image that the leadership development staff is creating a laboratory setting, which can cause a problem for some administrators and executives. To avoid this stigma, some organizations run a program using pilot

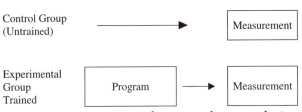

Figure 5-2. Post-test only, control group design.

participants as the experimental group and do not inform the non-participating control group.

Advantages and Disadvantages

The control group process does have some inherent problems that may make it difficult to apply in practice. The first major problem is that the process is inappropriate for many situations. For some types of leadership development programs, it is not proper to withhold development from one particular group while leadership development is given to another. This is particularly important for critical skills that are needed immediately on the job.

This particular barrier keeps many control groups from being implemented. Management is not willing to withhold leadership development in one area to see how it works in another. However, in practice, there are many opportunities for a natural control group agreement to develop in situations where leadership development is implemented throughout an organization. If it will take several months for everyone in the organization to receive the leadership development, there may be enough time for a parallel comparison between the initial group participating in the program and the last group participating in the program. In these cases, it is critical to ensure that the groups are matched as closely as possible so that the first two groups are very similar to the last two groups. These naturally occurring control groups often exist in major leadership development program implementation. The challenge is to address this issue early enough to influence the implementation schedule so that similar groups can be used in the comparison.

The second major problem is the selection of the groups. From a practical perspective it is virtually impossible to have identical control and experimental groups. Dozens of factors can affect employee performance, some of them individual and others contextual. To tackle the issue on a practical basis, it is best to select three to five variables that will have the greatest influence on performance.

A third problem with the control group arrangement is contamination, which can develop when participants in the leadership development program instruct others in the control group. Sometimes the reverse situation occurs when members of the control group model the behavior from the trained group. In either case, the experiment becomes contaminated because the influence filters to the control group. This can be minimized by ensuring that control groups and experimental groups are at different locations, have different shifts, or are on different floors in the same building. When this is not possible, it is sometimes helpful to explain to both groups that one group will participate in a leadership development program now and another will participate at a later date. Also, it may be helpful to appeal to the sense of responsibility of those participating in the program and ask them not to share the information with others.

Closely related to the previous problem is the issue of time. The longer a control group and experimental group comparison operates, the likelihood of other influences affecting the results increases. More variables will enter into the situation, contaminating the results. On the other end of the scale, there must be enough time so that a clear pattern can emerge between the two groups. Thus, the timing for control group comparisons must strike a delicate balance of waiting long enough for their performance differences to show, but not too long so that the results become seriously contaminated.

A fifth problem occurs when the different groups function under different environmental influences. Because they may be in different locations, the groups may have different environmental influences. Sometimes the selection of the groups can help prevent this problem from occurring. Also, using more groups than necessary and discarding those with some environmental differences is another tactic.

A sixth problem with using control groups is that it may appear to be too research oriented for most business organizations. For example, management may not want to take the time to experiment before proceeding with a program or they may not want to withhold leadership development from a group just to measure the impact of an experimental program. Because of this concern, some leadership development practitioners do not entertain the idea of using control groups. When the process is used, however, some organizations conduct it with pilot participants as the experimental group and nonparticipants as the control group. Under this arrangement, the control group is not informed of their control group status.

Because this is an effective approach for isolating the impact of a leadership development program, it should be considered as a strategy when a major ROI impact study is planned. In these situations it is important for the program impact to be isolated to a high level of accuracy; the primary advantage of the control group process is accuracy. About one-third of the more than 100 published studies on the ROI methodology use the control group process.

TREND LINE ANALYSIS

Another useful technique used for approximating the impact of a leadership development program is trend line analysis. With this approach, a trend line is drawn using previous performance as a base and extending the trend into the future. When a leadership development program is conducted, actual performance is compared to projected value, i.e., the trend line. Any improvement of performance over what the trend line predicted can then be reasonably attributed to the leadership development program, if two conditions are met:

1. The trend that has developed prior to the program is expected to continue if the program had not been implemented to alter it (i.e., if the leadership development program had not been implemented, would this trend continue on the same path established before the leadership development program?). The process owner(s) should be able to provide input to reach this conclusion. If the answer is "no," the trend line analysis will not be used. If the answer is "yes," the second condition is considered.

2. No other new variables or influences entered the process after the leadership development program was conducted. The key word is "new," realizing that the trend has been established because of the influences already in place, and no additional influences enter the process beyond the leadership development program. If the answer is "yes," another method would have to be used. If the answer is "no," the trend line analysis develops a reasonable estimate of the impact of leadership development.

Figure 5-3 shows an example of this trend line analysis taken from a shipping department in a large distribution company. The percent reflects the level of actual shipments compared to scheduled shipments. Data are presented before and after a team-leadership development program, which was conducted in July. As shown in Figure 5-3, there was an upward trend on data prior to conducting the program. Although the program apparently had a dramatic effect on shipment productivity, the trend line shows that improvement would have continued anyway, based on the trend that had been established previously. It is tempting to measure the improvement by comparing the average six-month shipments prior to the program (87.3 percent) to the average of six months after the program (94.4 percent) yielding a 6.9 percent difference. However, a more accurate comparison

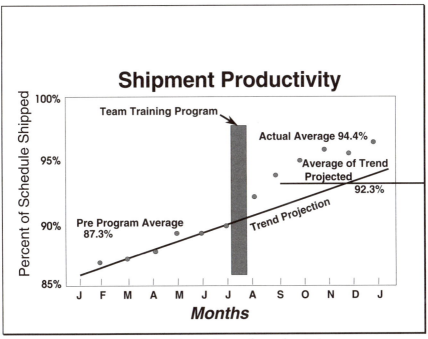

Figure 5-3. Trend line of productivity.

is the six-month average after the program compared to the trend line (92.3 percent). In this example, the difference is 2.1 percent. In this case, the two conditions outlined earlier were met (yes on the first; no on the second). Thus, using this more modest measure increases the accuracy and credibility of the process to isolate the impact of the program.

Preprogram data must be available before this technique can be used and data should have some reasonable degree of stability. If the variance of data is high, the stability of the trend line becomes an issue. If this is an extremely critical issue and the stability cannot be assessed from a direct plot of data, more detailed statistical analyses can be used to determine if data are stable enough to make the projection (Salkind, 2000).

The trend line, projected directly from historical data using a straight edge, may be acceptable. If additional accuracy is needed, the trend line can be projected with a simple routine, available in many calculators and software packages, such as Microsoft Excel™.

The use of trend line analysis becomes more dramatic and convincing when a measure, moving in an undesirable direction, is completely turned around by the program.

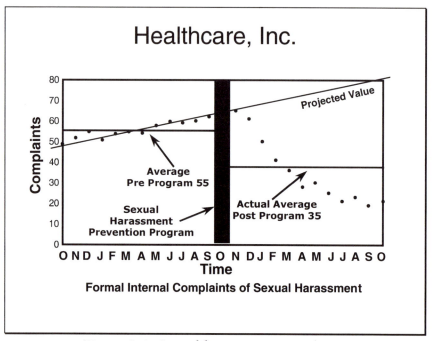

Figure 5-4. Sexual harassment complaints.

A primary disadvantage of this trend line approach is that it is not always accurate. The use of this approach assumes that the events that influenced the performance variable prior to the program are still in place after the program, except for the implementation of the development program (i.e., trends that were established prior to leadership development will continue in the same relative direction). Also, it assumes that no new influences entered the situation at the time the program was conducted. This is seldom the case.

The primary advantage of this approach is that it is simple and inexpensive. If historical data are available, a trend line can be drawn quickly and differences estimated. While not exact, it does provide a very quick assessment of leadership development's potential impact. About 15 percent of the more than 100 published studies on the ROI methodology use the trend line analysis technique. When other variables enter the situation, additional analysis is needed.

FORECASTING METHODS

A more analytical approach to trend line analysis is the use of forecasting methods, which predict a change in performance variables.

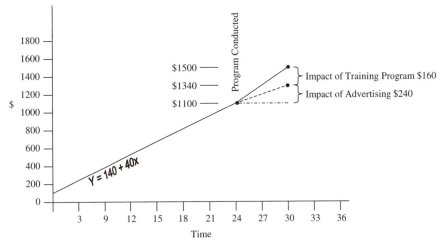

Figure 5-5. Daily sales versus advertising.

This approach represents a mathematical interpretation of the trend line analysis discussed earlier when other variables entered the situation at the time of the leadership development program. The basic premise is that the actual performance of a measure, related to leadership development, is compared to the forecasted value of that measure. The forecasted value is based on the other influences. A linear model, in the form of $y = ax + b$, is appropriate when only one other variable influences the output performance and that relationship is characterized by a straight line. Instead of drawing the straight line, a linear equation is developed, which calculates a value of the anticipated performance improvement.

A major disadvantage with this approach occurs when several variables enter the process. The complexity multiplies and the use of sophisticated statistical packages for multiple variable analyses is necessary. Even then, a good fit of data to the model may not be possible. Unfortunately, some organizations have not developed mathematical relationships for output variables as a function of one or more inputs. Without them, the forecasting method is difficult to use.

The primary advantage of this process is that it can predict business performance measures accurately without leadership development if appropriate data and models are available. The presentation of specific methods is beyond the scope of this book and is contained in other works (Armstrong, 2001). Approximately 5 percent of published studies on the ROI methodology utilize the forecasting technique.

PARTICIPANT ESTIMATE OF LEADERSHIP DEVELOPMENT'S IMPACT

An easily implemented method used to isolate the impact of a leadership development program is to obtain information directly from program participants. The effectiveness of this approach rests on the assumption that participants are capable of determining or estimating how much of a performance improvement is related to the leadership development program. Because their actions have produced the improvement, participants may have very accurate input on the issue. They should know how much of the change was caused by applying what they have learned in the program. Although an estimate, this value will typically have credibility with management because participants are at the center of the change or improvement.

When using this technique, several assumptions are made.

- A leadership development program has been conducted with a variety of different activities, exercises, and learning opportunities all focused on improving performance.
- One or more business measures have been identified prior to leadership development and have been monitored following the process. Data monitoring has revealed an improvement in the business measure.
- There is a need to link the leadership development program to the specific amount of performance improvement and develop the monetary impact of the improvement. This information forms the basis for calculating the actual ROI.

With these assumptions, the participants can pinpoint the actual results linked to the leadership development program and provide data necessary to develop the ROI. This can be accomplished using a focus group or with a questionnaire.

Focus Group Approach

The focus group works extremely well for this challenge if the group size is relatively small—in the 8–12 range. If much larger, the groups should be divided into multiple groups. Focus groups provide the opportunity for members to share information equally, avoiding domination by any one individual. The process taps the input, creativity, and reactions of the entire group.

The meeting should take about one hour (slightly more if there are multiple factors affecting the results or there are multiple business measures). The facilitator should be neutral to the process (i.e., the same individual conducting the leadership development should not conduct this focus group). Focus group facilitation and input must be objective.

The task is to link the business results of the leadership development program to business performance. The group is presented with the improvement and they provide input on isolating the effects of the leadership development program.

The following steps are recommended to arrive at the most credible value for leadership development impact.

Step 1: Explain the task. The task of the focus group meeting is outlined. Participants should understand that there has been improvement in performance. While many factors could have contributed to the performance, the task of this group is to determine how much of the improvement is related to the leadership development program.

Step 2: Discuss the rules. Each participant should be encouraged to provide input, limiting his or her comments to two minutes (or less) for any specific issue. Comments are confidential and will not be linked to a specific individual.

Step 3: Explain the importance of the process. The participant's role in the process is critical. Because it is their performance that has improved, the participants are in the best position to indicate what has caused this improvement; they are the experts in this determination. Without quality input, the contribution of this leadership development program (or any other processes) may never be known.

Step 4: Select the first measure and show the improvement. Using actual data, show the level of performance prior to and following leadership development; in essence, the change in business results—the Δ—is reported.

Step 5: Identify the different factors that have contributed to the performance. Using input from experts—others who are knowledgeable about the improvements—identify the factors that have influenced the improvement (e.g., the volume of work has changed, a new system has been implemented, or technology has been enhanced). If these are known, they are listed as the factors that may have contributed to the performance improvement.

Step 6: The group is asked to identify other factors that have contributed to the performance. In some situations, only the participants know other influencing factors and those factors should surface at this time.

Step 7: Discuss the linkage. Taking each factor one at a time, the participants individually describe the linkage between that factor and the business results. For example, for the leadership development influence, the participants would describe how the leadership development program has driven the actual improvement by providing examples, anecdotes, and other supporting evidence. Participants may require some prompting to provide comments. If they cannot provide dialogue of this issue, there is a good chance that the factor had no influence.

Step 8: The process is repeated for each factor. Each factor is explored until all the participants have discussed the linkage between all the factors and the business performance improvement. After this linkage has been discussed, the participants should have a clear understanding of the cause-and-effect relationship between the various factors and the business improvement.

Step 9: Allocate the improvement. Participants are asked to allocate the percent of improvement to each of the factors discussed. Participants are provided a pie chart, which represents a total amount of improvement for the measure in question, and are asked to carve up the pie, allocating the percentages to different improvements with a total of 100 percent. Some participants may feel uncertain with this process, but should be encouraged to complete this step using their best estimate. Uncertainty will be addressed later in the meeting.

Step 10: Provide a confidence estimate. The participants are then asked to review the allocation percentages and, for each one, estimate their level of confidence in the allocation estimate. Using a scale of 0–100 percent, where 0 percent represents no confidence and 100 percent is certainty, participants express their level of certainty with their estimates in the previous step. A participant may be more comfortable with some factors than others so the confidence estimate may vary. This confidence estimate serves as a vehicle to adjust results.

Step 11: Participants are asked to multiply the two percentages. For example, if an individual has allocated 35 percent of the improvement to leadership development and is 80 percent confident, he or she would multiply 35 percent × 80 percent, which is 28 percent. In essence, the participant is suggesting that at least 28 percent of the teams' business improvement is linked to the leadership development program. The confidence estimate serves as a conservative discount factor, adjusting for the error of the estimate. The pie charts with the calculations are collected without names and the

Table 5-1
Example of a Participant's Estimation

Factor influencing improvement	Percent of improvement caused by	Confidence expressed as a percent
1. Leadership development program	50	70
2. Change in procedures	10	80
3. Adjustment in standards	10	50
4. Revision to incentive plan	20	90
5. Increased management attention	10	50
Total	100%	

calculations are verified. Another option is to collect pie charts and make the calculations for the participants.

Step 12: Report results. If possible, the average of the adjusted values for the group is developed and communicated to the group. Also, the summary of all of the information should be communicated to the participants as soon as possible.

Participants who do not provide information are excluded from the analysis. Table 5-1 illustrates this approach with an example of one participant's estimations.

The participant allocates 50 percent of the improvement to leadership development. The confidence percentage is a reflection of the error in the estimate. A 70 percent confidence level equates to a potential error range of ±30 percent (100 percent − 70 percent = 30 percent). The 50 percent allocation to leadership development could be 30 percent more (50 percent + 15 percent = 65 percent) or 30 percent less (50 percent − 15 percent = 35 percent) or somewhere in between. Thus, the participant's allocation is in the range of 35 to 65 percent. In essence, the confidence estimate frames an error range. To be conservative, the lower side of the range is used (35 percent).

This approach is equivalent to multiplying the factor estimate by the confidence percentage to develop a usable leadership development factor value of 35 percent (50 percent × 70 percent). This adjusted percentage is then multiplied by the actual amount of the improvement (postprogram minus preprogram value) to isolate the portion attributed to the leadership development program. The adjusted improvement is now ready for conversion to monetary values and, ultimately, used in developing the return on investment.

This approach provides a credible way to isolate the effects of a leadership development program when other methods will not work. It is often regarded as the low-cost solution to the problem because it takes only a few focus groups and a small amount of time to arrive at this conclusion. In most of these settings, the actual conversion to monetary value is not conducted by the group, but developed in another way. For most data, the monetary value may already exist as a standard, acceptable value. The issue of converting data to monetary value is detailed in the next chapter. However, if participants must provide input on the value of data, it can be approached in the same focus group meeting as another phase of the process, where the participants provide input into the actual monetary value of the unit. To reach an accepted value, the steps are very similar to the steps for isolation.

Questionnaire Approach

Sometimes focus groups are not available or are considered unacceptable for the use of data collection. The participants may not be available for a group meeting or the focus groups become too expensive. In these situations, it may be helpful to collect similar information via a questionnaire. With this approach, participants must address the same issues as those addressed in the focus group, but now on a series of impact questions imbedded into a follow-up questionnaire.

The questionnaire may focus solely on isolating the effects of a leadership development program, as detailed in the previous example, or it may focus on the monetary value derived from the program, with the isolation issue being only a part of data collected. This is a more versatile approach for using questionnaires when it is not certain exactly how participants will provide business impact data. In some programs, the precise measures influenced by the program may not be known. This is sometimes the case in programs involving leadership, team building, communications, negotiations, problem solving, innovation, and other types of leadership development and performance improvement initiatives. In these situations, it is helpful to obtain information from participants on a series of impact questions, showing how they have used what they have learned and the subsequent impact in the work unit. It is important for participants to know about these questions before they receive the questionnaire. The surprise element can be disastrous in data collection. The recommended series of impact questions are:

1. How have you and your job changed as a result of attending this program (skills and knowledge application)?
2. What impact do these changes bring to your work or work unit?
3. How is this impact measured (specific measure)?
4. How much did this measure change after you participated in the program (monthly, weekly, or daily amount)?
5. What is the unit value of the measure?
6. What is the basis for this unit value? Please indicate the assumptions made and the specific calculations you performed to arrive at the value.
7. What is the annual value of this change or improvement in the work unit (for the first year)?
8. Recognize that many other factors influence output results in addition to leadership development; please identify the other factors that could have contributed to this performance.
9. What percent of this improvement can be attributed directly to the application of skills and knowledge gained in the program? (0–100 percent).
10. What confidence do you have in the aforementioned above estimate and data, expressed as a percent? (0 percent = no confidence; 100 percent = certainty)
11. What other individuals or groups could estimate this percentage or determine the amount?

Perhaps an illustration of this process can reveal its effectiveness and acceptability. In a large global organization, the impact of a leadership program for new managers was being assessed. Because the decision to calculate the impact of leadership development was made after the program had been conducted, the control group arrangement was not feasible as a method to isolate the effects of leadership development. Also, before the program was implemented, no specified business impact data (Level 4) were identified that was directly linked to the program. Participants may drive one or more of a dozen business performance measures. Consequently, it was not appropriate to use trend line analysis. Participants' estimates proved to be the most useful way to assess the impact of leadership development on the business performance. In a detailed follow-up questionnaire, participants were asked a variety of questions regarding the applications of what was learned from the program. As part of the program, the individuals were asked to develop action plans and implement them, although there was no specific follow-up plan needed. The series of impact questions listed above provided an estimation of the impact.

Although this series of questions is challenging, when set up properly and presented to participants in an appropriate way, they can be very effective for collecting impact data. Table 5-2 shows a sample of the calculations from these questions for this particular program. In this snapshot of data, the input from seven participants is presented. The total value for the program would be the total of the input from all who provided data.

Although this is an estimate, the approach has considerable accuracy and credibility. Four adjustments are used effectively to reflect a conservative approach:

1. The individuals who do not respond to the questionnaire or provide usable data on the questionnaire are assumed to have no improvements. This is probably an overstatement, as some individuals will have improvements, but not report them on the questionnaire.
2. Extreme data and incomplete, unrealistic, and unsupported claims are omitted from the analysis, although they may be included in the intangible benefits.
3. Because only annualized values are used, it is assumed that there are no benefits from the program after the first year of implementation. In reality, a leadership development program should be expected to add value for several years after the program has been conducted.
4. The confidence level, expressed as a percent, is multiplied by the improvement value to reduce the amount of the improvement by the potential error.

When presented to senior management, the results of this impact study were perceived to be an understatement of the program's success. Data and the process were considered credible and accurate.

Collecting an adequate amount of quality data from the series of impact questions is the critical challenge with this process. Participants must be primed to provide data, which can be accomplished in several ways.

- Participants should know in advance that they are expected to provide this type of data along with an explanation of why this is needed and how it will be used.
- Ideally, participants should see a copy of this questionnaire and

Table 5-2
Sample of Input from Participants in a Leadership Program
for New Managers

Participant number	Annual improvement value ($)	Basis for value	Confidence (%)	Isolation factor (%)	Adjusted value ($)
11	36,000	Improvement in efficiency of group. $3000 month × 12 (group estimate)	85	50	15,300
42	90,000	Turnover reduction. Two turnover statistics per year. Base salary × 1.5 = 45,000	90	40	32,400
74	24,000	Improvement in customer response time (8 to 6 hours). Estimated value: $2000/month	60	55	7,920
55	2,000	5% improvement in my effectiveness ($40,500 × 5%)	75	50	750
96	10,000	Absenteeism reduction (50 absences per year × $200)	85	75	6,375
117	8,090	Team project completed 10 days ahead of schedule. Annual salaries $210,500 = $809 per day × 10 days	90	45	3,279
118	159,000	Under budget for the year by this amount	100	30	47,700

discuss it while they are involved in the leadership development program. If possible, a verbal commitment to provide data should be obtained at that time.

- Participants could be reminded of the requirement prior to the time to collect data. The reminder should come from others involved in the process—even the immediate manager.
- Participants could be provided with examples of how the questionnaire can be completed, using most-likely scenarios and typical data.
- The immediate manager could coach participants through the process.
- The immediate manager could review and approve data.

These steps help keep the data collection process, with its chain of impact questions, from being a surprise. It will also accomplish three critical tasks.

1. *The response rate will increase.* Because participants commit to provide data during the session, a greater percentage will respond.
2. *The quantity of data will improve.* Participants will understand the chain of impact and understand how data will be used. They will complete more questions.
3. *The quality of data is enhanced.* With up-front expectations, there is greater understanding of the type of data needed and improved confidence in data provided. Perhaps subconsciously, participants begin to think through consequences of leadership development and specific impact measures. The result: improved quality of input.

Advantages and Disadvantages

Participant estimation is a critical technique used to isolate the effect of leadership development; however, the process has some disadvantages. It is an estimate and, consequently, does not have the accuracy desired by some leadership development managers. Also, input data may be unreliable because some participants are incapable of providing these types of estimates. They might not be aware of exactly which factors contributed to the results or they may be reluctant to provide data. If the questions come as a surprise, data will be scarce.

Several advantages make this strategy attractive. It is a simple process, understood easily by most participants and by others who review evaluation data. It is inexpensive, takes very little time and analysis, and thus results in an efficient addition to the evaluation process. Estimates originate from a credible source—the individuals who actually produced the improvement.

The advantages seem to offset the disadvantages. Isolating the effects of leadership development will never be precise and this estimate may be accurate enough for most clients and management groups. The process is appropriate when the participants are managers, supervisors, team leaders, sales associates, engineers, and other professional and technical employees.

This technique is the fallback isolation strategy for many types of programs. If nothing else works, this method is used. A fallback approach is needed if the effect of the leadership development program is always isolated. The reluctance to use the process often rests with trainers, leadership development managers, learning specialists, and performance improvement specialists. They are reluctant to use a technique that is not an airtight case. Estimates are typically avoided. However, the primary audience for data (the sponsor or senior manager) will readily accept this approach. Living in an ambiguous world, they understand that estimates have to be made and may be the only way to approach this issue. They understand the challenge and appreciate the conservative approach, often commenting that the actual value is probably greater than the value presented. When organizations begin to use this routinely, it sometimes becomes the method of choice for isolation. Because of this, approximately 50 percent of the more than 100 published studies on the ROI methodology use this as a technique to isolate the effects of a program.

Management Estimate of Leadership Development's Impact

In lieu of (or in addition to) participant estimates, the participants' supervisor may be asked to provide the extent of leadership development's role in producing a performance improvement. In some settings, participants' supervisors may be more familiar with the other factors influencing performance. Consequently, they may be better equipped to provide estimates of impact. The recommended questions to ask supervisors, after describing the improvement caused by the participants, are:

1. In addition to leadership development, what other factors could have contributed to this success?
2. What percent of the improvement in performance measures of the participant resulted from the leadership development program (0–100 percent)?
3. What is the basis for this estimate?
4. What is your confidence in this estimate, expressed as a percentage? (0 percent = no confidence; 100 percent = complete confidence)
5. What other individuals or groups would know about this improvement and could estimate this percentage?

These questions are similar to those in the participant's questionnaire. Supervisor estimates should be analyzed in the same manner as participant estimates. To be more conservative, estimates may be adjusted by the confidence percentage. If feasible, it is recommended that inputs be obtained from both participants and supervisors. When participants' estimates have been collected, the decision of which estimate to use becomes an issue. If there is some compelling reason to think that one estimate is more credible than another, it should be used. The most conservative approach is to use the lowest value and include an appropriate explanation. Another potential option is to recognize that each source has its own unique perspective and that an average of the two is appropriate, placing an equal weight on each input.

In some cases, upper management may estimate the percent of improvement that should be attributed to the leadership development program. While this process is very subjective, the input is received from the individuals who often provide or approve funding for the program. Sometimes their level of comfort with the process is the most important consideration.

This approach has the same disadvantages as participant estimates. It is subjective and, consequently, may be viewed with skepticism. Also, supervisors and managers may be reluctant to participate or be incapable of providing accurate impact estimates. In some cases, they may not know about other factors that contributed to the improvement.

The advantages of this approach are similar to the advantages of participant estimation. It is simple and inexpensive and enjoys an acceptable degree of credibility because it comes directly from the supervisors of those individuals who received the leadership development. When combined with participant estimation, the credibility is enhanced considerably. Also, when factored by the level of confidence, its value further increases.

In some situations, the leadership development program impact will be large, providing a very high ROI. Top managers may feel more comfortable making an adjustment in actual data. In essence, they are applying their discount factor for an unknown factor, although attempts have been made to identify each factor. While there is no scientific basis for this technique, it provides some assurance that data are discounted appropriately.

Subordinate Input on Leadership Development's Impact

In some situations, the subordinates of managers participating in a leadership development program will provide input concerning the extent of impact. Although they will not usually be able to estimate how much of an improvement can be attributed to the program, they can provide input in terms of what other factors might have contributed to the improvement. This approach is appropriate in programs in which leaders are implementing work unit changes or implementing new policies or procedures. Each manager's employees provide input about changes that have occurred since the manager participated in the leadership development program. They help determine the extent to which other factors have changed in addition to manager behavior. Subordinate input is usually obtained through surveys or interviews.

This approach has some disadvantages. Data from subordinates are subjective and may be questionable because of the possibility for biased input. Also, in some cases the subordinates may have difficulty determining changes in the work climate. This approach does offer a useful way to isolate the impact of the program from other influences. In some cases, subordinates are aware of the factors that caused changes in their work units, and they can provide input about the magnitude or quantity of these changes. When combined with other methods that isolate impact, this process has increased credibility.

Calculating the Impact of Other Factors

Although not appropriate in all cases, there are some situations where it may be feasible to calculate the impact of factors (other than leadership development) that influenced the improvement and then conclude that leadership development is credited with the remaining portion. In this approach, leadership development takes credit for improvement that cannot be attributed to other factors.

This method is appropriate when the other factors are easily identified and the appropriate mechanisms are in place to calculate their impact on the improvement. In some cases it is just as difficult to estimate the impact of other factors as it is for the impact of the leadership development program, leaving this approach less advantageous. This process can be very credible if the method used to isolate the impact of other factors is credible.

USING THE TECHNIQUES

With several techniques available to isolate the impact of leadership development, selecting the most appropriate techniques for the specific program can be difficult. Some techniques are simple and inexpensive, whereas others are more time-consuming and costly. When attempting to make the selection decision, several factors should be considered:

- feasibility of the technique
- accuracy provided with the technique, when compared to the accuracy needed
- credibility of the technique with the target audience
- specific cost to implement the technique
- the amount of disruption in normal work activities as the technique is implemented
- participant, staff, and management time needed with the particular technique

Multiple techniques or sources for data input should be considered because two sources are usually better than one. When multiple sources are used, a conservative method is recommended to combine the inputs. A conservative approach builds acceptance. The target audience should always be provided with explanations of the process and the various subjective factors involved. Multiple sources allow an organization to experiment with different techniques and build confidence with a particular technique. For example, if management is concerned about the accuracy of participants' estimates, a combination of a control group arrangement and participants' estimates could be attempted to check the accuracy of the estimation process.

It is not unusual for the ROI in leadership development and development to be extremely large. Even when a portion of the improvement is allocated to other factors, the numbers are still impressive in many situations. The audience should understand that although every effort was made to isolate the impact, it is still a figure that is not precise and may contain error. It represents the best estimate of the impact given the constraints, conditions, and resources available. Chances are it is more accurate than other types of analyzes regularly utilized in other functions within the organization.

FINAL THOUGHTS

This chapter presented a variety of techniques that isolate the effects of a leadership development program. The techniques represent the most effective approaches to tackle this issue and are used by some of the most progressive organizations. Too often results are reported and linked to leadership development without any attempt to isolate the portion of results that can be attributed to the leadership development program. It is impossible to link leadership development to business impact if this issue is ignored. If the leadership development function is to continue to improve its professional image, as well as meet its responsibility for obtaining results, this issue must be addressed early in the process.

CASE STUDY—PART D
INTERNATIONAL CAR RENTAL

Isolating the Impact of the Leadership Challenge

The method of isolation proved to be a challenge. Because the managers may represent different functional areas, there was no finite set of measures that could be linked to the program for each participant. Essentially, each manager could have a different measure as he or she focused on a particular business need in the work unit. Consequently, the use of a control group was inappropriate. In addition, trend line analysis and forecasting proved to be inappropriate for the same reason. Therefore, the team had to collect estimations directly from participants on the questionnaire. The follow-up questionnaire presented in Chapter 4, Figure 4-4 lists the questions used to isolate the impact of the program. Question 31 isolates the effects of this program using an estimate. Question 32 adjusts for the error

ROI ANALYSIS PLAN

Program: ___Leadership Challenge___   Responsibility: ___L&D Staff___   Date: _____

Data Items (Usually Level 4)	Methods for Isolating the Effects of the Program/Process	Methods of Converting Data to Monetary Values	Cost Categories	Intangible Benefits	Communication Targets for Final Report	Other Influences/Issues During Application	Comments
Varies, depending on measures selected	• Participant estimate	• Standard value • Expert value • Participant estimate	• Needs Assessment (Prorated) • Program Dev. (Prorated) • Facilitation fees • Prog materials • Facilitation & coordination • Meals and refreshments • Facilities • Participant salaries & benefits for time away from work • Mgrs salaries & benefit for time involved in program • Cost of overhead • Evaluation	• Job satisfaction for first level managers • Job satisfaction for team members • Improved teamwork • Improved communication	• Participants (first level managers) • Participants' managers • Senior executives • L&D staff • Prospective participants • Learning & development council members	• Several process improvement initiatives are on-going during this program implementation	• Must gain commitment to provide data • A high response rate is needed

Figure 5-6. Completed ROI Analysis Plan.

of the estimate. The challenge is to ensure that the participants are committed to submit data for this isolation.

ROI Analysis Plan

The completed ROI analysis form, Figure 5-6, contains several other important planning issues for the study. Methods for converting data and standard cost categories were included, anticipated intangible benefits were detailed, and the audiences for communication defined.

DISCUSSION QUESTIONS

1. How can data be converted to monetary value?
2. What period of time should be used for the monetary benefits? Three months? Six months? One year? Two years?

REFERENCES

Alliger, G.M., and Janak, E.A. "Kirkpatrick's Levels of Leadership Development Criteria: Thirty Years Later." *Personnel Psychology*, Vol. 42, 1989, pp. 331–342.

Armstrong, J.S. (Ed.). *Principles of Forecasting: A Handbook for Researchers and Practitioners*. Boston, MA: Kluwer Academic Publishers, 2001.

Bassi, L.J., and Lewis, E.M. *Linking Leadership Development and Performance: Benchmarking Results*. Alexandria, VA: American Society for Leadership Development, 1999.

Brinkerhoff, R.O., and Dressler, D. "Using Evaluation to Build Organizational Performance and Learning Capability: A Strategy and a Method," *Performance Improvement*, July 2002.

Kirkpatrick, D. *Evaluating Leadership Development Programs: The Four Levels*, 2nd ed. San Francisco, CA: Berrett-Koehler Publishers, 1998.

Phillips, P.P., and Phillips, J.J. "Evaluating the Impact of a Graduate Program in a Federal Agency," *In Action: Measuring ROI in the Public Sector*, Phillips, P.P. (Ed.). Alexandria, VA: American Society for Leadership Development, 2002, pp. 149–172.

Riley, T., Davani, H., Chason, P., and Findley, K. "Practices and Pitfalls: A Practitioner's Journey Into Level 3 Evaluation," *Performance Improvement*, May/June 2002.

Russ-Eft, D., and Preskil, H. *Evaluation in Organizations: A Systematic Approach to Enhancing Learning, Performance, and Change*. Cambridge, MA: Perseus Publishing, 2001.

Phillips, J.J. The Handbook of Trading Evaluation and Measurement Methods, 3rd Edition. Boston, MA: Butterworth Heinemann, 1997.

Salkind, N.J. *Statistics for People Who (Think They) Hate Statistics*. Thousand Oaks, CA: Sage Publications, Inc., 2000.

Wang, G. "Control Group Methods for HPT Program Evaluation and Measurement," *Performance Improvement Quarterly*, 15(2), 2002, pp. 32–46.

Wang, G., Dou, Z., and Lee, N. "A Systems Approach to Measuring Return on Investment (ROI) for HRD Interventions." *Human Resource Development Quarterly*, 13(2), 2002, pp. 203–224.

CHAPTER 6

Converting Business Measures to Monetary Values

Traditionally, leadership impact studies stop with a tabulation of business impact, which is a Level 4 evaluation. In those situations, a leadership development program is considered successful if it produced improvements such as productivity increases, quality enhancements, absenteeism reductions, or customer satisfaction improvements. While these results are important, it is more insightful to convert the data to monetary value and show the total impact of the improvement. The monetary value is essential to compare the cost of the program to develop the ROI for the leadership scorecard. This is the ultimate level of evaluation. This chapter shows how leading organizations are moving beyond just tabulating business results and are adding another step of converting business measures to monetary value.

PRELIMINARY ISSUES

Sorting out Hard and Soft Data

After collecting performance data, many organizations find it helpful to divide data into hard and soft categories. Hard data are the traditional measures of organizational performance. They are objective, easy to measure, and easy to convert to monetary values. Hard data are often very common measures, achieve high credibility with management, and are available in every type of organization. They are destined to be converted to monetary value and included in the ROI formula.

Table 6-1
Examples of Hard Data

Output	Time
Units produced	Equipment downtime
Items assembled	Overtime
Items sold	On time shipments
Forms processed	Time to project completion
Loans approved	Processing time
Inventory turnover	Cycle time
Patients	Meeting schedules
Applications processed	Repair time
Productivity	Efficiency
Work backlog	Work stoppages
Shipments	Order response time
New accounts opened	Late reporting
	Lost time days

Costs	Quality
Budget variances	Scrap
Unit costs	Rejects
Cost by account	Error rates
Variable costs	Rework
Fixed costs	Shortages
Overhead costs	Deviation from standard
Operating costs	Product failures
Number of cost reductions	Inventory adjustments
Accident costs	Percent of tasks completed properly
Sales expense	Number of accidents

Hard data represent the output, quality, cost, and time of work-related processes. Table 6-1 shows a sampling of typical hard data under these four categories. Almost every department or unit will have hard-data performance measures. For example, a government office approving applications for work visas in a foreign country will have these four measures among its overall performance measurement: the number of applications processed (output), cost per application processed (cost), the number of errors made processing applications (quality), and the time it takes to process and approve an application (time). In most situations, leadership development programs for leaders in a work unit should be linked to one or more hard data measures.

Because many leadership development programs are designed to develop soft skills, soft data are needed in evaluation. Soft data are usually subjective, sometimes difficult to measure, almost always difficult to convert to monetary values, and are behaviorally oriented. When compared to hard data, soft data are usually less credible as a performance measure. Soft data measures may or may not be converted to monetary values.

Soft data items can be grouped into several categories; Table 6-2 shows one such grouping. Measures such as employee turnover,

Table 6-2
Examples of Soft Data

Work habits	Customer satisfaction
Absenteeism	Churn rate
Tardiness	Number of satisfied customers
Visits to the dispensary	Customer satisfaction index
First aid treatments	Customer loyalty
Violations of safety rules	Customer complaints
Excessive breaks	

Work climate	Development/advancement
Number of grievances	Number of promotions
Number of discrimination charges	Number of pay increases
Employee complaints	Number of training programs attended
Job satisfaction	Requests for transfer
Employee turnover	Performance appraisal ratings
Litigation	Increases in job effectiveness

Job attitudes	Initiative
Job satisfaction	Implementation of new ideas
Organizational commitment	Successful completion of projects
Perceptions of job responsibilities	Number of suggestions implemented
Employee loyalty	Number of goals
Increased confidence	

absenteeism, and grievances appear as soft data items, not because they are difficult to measure, but because it is difficult to accurately convert them to monetary values.

General Steps to Convert Data

Before describing the techniques to convert either hard or soft data to monetary values, the general steps used to convert data in each strategy are briefly summarized. These steps should be followed for each data conversion.

Focus on a unit of measure. First, identify a unit of improvement. For output data, the unit of measure is the item produced, service provided, or sale consummated. Time measures are varied and include items such as the time to complete a project, cycle time, or customer response time. The unit is usually expressed as minutes, hours, or days. Quality is a common measure, and the unit may be one error, reject, defect, or rework item. Soft data measures are varied, and the unit of improvement may include items such as a grievance, an absence, an employee turnover statistic, or a change of one point in the customer satisfaction index.

Determine a value of each unit. Place a value (V) on the unit identified in the first step. For measures of production, quality, cost, and time, the process is relatively easy. Most organizations have records or reports reflecting the value of items such as one unit of production or the cost of a defect. Soft data are more difficult to convert to a value, as the cost of one absence, one grievance, or a change of one point in the employee attitude survey is often difficult to pinpoint. The techniques used in this chapter provide an array of possibilities to make this conversion. When more than one value is available, either the most credible or the lowest value is used.

Calculate the change in performance data. The change in output data is developed after the effects of training have been isolated from other influences. The change (ΔP) is the performance improvement, measured as hard or soft data, which is directly attributable to the training program. The value may represent the performance improvement for an individual, a team, a group, or several groups of participants.

Determine an annual amount for the change. Annualize the ΔP value to develop a total change in the performance data for one year. Using a year has become a standard approach with many organizations that wish to capture the total benefits of a training program. Although the benefits may not be realized at the same level for an entire year, some programs will continue to produce benefits beyond one year. In some cases, the stream of benefits may involve several years. However, using one year of benefits is considered a conservative approach.

Calculate the total value of the improvement. Develop the total value of improvement by multiplying the annual performance change (ΔP) by the unit value (V) for the complete group in question. For example, if one group of participants for a program is being evaluated, the total value will include total improvement for all participants in the group. This value for annual program benefits is then compared to the cost of the program, usually through the return on investment formula.

Techniques for Converting Data to Monetary Values

An example taken from a leadership development program at a manufacturing plant describes the five-step process of converting data to monetary values. This program was developed and implemented after a needs assessment revealed that a lack of teamwork was causing an excessive number of grievances. Thus, the actual number of grievances resolved at Step 2 in the grievance process was selected as an output measure. Table 6-3 shows the steps taken to assign a monetary value to data arrived at a total program impact of $546,000.

Ten techniques are available to convert data to monetary values. Some techniques are appropriate for a specific type of data or data category, whereas others can be used with virtually any type of data. The leadership development staff's challenge is to select the particular strategy that best matches the type of data and situation. Each strategy is presented next, beginning with the most credible approach.

Converting Output Data to Contribution

When a leadership development program has produced a change in output, the value of the increased output can usually be determined from the organization's accounting or operating records. For organizations operating on a profit basis, this value is usually the marginal profit contribution of an additional unit of production or unit of service provided. For example, a production team in a major appliance manufacturer is able to boost the production of small

Table 6-3
An Example Illustrating Steps to Convert Data to Monetary Values

Setting: Leadership development program in a manufacturing plant

Step 1 Focus on a unit of improvement
One grievance reaching Step 2 in the four-step grievance resolution process

Step 2 Determine a value of each unit
Using internal experts, the labor relations staff, the cost of an average grievance was estimated to be $6500 when considering time and direct costs (V = $6500)

Step 3 Calculate the change in performance data
Six months after the program was completed, total grievances per month reaching Step 2 declined by 10. Seven of the 10 grievance reductions were related to the program as determined by supervisors (isolating the effects of training)

Step 4 Determine an annual amount for the change
Using the six-month value, 7 per month yields an annual improvement of 84 ($\Delta P = 84$) for the first year

Step 5 Calculate the annual value of the improvement
Annual value = $\Delta P \times V$
= $84 \times \$6500$
= $546,000

refrigerators with a series of comprehensive training programs. The unit of improvement, therefore, is the profit margin of one refrigerator. In organizations that are performance rather than profit driven, this value is usually reflected in the savings accumulated when an additional unit of output is realized for the same input requirements. For example, in a visa section of a government office, an additional visa application is processed at no additional cost. Thus, an increase in output translates into a cost savings equal to the unit cost of processing a visa.

The formulas and calculations used to measure this contribution depend on the organization and its records. Most organizations have this type of data readily available for performance monitoring and goal setting. Managers often use marginal cost statements and sensitivity analyses to pinpoint the value associated with changes in output (Boulton *et al.*, 2002). If data are not available, the leadership development staff must initiate or coordinate the development of appropriate values.

Table 6-4
Loan Profitability Analysis

Profit component	Unit value
Average loan size	$15,500
Average loan yield	9.75%
Average cost of funds (including branch costs)	5.50%
Direct costs for consumer lending	0.82%
Corporate overhead	1.61%
Net profit per loan	**1.82%**

In one case involving a commercial bank, a leadership develop-ment program for consumer loan managers was conducted that resulted in additional consumer loan volume (output). To measure the return on investment in the program, it was necessary to calcu-late the value (profit contribution) of one additional consumer loan. This was a relatively easy item to calculate from the bank's records (Phillips, 2000). As shown in Table 6-4, several components went into this calculation.

The first step was to determine the yield, which was available from bank records. Next, the average spread between the cost of funds and the yield received on the loan was calculated. For example, the bank could obtain funds from depositors at 5.5 percent on average, including the cost of operating the branches. The direct costs of making the loan, such as salaries of employees directly involved in consumer lending and advertising costs for consumer loans, had to be subtracted from this difference. Historically, these direct costs amounted to 0.82 percent of the loan value. To cover overhead costs for other corporate functions, an additional 1.61 percent was sub-tracted from the value. The remaining 1.82 percent of the average loan value represented the bank's profit margin on a loan.

The good news about this strategy is that standard values are available for many of the measures. The challenge is to quickly find the appropriate and credible value. As the previous example illus-trates, the value was already developed for other purposes. This value was then used in the evaluation of the training program. Table 6-5 provides additional details on the common measures of output data, showing how they are typically developed and some of the comments concerning them. As Table 6-5 illustrates, standard values are almost always available in the organization. However, if no value

Table 6-5
Common Measures and the Methods to Convert Output to
Monetary Values

Output measures	Example	Technique	Comments
Production unit	One unit assembled	Standard value	Available in almost every manufacturing unit
Service unit	Packages delivered on time	Standard value	Developed for most service providers when it is a typical service delivery unit
Sales	Monetary increase in revenue	Standard value (profit margin)	The profit from one additional dollar of sales is a standard item
Market share	10% increase in market share in one year	Standard value	Margin of increased sales
Productivity measure	10% change in productivity index	Standard value	This measure is very specific to the type of production or productivity measured. It may include per unit of time

has been developed for a particular measure, one of the techniques listed in the chapter can be used to develop the value.

CALCULATING THE COST OF QUALITY

Quality is a critical issue, and its cost is an important measure in most manufacturing and service firms. For some quality measures, the task is easy. For example, if quality is measured with a defect rate, the value of the improvement is the cost to repair or replace the product. The most obvious cost of poor quality is the scrap or waste generated by mistakes. Defective products, spoiled raw materials, and discarded paperwork are all the results of poor quality. This scrap or waste translates directly into a monetary value. For example, in a production environment, the cost of a defective product is the total cost incurred to the point the mistake is identified minus the salvage value.

Employee mistakes and errors can cause expensive rework. The most costly rework occurs when a product is delivered to a customer and must be returned for correction. The cost of rework includes both labor and direct costs. In some organizations, the cost of rework can be as much as 35 percent of operating costs (Campanella, 1999). In one example of a program involving customer service training for dispatchers in an oil company, a measure of rework is the number of pullouts. A pullout occurs when a delivery truck cannot fill an order for fuel at a service station. The truck returns to the terminal for an adjustment to the order. Tabulating the cost of a sample of actual pullouts develops the average cost of the pullout. The cost elements include driver time involved, the cost of the truck, the cost of terminal use, and an estimate of administrative costs.

Perhaps the costliest element of unacceptable quality is customer and client dissatisfaction. In some cases, serious mistakes can result in lost business. Customer dissatisfaction is difficult to quantify, and attempts to arrive at a monetary value may be impossible using direct methods. Usually the judgment and expertise of sales, marketing, or quality managers may be the best technique to measure the impact of dissatisfaction. A growing number of quality experts are now measuring customer and client dissatisfaction with market surveys (Johnson and Gustafsson, 2000). However, other strategies discussed in this chapter may be more appropriate to measure the cost of customer dissatisfaction.

The good news about quality measures is that there has been much effort to develop the value for improving the particular measure. This is due in part to total quality management, continuous process improvement, and six sigma. All of these processes have focused on individual quality measures and the cost of quality. Consequently, specific standard values have been developed. If standard values are not available for any of the quality measures, one of the techniques in this chapter can be used to develop the value.

Converting Employee Time

Reduction in employee time is a common objective for performance improvement programs. In a team environment, a program could enable the team to perform tasks in a shorter time frame, or with fewer people. On an individual basis, time management workshops are designed to help professional, sales, supervisory, and managerial employees save time in performing daily tasks. The value of the time saved is an important measure of the program's success, and this conversion is a relatively easy process.

The most obvious time savings are from labor reduction costs in performing work. The monetary savings is found by multiplying the hours saved times the labor cost per hour. For example, after attending a personal productivity program, leaders estimated that each saves an average of 74 minutes per day, worth $31.25 per day or $7500 per year (Stamp, 1992). This time savings was based on the average salary plus benefits for the typical participant.

The average wage with a percent added for employee benefits will suffice for most calculations. However, employee time may be worth more. For example, additional costs in maintaining an employee (office space, furniture, telephone, utilities, computers, secretarial support, and other overhead expenses) could be included in the average labor cost. Thus, the average wage rate may escalate quickly to a large number. However, the conservative approach is to use the salary plus employee benefits.

In addition to the labor cost per hour, other benefits can result from a time savings. These include improved service, avoidance of penalties for late projects, and the creation of additional opportunities for profit. These values can be estimated using other methods discussed in this chapter.

A word of caution is in order when the time savings are developed. Time savings are only realized when the amount of time saved translates into an additional contribution. If a leadership development program results in a savings in manager time, a monetary value is realized only if the manager used the additional time in a productive way. If a team-based program generates a new process that eliminates several hours of work each day, the actual savings will be realized only if there is a cost savings from a reduction in employees, a reduction in overtime pay, or increased productivity. Therefore, an important preliminary step in developing time savings is to determine if a "true" savings will be realized (Harbour, 1996).

Using Historical Costs

Sometimes historical records contain the value of a measure in, and reflect the cost (or value) of a unit of improvement. This strategy involves identifying the appropriate records and tabulating the actual cost components for the item in question.

In one example, a large city tackled an absenteeism problem with its city bus drivers (Phillips and Stone, 2002). Using a project based leadership development program, a group of leaders developed and implemented two solutions to reduce absenteeism. The HR vice president was interested in showing the return on investment for the program. To show the impact of the absenteeism reduction, the cost of one absence was needed. As part of the study, the external consulting firm developed a detailed cost of an absence, considering the full costs of a driver pool maintained to cover an unexpected absence. All of the costs were calculated in a fully loaded profile to present the cost of an absence. As this impact study revealed, the time to develop historical costs is sometimes expensive, leaving the researchers often looking for an easier way. Consequently, using historical cost data may not be the technique of choice because of the time and effort involved. In those situations, one or more of the techniques listed in the remainder of the chapter should be used.

Using Internal and External Experts' Input

When faced with converting soft data items for which historical records are not available, it might be feasible to consider input from experts. With this approach, internal experts provide the cost (or value) of one unit of improvement. The individuals who have knowledge of the situation and the respect of the management group are often the best prospects for expert input. These experts must understand the processes and be willing to provide estimates as well as the assumptions used in arriving at the estimate. When requesting input from experts, it is best to explain the full scope of what is needed, providing as many specifics as possible. Most experts have their own methodology to develop this value.

An example will help clarify this approach. In one manufacturing plant, a leadership development program was designed to reduce the number of grievances filed at Step 2 (see Table 6-3). This is the step in which the grievance is recorded in writing and becomes a measurable soft data item. Except for the actual cost of settlements and direct external costs, the company had no records of the total costs of grievances (i.e., there were no data for the time required to resolve a grievance). Therefore, an estimate was needed from an expert. The manager of labor relations, who had credibility with senior management and thorough knowledge of the grievance process, provided an estimate of the cost. He based his estimate on the average settlement when a grievance was lost, the direct costs related to the grievances (arbitration, legal fees, printing, research), the estimated amount of supervisory, staff, and employee time associated with the grievance, and a factor for reduced morale and other "soft" consequences. Although not a precise figure, this internal estimate was appropriate for this analysis and had adequate credibility with management.

When internal experts are not available, external experts are sought. External experts must be selected based on their experience with the unit of measure. Fortunately, many experts are available who work directly with important measures such as creativity, innovation, employee attitudes, customer satisfaction, employee turnover, absenteeism, and grievances. They are often willing to provide estimates of the cost (or value) of these items. Because the credibility of the value is related directly to his or her reputation, the credibility and reputation of the expert are critical.

Sometimes one or more techniques may be used in a complementary way to develop the costs. Consider, for example, the process for developing the cost of a sexual harassment complaint (Phillips and Hill, 2001). In this case study, the cost of a formal complaint filed with the vice president of human resources was developed. In this analysis, the assumption was made that if no complaints were filed, there would be no costs of sexual harassment communication, investigation, and defense. Consequently, two approaches were used to arrive at the cost of a complaint. First, the direct cost was captured for an entire year of all activities and processes connected with sexual harassment. This figure was taken directly from the cost statements. Second, the other cost values were estimated (e.g., time of the staff and management involved in these activities) using input from internal experts, the EEOC, and affirmative action staff. Figure 6-1 shows how these two values were combined to yield a total value of $852,000 for 35 complaints, which yielded an approximate value of $24,000 for a complaint.

USING VALUES FROM EXTERNAL DATABASES

For some soft data items, it may be appropriate to use estimates of the cost (or value) of one unit based on the research of others. This strategy taps external databases that contain studies and research projects focusing on the cost of data items. Fortunately, many databases are available that report cost studies of a variety of data items related to leadership development programs. Data are available on the cost of turnover, absenteeism, grievances, accidents,

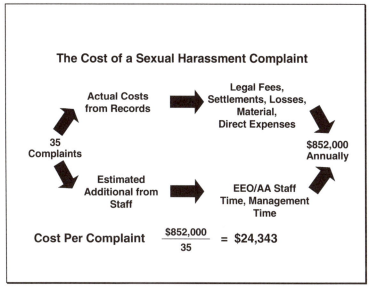

Figure 6-1. Converting data using historical costs and expert input.

and even customer satisfaction. The difficulty lies in finding a database with studies or research efforts for a situation similar to the program under evaluation. Ideally, data would come from a similar setting in the same industry, but that is not always possible. Sometimes data on all industries or organizations would be sufficient, perhaps with an adjustment to fit the industry under consideration.

An example illustrates the use of this process. A leadership development program was designed to reduce the turnover of branch employees in a regional banking group (Phillips and Phillips, 2002). To complete the evaluation and calculate the ROI, the cost of turnover was needed. To develop the turnover value internally, several costs would have to be identified, including the cost of recruiting, employment processing, orientation, training new employees, lost productivity while a new employee is trained, quality problems, scheduling difficulties, and customer satisfaction problems. Additional costs include regional manager time to work with the turnover issues and, in some cases, exit costs of litigation, severance, and unemployment. Obviously, these costs are significant. Most leadership development managers do not have the time to calculate the cost of turnover, particularly when it is needed for a one-time event such as evaluating a training program. In this example, turnover cost studies in the same industry placed the value at about 1.1 to 1.25 times the average annual salaries of the employees. Most turnover cost studies report the cost of turnover as a multiple of annual base salaries. In this example, management decided to be conservative and adjusted the value downward to 0.9 of the average base salary of the employees.

USING ESTIMATES FROM PARTICIPANTS

In some situations, program participants estimate the value of a soft data improvement. This strategy is appropriate when participants are capable of providing estimates of the cost (or value) of the unit of measure improved by applying the skills learned in the program. When using this approach, participants should be provided with clear instructions, along with examples of the type of information needed. The advantage of this approach is that individuals closest to the improvement are often capable of providing the most reliable estimates of its value.

An example illustrates this process. A group of team leaders attended an interpersonal skills program, "Improving Work Habits," which was designed to lower the absenteeism rate of the employees in their work units. Successful application of the program should result in a reduction in absenteeism. To calculate the ROI for the program, it was necessary to determine the average value of one absence in the company. As is the case with most organizations, historical records for the cost of absenteeism were not available. Experts were not available, and external studies were sparse for this particular industry. Consequently, supervisors (program participants) were asked to estimate the cost of an absence.

In a group-interview format, each participant was asked to recall the last time an employee in his or her work group was unexpectedly absent and describe what was necessary to compensate for the absence. Because the impact of an absence will vary considerably from one employee to another within the same work unit, the group listened to all explanations. After reflecting on what must be done when an employee is absent, each supervisor was asked to provide an estimate of the average cost of an absence in the company. Although some supervisors are reluctant to provide estimates, with prodding and encouragement they will usually provide a value. The values are averaged for the group, and the result is the cost of an absence to be used in evaluating the program. Although this is an estimate, it is probably more accurate than data from external studies, calculations using internal records, or estimates from experts. Also, because it comes from supervisors who deal with the issue daily, it will usually have credibility with senior management.

Using Estimates from Immediate Managers

In some situations, participants may be incapable of placing a value on the improvement. Their work may be so far removed from the output of the process that they cannot reliably provide estimates. In these cases, the managers of participants may be capable of providing estimates. Consequently, they may be asked to provide a value for a unit of improvement linked to the program.

In other situations, supervisors are asked to review and approve participants' estimates. After the program is completed, participants estimated the value of their improvements that were directly related to their participation in the program. Their immediate managers are then asked to review the estimates and the process used by the participants to arrive at the estimates. Supervisors could confirm, adjust, or discard the values provided by the participants.

In some situations, senior management provides estimates of the value of data. With this approach, senior managers interested in the process or program are asked to place a value on the improvement based on their perception of its worth. This approach is used in situations in which it is very difficult to calculate the value or other sources of estimation are unavailable or unreliable. Although this process is subjective, it does have the benefit of ownership from senior executives, the same executives who approved the program budget.

Linking with Other Measures

When standard values, records, experts, and external studies are unavailable, a feasible approach might be developing a relationship between the measure in question and some other measure that may be converted easily to a monetary value. This approach involves identifying, if possible, existing relationships showing a strong correlation between one measure and another with a standard value.

For example, the classical relationship depicted in Figure 6-2 shows a correlation between increasing job satisfaction and employee turnover. In a consulting project designed to improve job satisfaction, a value is needed for changes in the job satisfaction index. A predetermined relationship showing the correlation

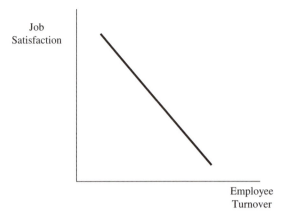

Figure 6-2. Relationship between job satisfaction and turnover.

between improvements in job satisfaction and reductions in turnover can link the changes directly to turnover. Using standard data or external studies, the cost of turnover can easily be developed as described earlier. Thus, a change in job satisfaction is converted to a monetary value, or at least an approximate value. It is not always exact because of the potential for error and other factors, but the estimate is sufficient for converting data to monetary values.

In some situations, a chain of relationships may be established to show the connection between two or more variables. In this approach, a measure that may be difficult to convert to a monetary value is linked to other measures that, in turn, are linked to measures on which a value can be placed. Ultimately these measures are traced to a monetary value that is often based on profits. Figure 6-3 shows the model used by Sears, one of the world's largest retail store chains (Ulrich, 1998). The model connects job attitudes (collected directly from the employees) with customer service, which is related directly to revenue growth. The rectangles in the chart represent survey information, whereas the ovals represent hard data. The shaded measurements are collected and distributed in the form of Sears total performance indicators.

As the model shows, a 5-point improvement in employee attitudes will drive a 1.3-point improvement in customer satisfaction. This, in turn, drives a 0.5 percent increase in revenue growth. Thus, if employee attitudes at a local store improved by 5 points, and previous revenue growth was 5 percent, the new revenue growth would be 5.5 percent.

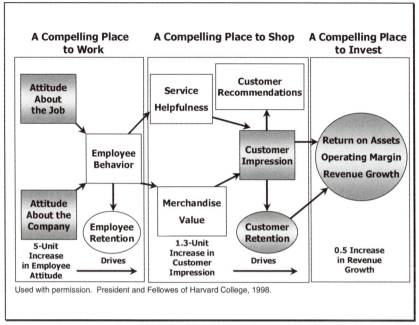

Figure 6-3. Linkage of job satisfaction and revenue.

These links between measures, often called the *service-profit chain*, create a promising way to place monetary values on hard-to-quantify measures.

USING LEADERSHIP DEVELOPMENT STAFF ESTIMATES

The final technique for converting data to monetary values is to use leadership development staff estimates. Using all the available information and experience, the staff members most familiar with the situation provide estimates of the value. Although the staff may be capable of providing accurate estimates, this approach may be perceived as being biased, as the leadership development staff wanted it to be large (a motive). It should be used only when other approaches are not available.

SELECTING THE APPROPRIATE MEASURES

With so many techniques available, the challenge is to select one or more techniques appropriate to the situation. The following guidelines can help determine the proper selection.

Use the technique appropriate for the type of data. Some techniques are designed specifically for hard data, whereas others are more appropriate for soft data. Consequently, the type of data will often dictate the strategy. Hard data, while always preferred, are not always available. Soft data are often required, and thus must be addressed with the techniques appropriate for soft data.

Move from most accurate to least accurate techniques. The techniques are presented in order of accuracy and credibility, beginning with the most credible. Standard, accepted values are most credible; leadership development staff estimates are least credible. Working down the list, each technique should be considered for its feasibility in the situation. The technique with the most accuracy and credibility is recommended.

Consider availability and convenience when selecting the technique. Sometimes the availability of a particular source of data will drive the selection. In other situations, the convenience of a technique may be an important factor in its selection.

When estimates are sought, use the source with the broadest perspective on the issue. To improve the accuracy of an estimate, the broadest perspective on the issue is needed. The individual providing an estimate must be knowledgeable of all the processes and the issues surrounding the value of the data item.

Use multiple techniques when feasible. Sometimes it is helpful to have more than one technique for obtaining a value for data. When multiple sources are available, more than one source should be used to serve as a comparison or to provide another perspective. When multiple sources are used, data must be integrated using a convenient decision rule, such as the lowest value, a preferred approach because of the conservative nature of the lowest value.

By most conservative, it is the approach that yields the lowest ROI. Thus, if the benefits are in consideration (numerator), it is the value that yields that lowest ROI.

Minimize the amount of time required to select and implement the appropriate technique. As with other processes, it is important to keep the time invested as low as possible so that the total time and effort for the ROI do not become excessive. Some strategies can be implemented with less time than others. This block in the ROI model can quickly absorb more time than the remainder of all the steps. Too much time at this step can dampen an otherwise enthusiastic attitude about the process.

Accuracy and Credibility of Data

The Credibility Problem

The techniques presented in this chapter assume that each data item collected and linked with leadership development can be converted to a monetary value. Although estimates can be developed using one or more of these techniques, the process of converting data to monetary values may lose credibility with the target audience, who may doubt its use in analysis. Very subjective data, such as a change in employee morale or a reduction in the number of employee conflicts, are difficult to convert to monetary values. The key question for this determination is this: "Could these results be presented to senior management with confidence?" If the process does not meet this credibility test, data should not be converted to monetary values and instead listed as an intangible benefit. Other data, particularly hard data items, could be used in the ROI calculation, leaving the very subjective data as intangible improvements.

When converting data to monetary value, it is important to be consistent in the approach. Specific rules for making conversions will ensure this consistency and, ultimately, enhance the reliability of the study. When it is questionable if a data item should be converted, a four-part test is suggested, starting with the question "Is there a standard value?" If the answer is yes, it is used; if not, the next part of the test is considered. The next question "Is there a method available to convert data to monetary value?" If this answer is no, the item is listed as an intangible. If it can be converted using one of the methods in this chapter, the next step is considered. The next question is "Can the conversion be accomplished with minimum resources?" If the answer is no, the item should be considered an intangible; if yes, the final step is considered. The last question is "Can the conversion process be described to an executive audience and obtain their buy-in in two minutes?" If yes, the value can be placed in the ROI calculation; if no, it is listed as an intangible. These guidelines are very critical in converting data consistently. The important point is to be consistent and methodical when converting data.

The accuracy of data and the credibility of the conversion process are important concerns. Leadership development professionals sometimes avoid converting data because of these issues. They are more comfortable in reporting that a leadership development program resulted in reducing absenteeism from 6 to 4 percent without attempting to place a value on the improvement. They assume that each person receiving the information will place a value on the absenteeism reduction. Unfortunately, the target audience may know little about the cost of absenteeism and will usually underestimate the actual value of the improvement. Consequently, there should be some attempt to include this conversion in the ROI analysis.

How the Credibility of Data Is Influenced

When ROI data are presented to selected target audiences, its credibility will be an issue. The degree to which the target audience will believe the data will be influenced by the following factors.

Reputation of the source of data. The actual source of data represents the first credibility issue. How credible is the individual or groups providing data? Do they understand the issues? Are they knowledgeable of all the processes? The target audience will often place more credibility on data obtained from those who are closest to the source of the actual improvement or change.

Reputation of the source of the study. The target audience scrutinizes the reputation of the individual, group, or organization presenting the data. Do they have a history of providing accurate reports? Are they unbiased with their analyses? Are they fair in their presentation? Answers to these and other questions will form an impression about the reputation.

Audience bias. The audience may have a bias—either positive or negative—to a particular study or data presented from the study. Some executives have a positive feeling about a particular program and will need less data to convince them of its value. Other executives may have negative bias toward the program and will need more data to make this comparison. The potential bias of the audience should be understood so that data can be presented to counter any attitude.

Motives of the evaluators. The audience will look for motives of the person(s) conducting the study. Do the individuals presenting the data have an axe to grind? Do they have a personal interest in creating a favorable or unfavorable result? Are the stakes high if the study is unfavorable? These and other issues will cause the target audience to examine motives.

Methodology of the study. The audience will want to know specifically how the research was conducted. How were the calculations made? What steps were followed? What processes were used? A lack of information on the methodology will cause the audience to become wary and suspicious of the results. They will substitute their own perception of the methodology.

Assumptions made in the analysis. The audience will try to understand the assumptions made in the analysis. What are the assumptions in the study? Are they standard? How do they compare with other assumptions in other studies? When assumptions are omitted, the audience will substitute their own, often-unfavorable assumptions. In ROI studies, conservative guiding principles influence calculations and conclusions.

Realism of the outcome data. Impressive ROI values could cause problems. When outcomes appear to be unrealistic, it may be difficult for the target audience to believe them. Huge claims often fall on deaf ears, causing reports to be thrown away before they are reviewed.

Types of data. The target audience will usually have a preference for hard data. They are seeking business performance data tied to output, quality, costs, and time. These measures are usually easily understood and closely related to organizational performance. Conversely, soft data are sometimes viewed suspiciously from the outset, as many senior executives are concerned about its soft nature and limitations on the analysis.

Scope of analysis. The smaller the scope, the more credible the data. Is the scope of the analysis narrow? Does it involve just one group or all of the employees in the organization? Limiting the study to a small group, or series of groups, of employees makes the process more accurate and believable.

Collectively, these factors will influence the credibility of a leadership development scorecard and provide a framework from which to develop the evaluation report. Thus, when considering each of the issues, the following key points are suggested for developing a leadership development scorecard report and presenting it to the management group:

- Use the most credible and reliable source for estimates.
- Present the material in an unbiased, objective way.
- Be prepared for the potential bias of the audience.
- Fully explain the methodology used throughout the process, preferably on a step-by-step basis.
- Define the assumptions made in the analysis and compare them to assumptions made in other similar studies.

- Consider factoring or adjusting output values when they appear to be unrealistic.
- Use hard data whenever possible and combine with soft data if available.
- Keep the scope of the analysis very narrow. Conduct the impact with one or more groups of participants in the program instead of all participants or all employees.

Making Adjustments

Two potential adjustments should be considered before finalizing the monetary value. In some organizations where soft data are used and values are derived with imprecise methods, senior management is sometimes offered the opportunity to review and approve data. Because of the subjective nature of this process, management may factor (reduce) data so that the final results are more credible.

The other adjustment concerns the time value of money. Since an investment in a program is made at one time period and the return is realized in a later time period, a few organizations adjust the program benefits to reflect the time value of money, using discounted cash flow techniques. The actual monetary benefits of the program are adjusted for this time period. The amount of this adjustment, however, is usually small compared with the typical benefits realized from leadership development programs.

FINAL THOUGHTS

In conclusion, organizations are attempting to be more aggressive when defining the monetary benefits of leadership development. Progressive leadership development managers are no longer satisfied with reporting business performance results from programs. Instead, they are taking additional steps to convert business results data to monetary values and compare them with the program's cost to develop the ultimate level of evaluation, the return on investment. This chapter presented ten specific techniques to convert business results to monetary values, offering an array of possibilities to fit any situation and program.

CASE STUDY—PART E
INTERNATIONAL CAR RENTAL

CONVERTING BUSINESS MEASURES TO MONETARY VALUES

Data conversion comes directly from participants as they are asked to identify or estimate the value of their data. During review of the data collection instrument at the end of the program, participants were reminded that standard monetary values are available for many of the data items. Also, internal experts, who work routinely with the measure, are available to provide a value. They could be contacted to provide an estimate. Finally, in some cases, the participants could estimate it using the knowledge of the particular measure and the impact of it on the work unit. Because there are so many measures to convert to monetary values, it would be impossible to use most of the other data conversion techniques. On the follow-up questionnaire provided in Chapter 4, Figure 4-4, question 27 asks the participant to provide data and question 28 provides the basis for the value. One year of benefits was used in the analysis to be standard, consistent, and conservative.

Twenty-nine questionnaires were returned for an 81 percent response rate. Participants provided rich data indicating success at levels 1, 2, 3, and 4. Although significant improvements were indicated at levels 1, 2, and 3, only business impact data (Level 4) are shown in Figure 6-4. Figure 6-4 shows specific improvements identified directly from the questionnaire, by participant number, for the first 15 participants. The remaining 14 participants are included as a total. Usually, each participant provided improvements on two

Participant Number	Q30 Annual Improvement	Q26 Measure	Q31 Contribution from Program	Q32 Confidence Estimate	Total Monetary Benefits Q30xQ31xQ32 Adjusted Value
1	$ 13,100	Sales	60%	80%	$ 6,288
3	41,200	Productivity	75%	95%	29,355
4	5,300	Sales	80%	90%	3,816
6	7,210	Cost	70%	70%	3,533
9	4,215	Efficiency	40%	75%	1,265
10	17,500	Quality	35%	60%	3,675
12	11,500	Time	60%	80%	5,520
14	3,948	Time	70%	80%	2,212
15	14,725	Sales	40%	70%	4,123
17	6,673	Efficiency	50%	60%	2,002
18	12,140	Costs	100%	100%	12,140
19	17,850	Sales	60%	70%	7,497
21	13,920	Sales	50%	80%	5,568
22	15,362	Cost	40%	90%	5,530
23	18,923	Sales	60%	75%	8,515
				Total for the items above	$ 101,039
				Total for the next 14 items	$ 84,398
				Total for 2nd measure	$ 143,764
				Total Benefits	$ 329,201

Figure 6-4. Business impact results.

measures. The total for the second measure is shown at the bottom of Figure 6-4.

DISCUSSION QUESTIONS

1. Which specific costs should be included when tabulating the overall cost of the leadership challenge program?

REFERENCES

Boulton, R.E.S., Libert, B.D., and Samek, S.M. *Cracking the Value Code: How Successful Businesses Are Creating Wealth in the New Economy.* New York: Harper Business, 2000.

Campanella, J. (Ed.). *Principles of Quality Costs.* 3rd ed. Milwaukee, WI: American Society for Quality, 1999.

Harbour, J.L. *Cycle Time Reduction: Designing and Streamlining Work for High Performance.* New York: Quality Resources, 1996.

Johnson, M.D., and Gustafsson, A. *Improving Customer Satisfaction, Loyalty, and Profit: An Integrated Measurement and Management System.* San Francisco, CA: Jossey-Bass, 2000.

Phillips, J.J. *The Consultant's Scorecard: Tracking Results and Bottom-Line Impact of Consulting Projects.* New York: McGraw-Hill, 2000.

Phillips, J.J., and Hill, D. "Sexual Harassment Prevention," *The Human Resources Scorecard: Measuring the Return on Investment.* Boston, MA: Butterworth-Heinemann, 2001, pp. 354–372.

Phillips, J.J., and Stone, R.D. "Absenteeism Reduction Program" *In Action: Measuring ROI in the Public Sector.* Alexandria, VA: American Society for Training and Development, 2002, pp. 221–234.

Phillips, P.P., and Phillips, J.J. "A Strategic Approach to Retention Improvement," *In Action: Retaining Your Best Employees,* P.P. Phillips (Ed.). Alexandria, VA: American Society for Training and Development, 2002.

Phillips, P.P. "Executive Leadership Development," *The Human Resources Scorecard: Measuring the Return on Investment.* Boston, MA: Butterworth-Heinemann, 2001, pp. 449–476.

Stamp, D. *The Workplace of the 21st Century.* Bellevue, WA: Priority Management Systems, 1992.

Ulrich, D. (Ed.). *Delivering Results.* Boston, MA: Harvard Business School, 1998.

CHAPTER 7

Tabulating Leadership Development Program Costs

The cost of providing leadership development programs is increasing—creating more pressure for leadership development managers to know how and why money is spent. The total cost of leadership development is required, which means that the cost profile goes beyond the direct costs and includes all indirect costs. Fully loaded cost information is used to manage resources, develop standards, measure efficiencies, and examine alternative delivery processes.

Tabulating program costs is an essential step in developing the ROI calculation for the leadership development scorecard, and these costs are used as the denominator in the ROI formula. It is just as important to focus on costs as it is on benefits. In practice, however, costs are often captured more easily than benefits. This chapter explores costs accumulation and tabulation steps, outlines the specific costs that should be captured, and presents economical ways to develop costs.

Cost Strategies

Importance of Costs

Many influences have caused the increased attention now given to monitoring leadership development costs accurately and thoroughly. Every organization should know approximately how much money it spends on leadership development. Many organizations calculate this expenditure and make comparisons with that of other organizations, although comparisons are difficult to make because of the different bases for cost calculations. Some organizations calculate leadership development costs as a percentage of payroll costs and set targets for increased investment.

An effective system of cost monitoring enables an organization to calculate the magnitude of total leadership development expenditures. Collecting this information also helps top management answer two important questions:

1. How much should we spend on leadership development?
2. How much do we spend on leadership development compared with other organizations?

The leadership development staff should know the relative cost effectiveness of programs and their components. Monitoring costs by program allows the staff to evaluate the relative contribution of a program and to determine how those costs are changing. If a program's cost rises, it might be appropriate to reevaluate the program's impact and overall success. It may be useful to compare specific components of costs with those of other programs or organizations. For example, the cost per participant for one program could be compared with the cost per participant for a similar program. Huge differences may signal a problem. Also, costs associated with design, development, or delivery could be compared with those of other programs within the organization and used to develop cost standards.

Accurate costs are necessary to predict future costs. Historical costs for a program provide the basis for predicting future costs of a similar program or budgeting for a program. Sophisticated cost models make it possible to estimate or predict costs with reasonable accuracy.

When a return on investment or cost benefit analysis is needed for a specific program, costs must be developed. One of the most significant reasons for collecting costs is to obtain data for use in a benefits-versus-costs comparison. In this comparison, cost data are equally important as the program's economic benefits.

To improve the efficiency of the leadership development function, controlling costs is necessary. Competitive pressures place increased attention on efficiencies. Most leadership development departments have monthly budgets with cost projections listed by various accounts and, in some cases, by program. Cost monitoring is an excellent tool for identifying problem areas and taking corrective action. In the practical and classical management sense, the accumulation of cost data is a necessity.

Capturing costs is challenging because the figures must be accurate, reliable, and realistic. Although most organizations develop costs with much more ease than developing the economic value of benefits, the true cost of leadership development is often an elusive figure even in some of the best organizations. While the total leadership development direct budget is usually a number that is easily developed, it is more difficult to determine the specific costs of a program, including the indirect costs related to it. To develop a realistic ROI, costs must be accurate and credible. Otherwise, the painstaking difficulty and attention to the benefits will be wasted because of inadequate or inaccurate costs.

Pressure to Disclose all Costs

Today there is increased pressure to report all leadership development costs, or what is referred to as fully loaded costs. This takes the cost profile beyond the direct cost of leadership development and includes the time that participants are involved in leadership development, including their benefits and other overhead. For years, management has realized that there are many indirect costs of leadership development. Now they are asking for an accounting of these costs.

Fully Loaded Costs

The conservative approach to calculating the ROI has a direct connection to cost accumulation. With this approach, all costs that can be identified and linked to a particular program are included. The philosophy is simple: When in doubt in the denominator, put it in (i.e., if it is questionable whether a cost should be included, it is recommended that it be included, even if the cost guidelines for the organization do not require it). This parallels a rule for the numerator, which states, "when in doubt, leave it out" (i.e., if it is questionable whether a benefit should be included in the numerator, it should be omitted from the analysis). When an ROI is calculated and reported to target audiences the process should withstand even the closest scrutiny in terms of its accuracy and credibility. The only way to meet this test is to ensure that all costs are included. Of course, from a realistic viewpoint, if the controller or chief financial officer insists on not using certain costs, then it is best to leave them out.

The Danger of Costs without Benefits

It is dangerous to communicate the costs of leadership development without presenting benefits. Unfortunately, many organizations have fallen into this trap for years. Costs are presented to management in all types of ingenious ways, such as cost of the program, cost per employee, and cost per development hour. While these may be helpful for efficiency comparisons, it may be troublesome to present them without benefits. When most executives review leadership development costs, a logical question comes to mind: What benefit was received from the program? This is a typical management reaction, particularly when costs are perceived to be high. Because of this, some organizations have developed a policy of not communicating leadership development cost data for a specific program unless the benefits can be captured and presented along with the costs. Even if benefit data are subjective and intangible, they are included with cost data. This helps keep a balance with the two issues.

Policies and Guidelines

It may be helpful to detail the philosophy and policy on costs in guidelines for the leadership development staff and others who monitor and report costs. Cost guidelines detail specifically what costs are included with leadership development and how cost data are captured, analyzed, and reported. Cost guidelines can range from a 1-page document to a 50-page manual in a large, complex organization. The simpler approach is better. When fully developed, they should be reviewed by the finance and accounting staff. The final document serves as the guiding force in collecting, monitoring, and reporting costs. When an ROI is calculated and reported, costs are included in a summary form and the cost guidelines are referenced in a footnote or attached as an appendix.

COST TRACKING ISSUES

Sources of Costs

It can be helpful to first consider the sources of leadership development cost. There are three major categories of sources, as illustrated in Table 7-1. The leadership development staff expenses usually represent the greatest segment of costs and are sometimes transferred directly to the client or program sponsor. The second major cost category consists of participant expenses, both direct and indirect. These costs are not identified in many leadership development projects, but, nevertheless, reflect a significant amount. The third cost source is the payments made to external organizations.

Table 7-1
Sources of Costs

Source of costs	Cost reporting issues
1. Leadership development staff expenses	A. Costs are usually accurate B. Variable expenses may be underestimated
2. Participant expenses (direct and indirect)	A. Direct expenses are usually not fully loaded B. Indirect expenses are rarely included in costs
3. External expenses (equipment and services)	A. Sometimes understate B. May lack accountability

These include payments directly to hotels and conference centers, equipment suppliers, and services prescribed in the project. As Table 7-1 shows, some of these cost categories are understated. The finance and accounting records should be able to track and reflect the costs from these three different sources. The process presented in this chapter has the capability of tracking these costs, as well.

Leadership Development Process Steps and Cost

Another important way to consider leadership development costs is in the characteristics of how the project unfolds. Figure 7-1 shows the typical leadership development cycle, beginning with the initial analysis and assessment and progressing to the evaluation and reporting of the results. These functional process steps represent the typical flow of work. As a performance problem is addressed, a solution is developed or acquired and implemented in the organization. Implementation is often grouped with delivery. The entire process is routinely reported to the client or sponsor and evaluation is undertaken to show the project's success. There is also a group of costs to support the process—administrative support and overhead costs. To fully understand costs, the project should be analyzed in these different categories, as described later in this chapter.

Prorated vs Direct Costs

Usually all costs related to a program are captured and expensed to that program. However, three categories are usually prorated over several sessions of the same program. Needs assessment, design and development, and acquisition are all significant costs that should be

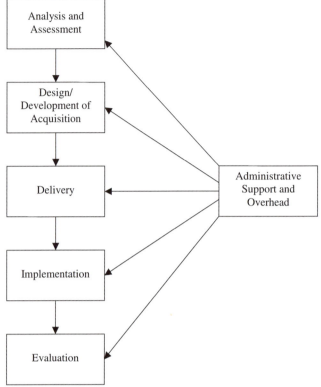

Figure 7-1. Leadership development functions and cost categories.

prorated over the shelf life of the program. Using a conservative approach, the shelf life should be very short. Some organizations will consider one year of operation for the program, others may consider two or three years. If there is some dispute about the specific time period to be used in the prorating formula, the shorter period should be used. If possible, the finance and accounting staff should be consulted.

Employee Benefits Factor

When presenting salaries for participants and leadership development staff associated with programs, the benefits factor should be included. This number is usually well known in the organization and used in other cost application. It represents the cost of all employee benefits expressed as a percent of base salaries. In some organizations this value is as high as 50 to 60 percent. In others, it may be as low as 25 to 30 percent. The average in the United States is approximately 38 percent (Nation's Business, 2002).

MAJOR COST CATEGORIES

The most important task is to define which specific costs are included in a tabulation of the program costs. This task involves decisions that will be made by the leadership development staff and usually approved by management. If appropriate, the finance and accounting staff may need to approve the list. Table 7-2 shows the recommended cost categories for a fully loaded, conservative approach to estimating costs. Each category is described.

Needs Assessment and Analysis

One of the most often overlooked items is the cost of conducting a needs assessment. In some programs, this cost is zero because the program is conducted without a needs assessment. However, as more organizations focus increased attention on needs assessment, this item will become a more significant cost in the future. All costs associated with the needs assessment should be captured to the fullest

Table 7-2
Leadership Development Program Cost Categories

Cost item	Prorated	Expensed
Needs assessment and analysis	✓	
Design and development	✓	
Acquisition	✓	
Delivery/implementation		✓
• Salaries/benefits—Facilitators		✓
• Salaries/benefits—Coordination		✓
• Program materials and fees		✓
• Travel/lodging/meals		✓
• Facilities		✓
• Participants salaries/benefits		✓
• Contact time		✓
• Travel time		✓
• Preparation time		✓
Evaluation		✓
Overhead/leadership development	✓	

extent possible. These costs include the time of staff members conducting the assessment, direct fees and expenses for external consultants who conduct the needs assessment, and internal services and supplies used in the analysis. The total costs are usually prorated over the life of the program. Depending on the type and nature of the program, the shelf life should be kept to a very reasonable number in the one- to two-year time frame. The exception would be very expensive programs that are not expected to change significantly for several years.

Design and Development Costs

One of the most significant items is the cost of designing and developing the program. These costs include internal staff time in both design and development and the purchase of supplies, videos, CD ROMs, and other material directly related to the program. It would also include the use of consultants. As with needs assessment costs, design and development costs are usually prorated, perhaps using the same time frame. One to two years is recommended unless the program is not expected to change for many years and the costs are significant.

When pilot programs are implemented, a prorating dilemma may surface. For expensive pilots, the complete design and development costs could be very significant. In this situation, prorating may not be an issue because the pilot is completely at risk. If all of those costs are included in the ROI analysis, it may be difficult, if not impossible, for a project to produce a positive ROI. The following rules can help work through this dilemma.

1. If the pilot project is completely at risk, all the costs should be placed in the ROI evaluation decision, (i.e., if the pilot does not have a positive ROI with all the costs included, it will not be implemented). In this scenario, it is best to keep the design and development costs to a minimum. Perhaps the program could be implemented without all of the "bells and whistles." The videos, CD ROMs, and other expensive development tools may be delayed until the use of skills and content are proven. This approach is often unreasonable.

2. If program implementation is not at risk, the cost of the development should be prorated over the anticipated life cycle. This is the approach taken in most situations. It is plausible to have a significant investment in the design and development of a

pilot when it is initiated, with the understanding that if it is not adding value, it can be adjusted, changed, or modified to add value. In these cases, a prorated development cost would be appropriate.

Regardless of the approach taken, these should be discussed before the evaluation begins. A dispute over prorating should not occur at the time the results are being tabulated. This discussion should also involve the sponsor of the program and a representative from finance and accounting.

Acquisition Costs

In lieu of development costs, many organizations purchase programs to use directly or in a modified format. The acquisition costs for these programs include the purchase price for the facilitator materials, train-the-trainer sessions, licensing agreements, and other costs associated with the right to deliver the program. These acquisition costs should be prorated using the same rationale given earlier; one to two years should be sufficient. If modification of the program is needed or some additional development is required, these costs should be included as development costs. In practice, many programs have both acquisition costs and development costs.

Delivery Costs

Usually the largest segment of leadership development costs would be those associated with delivery. Five major categories are included.

Salaries of facilitators and coordinators. The salaries of facilitators or program coordinators should be included. If a coordinator is involved in more than one program, the time should be allocated to the specific program under review. If external facilitators are used, all charges should be included for the session. The important issue is to capture all of the direct time of internal employees or external consultants who work directly with the program. The benefits factor should be included each time direct labor costs are involved. This factor is a widely accepted value, usually generated by the finance and accounting staff and in the 30 to 50 percent range.

Program materials and fees. Specific program materials, such as notebooks, textbooks, CD ROMs, case studies, exercises, and participant workbooks, should be included in the delivery costs, along with license fees, user fees, and royalty payments. Pens, paper, certificates, calculators, and personal copies of software are also included in this category.

Travel, lodging, and meals. Direct travel for participants, facilitators, or coordinators are included. Lodging and meals are included for participants during travel, as well as meals during the stay for the program. Refreshments should also be included.

Facilities. The direct cost of the facilities should be included. For external programs, this is the direct charge from the conference center, hotel, or motel. If the program is conducted in-house, the conference room represents a cost for the organization, then the cost should be estimated and included even if it is not the practice to include facilities' cost in other reports. The cost of internal facilities can easily be estimated by obtaining a room rental rate of the same size room at a local hotel. Sometimes this figure is available on a square foot basis from the finance and accounting staff (e.g., the value per square foot per day). In other situations, the cost of commercial real estate, on a square foot basis, could be determined locally from commercial real estate agents or the newspaper. The important point is to quickly come to a credible estimate for the value of the cost of the room.

This is an important issue that is often overlooked. Without encouragement from the finance and accounting staff, some leadership development staff members do not charge an amount for the use of internal facilities. The argument is that the room would be used regardless. However, the complete cost of leadership development should include the item because the room would probably not exist unless there was routine leadership development taking place. In the total cost picture, this is a very minor charge. It might have more value from the gesture than influencing the ROI calculation.

Participants' salaries and benefits. Salaries plus employee benefits of participants represent an expense that should be included. For situations where the program has been conducted, these costs can be estimated using average or midpoint values for salaries in typical job classifications. When a program is targeted for an ROI calculation, participants can provide their salaries directly and in a confidential manner.

For major leadership development programs, there may be a separate category for implementation. If the program involves meetings, follow-ups, manager reinforcement, and a variety of other activities beyond the specific leadership development program, an additional category for implementation may be appropriate. In some extreme examples, on-site coordinators are available to provide assistance and support for the program as it is implemented throughout the region, branch, or division. The total expense of these coordinators is implementation expenses that should be included. The specific cost categories for implementation are often mirrored in the delivery categories. However, in most situations, the implementation is considered part of the delivery and is placed in that category.

Evaluation

Usually the total evaluation cost is included in the program costs to compute the fully loaded cost. ROI costs include the cost of developing the evaluation strategy, designing instruments, collecting data, data analysis, and report preparation and distribution. Cost categories include time, materials, purchased instruments, or surveys. A case can be made to prorate the evaluation costs over several programs instead of charging the total amount as an expense. For example, if 25 sessions of a program are conducted in a three-year period and one group is selected for an ROI calculation, then the ROI costs could logically be prorated over the 25 sessions because the results of the ROI analysis should reflect the success of the other programs and will perhaps result in changes that will influence the other programs as well.

Overhead

A final charge is the cost of overhead, the additional costs in the leadership development function not directly related to a particular program. The overhead category represents any leadership development department cost not considered in the aforementioned calculations. Typical items include the cost of clerical support, departmental office expenses, salaries of training managers, and other fixed costs. Some organizations obtain an estimate for allocation by dividing the total overhead by the number of program participant training days or hours for the year. This becomes a standard value to use in calculations.

An example illustrates the simplicity of this approach. An organization with 50 training and development programs (including leadership development programs) tabulates all of the expenditures in the budget not allocated directly to a particular program ($548,061 in this example). This part of the budget is then viewed as total overhead, unallocated to specific training and development programs. The hours approach may be helpful if there is a significant amount of e-learning and participants are involved in programs an hour at a time. The allocation of days may be appropriate in others. Next, this number is divided by the total number of participant days or hours (e.g., if a 5-day program is offered 10 times a year, 50 days should be put in the total days category, or 400 hours for an 8-hour day). In this example, the total days were approximately 7400. The total unallocated overhead of $548,061 is divided by 7400 days to arrive at $74. Thus, an overhead amount of $74 is charged for overhead for each day of training. A 3-day leadership development program would be charged $222 for overhead. The amount is usually small and will have very little impact on the ROI calculation. The gesture of including the number as part of a fully loaded cost profile builds credibility with the sponsor and senior executives.

COST REPORTING

An example using an actual case study shows how the total costs are presented. Table 7-3 shows the cost for a major executive leadership development program (Phillips, 2001). This was a very extensive leadership program involving four one-week off-site training sessions with personal coaches and learning coaches assigned to the participants. Working in teams, participants tackled a project that was important to top executives. Each team reported the results to management. The project teams could hire consultants, as well. These costs are listed as project costs. Costs for the first group, involving 22 participants, are detailed in Table 7-3.

The issue of prorating costs was an important consideration. In this case, it was reasonably certain that a second group would be conducted. The analysis, design, and development expenses of $580,657 could, therefore, be prorated over two sessions. Consequently, in the actual ROI calculation, half of this number was used to arrive at the total value ($290,328). This left a total program cost of $2,019,598 to include in the analysis ($2,309,926 −$290,328). On a participant basis, this was $91,800 or $22,950 for each week of formal sessions. Although this program was very expensive, it was still close to a rough benchmark of weekly costs of several senior executive leadership programs.

COST ACCUMULATION AND ESTIMATION

There are two basic ways to accumulate costs. One is by a description of the expenditure such as labor, materials, supplies, and travel.

Table 7-3
Leadership Development Program Costs

Program costs	
Analysis/design/development	
External consultants	$525,330
Leadership development department	28,785
Management committee	26,542
Delivery	
Conference facilities (hotel)	142,554
Consultants/external	812,110
Leadership development department salaries and benefits (for direct work with the program)	15,283
Leadership development department travel expenses	37,500
Management committee (time)	75,470
Project costs ($25,000 × 4)	100,000
Participant salaries and benefits (class sessions) (average daily salary × benefits factor × number of program days)	84,564
Participant salaries and benefits (project work)	117,353
Travel and lodging for participants	100,938
Cost of materials (handouts, purchased materials)	6,872
Research and evaluation	
Research	110,750
Evaluation	125,875
Total costs	$2,309,926

These are expense account classifications. The other is by categories in the leadership development process or function such as program development, delivery, and evaluation. An effective system monitors costs by account categories according to the description of those accounts but also includes a method for accumulating costs by the leadership development process/functional category. Many systems stop short of this second step. While the first grouping sufficiently gives the total program cost, it does not allow for a useful comparison with other programs or indicate areas where costs might be excessive by relative comparisons.

Cost Classification Matrix

Costs are accumulated under both of these classifications. The two classifications are obviously related and the relationship depends on the organization. For instance, the specific costs that comprise the analysis part of a program may vary substantially with the organization.

An important part of the classification process is to define the kinds of costs in the account classification system that normally apply to the major process/functional categories. Table 7-4 is a matrix that represents the categories for accumulating all leadership development-related costs in the organization. Those costs, which normally are a part of a process/functional category, are checked in the matrix. Each member of the leadership development staff should know how to charge expenses properly. For example, equipment is rented to use in the development and delivery of a program. Should all or part of the cost be charged to development or should it be charged to delivery? More than likely the cost will be allocated in proportion to the extent in which the item was used for each category.

Cost Accumulation

With expense account classifications clearly defined and the process/functional categories determined, it is easy to track costs on individual programs. This is accomplished by using special account numbers and project numbers. An example illustrates the use of these numbers.

A project number is a three-digit number representing a specific leadership development program. For example:

New manager orientation	112
Management essentials	215
Strategic business leadership	418
Valuing diversity	791

Numbers are assigned to the process/functional breakdowns. Using the example presented earlier, the following numbers are assigned:

Analysis	1
Development	2
Delivery	3
Evaluation	4

Table 7-4
Cost Classification Matrix

Expense account classification	Process / functional categories			
	Analysis	Development	Delivery	Evaluation
00 Salaries and benefits —HRD staff	X	X	X	X
01 Salaries and benefits —Other staff		X	X	
02 Salaries and benefits —Participants			X	X
03 Meals, travel, and incidental expenses —HRD staff	X	X	X	X
04 Meals, travel, and accommodations —Participants			X	
05 Office supplies and expenses	X	X		X
06 Program materials and supplies		X	X	
07 Printing and copying	X	X	X	X
08 Outside services	X	X	X	X
09 Equipment expense allocation	X	X	X	X
10 Equipment—Rental		X	X	
11 Equipment— Maintenance			X	
12 Registration fees	X			
13 Facilities expense allocation			X	
14 Facilities rental			X	
15 General overhead allocation	X	X	X	X
16 Other miscellaneous expenses	X	X	X	X

Using the two-digit numbers assigned to account classifications in Table 7-4, an accounting system is complete. For example, if workbooks are reproduced for the valuing diversity workshop, the appropriate charge number for that reproduction is 07-3-791. The first two digits denote the account classification, the next digit the process/functional category, and the last three digits the project number. This system enables rapid accumulation and monitoring of leadership development costs. Total costs can be presented by:

- leadership development program (valuing diversity workshop),
- process/functional categories (delivery), and
- expense account classification (printing and reproduction).

Cost Estimation

The previous sections covered procedures for classifying and monitoring costs related to leadership development programs. It is important to monitor and compare ongoing costs with the budget or with projected costs. However, a significant reason for tracking costs is to predict the cost of future programs. Usually this goal is accomplished through a formal cost estimation method unique to the organization.

Some organizations use cost-estimating worksheets to arrive at the total cost for a proposed program. Figure 7-2 shows an example of a cost-estimating worksheet that calculates analysis, development, delivery, and evaluation costs. The worksheets contain a few formulas that make it easier to estimate the cost. In addition to these worksheets, current charge rates for services, supplies, and salaries are available. These data become outdated quickly and are usually prepared periodically as a supplement.

The most appropriate basis for predicting costs is to analyze the previous costs by tracking the actual costs incurred in all phases of a leadership development program from analysis to evaluation. This way, it is possible to see how much is spent on programs and how much is being spent in the different categories. Until adequate cost data are available, it is necessary to use the detailed analysis in the worksheets for cost estimation.

FINAL THOUGHTS

Costs are important for a variety of uses and applications. They help the leadership development staff manage the resources carefully, consistently, and efficiently. They also allow for comparisons between different elements and cost categories. Cost categorization can take several different forms; the most common are presented in this chapter. Costs should be fully loaded for leadership scorecard ROI calculation. From a practical standpoint, including certain cost items may be optional, based on the organization's guidelines and philosophy. However, because of the scrutiny involved in ROI calculations, it is recommended that all costs be included, even if it goes beyond the requirements of the company policy.

Analysis Costs		**Total**
Salaries & Employee Benefits--HRD Staff (No. of People x Average Salary x Employee Benefits Factor x No. of Hours on Project)		_____
Meals, Travel, and Incidental Expenses		_____
Office Supplies and Expenses		_____
Printing and Reproduction		_____
Outside Services		_____
Equipment Expenses		_____
Registration Fees		_____
General Overhead Allocation		_____
Other Miscellaneous Expenses		_____
Total Analysis Cost		_____
Development Costs		**Total**
Salaries & Employee Benefits (No. of People x Avg. Salary x Employee Benefits Factor x No. of Hours on Project)		_____
Meals, Travel, and Incidental Expenses		_____
Office Supplies and Expenses		_____
Program Materials and Supplies		_____
Videotape	_____	
CD-ROM	_____	
Books	_____	
Manuals and Materials	_____	
Other	_____	
Printing and Reproduction		_____
Outside Services		_____
Equipment Expense		_____
General Overhead Allocation		_____
Other Miscellaneous Expenses		_____
Total Development Cost		_____

Figure 7-2. Program-estimating worksheet.

Delivery Costs	Total	
Participant Costs (A)*		
Salaries & Employee Benefits (No. of Participants x Avg. Salary x Employee Benefits Factor x Hrs. or Days of Training Time)		*Use A, B, or C – Not a combination
Meals, Travel, & Accommodations (No. of Participants x Avg. Daily Expenses x Days of Training)		
Program Materials and Supplies		
Participant Replacement Costs (if applicable) (B)*		
Lost Production (Explain Basis) (C)*		
Facilitator Costs		
Salaries & Benefits		
Meals, Travel, & Incidental Expense		
Outside Services		
Facility Costs		
Facilities Rental		
Facilities Expense Allocation		
Equipment Expense		
General Overhead Allocation		
Other Miscellaneous Expense		
Total Delivery Costs		

Evaluation Costs	Total
Salaries & Employee Benefits--HRD Staff (No. of People x Avg. Salary x Employee Benefits Factor x No. or Hours on Project)	
Meals, Travel, and Incidental Expense	
Participant Costs	
Office Supplies and Expense	
Printing and Reproduction	
Outside Services	
Equipment Expense	
General Overhead Allocation	
Other Miscellaneous Expenses	
Total Evaluation Costs	
TOTAL PROGRAM COSTS	

Figure 7-2. (Continued)

CASE STUDY—PART F
INTERNATIONAL CAR RENTAL

Tabulating Costs

In tabulating the costs for the leadership challenge, the L&D staff took a conservative approach and ensured that the costs were fully loaded. Figure 7-3 illustrates the cost categories used as well as

Program Cost Summary

(36 Participants)

Cost Item	Cost
Needs Assessment (prorated over 4 years)	$ 900
Program Development (prorated over 3 years)	2,000
Program Materials ($120/participant)	4,320
Travel, Meals, and Lodging ($1,600/participant)	57,600
Facilitation and Coordination ($4,000/day)	32,000
Facilities and Refreshments ($890/day)	7,120
Participants Salaries (plus benefits) for time and program	37,218
Manager Salaries (plus benefits) for time involved in program	12,096
Training and Education Overhead (allocated)	2,500
ROI Evaluation	5,000
Total	$ 160,754

Figure 7-3. Fully loaded costs.

the total cost of the first two programs conducted for the 36 participants.

DISCUSSION QUESTIONS

1. Using a total benefit on both measures (Figure 6-4) and the fully loaded cost of the program, calculate the benefit cost ratio and the return on investment.
2. Are the impact and ROI data credible? Explain.

REFERENCES

Annual Employee Benefits Report, *Nation's Business*, January 2000.

Cascio, W.F. *Costing Human Resources: The Financial Impact of Behavior in Organizations*. Australia: South-Western College Publishing, 2000.

Kaplan, R.S., and Cooper, R. *Cost & Effect: Using Integrated Cost Systems to Drive Profitability and Performance.* Boston, MA: Harvard Business School Press, 1998.

Phillips, P.P. "Executive Leadership Development," *In The Human Resources Scorecard: Measuring the Return on Investment,* Boston, MA: Butterworth-Heinemann, 2001, pp. 449–476.

Young, S.D., and O'Byrne, S.F. *EVA® and Value-Based Management: A Practical Guide to Implementation.* New York: McGraw-Hill, 2001.

CHAPTER 8

Calculating the Return on Investment

The monetary values for program benefits, developed in Chapter 6, are combined with program cost data, developed in Chapter 7, to calculate the return on investment. This chapter explores approaches for developing the return on investment measure for the leadership scorecard, describing the various techniques, processes, and issues involved. Before presenting the formulas for calculating the ROI, a few basic issues are described. An adequate understanding of these issues is necessary to complete this major step in the ROI process. The uses and abuses of ROI are fully explored.

BASIC ROI ISSUES

Definitions

The term *return on investment* is often misused, sometimes intentionally. In some situations, a broad definition for ROI includes any benefit from the program. In these situations, ROI is a vague concept in which even subjective data linked to a program are included in the concept of the return. In this book, the return on investment is more precise and is meant to represent an actual value developed by comparing program costs to benefits. The two most common measures are the cost/benefit ratio and the ROI formula. Both are presented along with other approaches that calculate the return.

For many years, leadership development practitioners and researchers have sought to calculate the actual return on the investment for leadership development. If leadership development is considered an investment, not an expense, it is appropriate to place the leadership development investment in the same funding mechanism as other investments, such as the investment in equipment and facilities. Although these other investments are quite different, management often views them in the same way. Thus, it is critical to the success of the leadership development field to develop specific values that reflect the return on the investment.

Annualized Values

All of the formulas presented in this chapter use annualized values so that the first year impact of the program investment is developed. Using annual values is becoming a generally accepted practice for developing the ROI in many organizations. This approach is a conservative way to develop the ROI, as many short-term leadership development programs have added value in the second or third year. For long-term programs, annualized values are inappropriate and longer time frames need to be used. For example, in an ROI analysis of a program to send employees to the United States to obtain MBA degrees, a Singapore-based company used a seven-year time frame. The program itself required two years and a five-year impact, with postprogram data used to develop the ROI. However, for most programs lasting one day to one month, first year values are appropriate.

When selecting the approach to measure ROI, it is important to communicate to the target audience the formula used and the assumptions made to arrive at the decision to use it. This action can avoid misunderstandings and confusion surrounding how the ROI value was developed. Although several approaches are described in this chapter, two stand out as the preferred methods: the benefit/cost ratio and the basic ROI formula. These two approaches are described next along with the interpretation of ROI and a brief coverage of the other approaches.

Benefits/Costs Ratio

One of the earliest methods for evaluating leadership development investments is the benefit/cost ratio. This method compares the benefits of the program to the costs in a ratio. In formula form, the ratio is:

$$\text{BCR} = \frac{\text{Program benefits}}{\text{Program costs}}$$

In simple terms, the BCR compares the annual economic benefits of the program to the cost of the program. A BCR of 1 means that the benefits equal the costs. A BCR of two, usually written as $2:1$, indicates that for each dollar spent on the program, two dollars were returned as benefits.

The principal advantage of using this approach is that it avoids traditional financial measures so that there is no confusion when comparing leadership development investments with other investments in the company. Investments in plants, equipment, or subsidiaries, for example, are not usually evaluated with the benefit/cost method. Some leadership development executives prefer not to use the same method to compare the return on leadership development investments with the return on other investments. Consequently, the ROI for leadership development stands alone as a unique type of evaluation.

Unfortunately, there are no standards for what constitutes an acceptable benefit/cost ratio. A standard should be established within an organization, perhaps even for a specific type of program. However, a $1:1$ ratio is unacceptable for most programs, and in some organizations, a $1.25:1$ ratio is required, where 1.25 times the cost of the program is the benefit.

ROI Formula

Perhaps the most appropriate formula for evaluating leadership development investments is net program benefits divided by cost. The ratio is usually expressed as a percent when the fractional values are multiplied by 100. In formula form, the ROI becomes:

$$\text{ROI}(\%) = \frac{\text{Net program benefits}}{\text{Program costs}} \times 100$$

Net benefits are program benefits minus program costs. The ROI value is related to the BCR by a factor of one. For example, a BCR of 2.45 is the same as an ROI value of 145 percent. This formula is essentially the same as ROI in other types of investments. For example, when a firm builds a new plant, the ROI is found by dividing annual earnings by the investment. The annual earnings is comparable to net benefits (annual benefits minus the cost). The investment is comparable to program costs, which represent the investment in the program.

An ROI on a leadership development investment of 50 percent means that the costs are recovered and an additional 50 percent of the costs are reported as "earnings." A leadership development investment of 150 percent indicates that the costs have been re-covered and an additional 1.5 multiplied by the costs is captured as "earnings."

Using the ROI formula essentially places leadership development investments on a level playing field with other investments using the same formula and similar concepts. The ROI calculation is easily understood by key management and financial executives who regu-larly use ROI with other investments.

ROI INTERPRETATION

Choosing the Right Formula

What quantitative measure best represents top management goals? Many managers are preoccupied with the measures of sales, profits (net income), and profit percentages (the ratio of profits to dollar sales). However, the ultimate test of profitability is not the absolute amount of profit or the relationship of profit to sales. The critical test is the relationship of profit to invested capital. The most popular way of expressing this relationship is by means of a rate of return on investment (Anthony and Reece, 1983).

Profits can be generated through increased sales or cost savings. In practice, there are more opportunities for cost savings than profit. Cost savings can be generated when there is improvement in pro-ductivity, quality, efficiency, cycle time, or actual cost reduction. When reviewing almost 500 studies, the vast majority of the studies were based on cost savings. Approximately 85 percent of the studies had a payoff based on output, quality, efficiency, time, or cost reduc-tion. The other had a payoff based on sales increases, where the earn-ings are derived from the profit margin. This situation is important for nonprofits and public sector organizations where the profit opportunity is often unavailable. Most leadership development ini-tiatives will be connected directly to the cost-savings portion; thus ROIs can still be developed in those settings.

In the finance and accounting literature, return on investment is defined as net income (earnings) divided by investment. In the context of leadership development, net income is equivalent to net monetary benefits (program benefits minus program costs). Invest-ment is equivalent to program costs. The term investment is used in three different senses in financial analysis, thus giving three different ROI ratios: return on assets (ROA), return on owners' equity (ROE), and return on capital employed (ROCE).

Financial executives have used the ROI approach for centuries. Still, this technique did not become widespread in industry for judging operating performance until the early 1960s. Conceptually, ROI has innate appeal because it blends all the major ingredients of profitability in one number; the ROI statistic by itself can be compared with opportunities elsewhere (both inside or outside). Practically, however, ROI is an imperfect measurement that should be used in conjunction with other performance measurements (Horngren, 1982).

It is important for this formula (outlined earlier) to be utilized in the organization. Deviations from, or misuse of, the formula can create confusion not only among users, but also among the finance and accounting staff. The chief financial office (CFO) and the finance and accounting staff should become partners in the implementation of the ROI methodology. Without their support, involvement, and commitment, it is difficult for ROI to be used on a wide-scale basis. Because of this relationship, it is important that the same financial terms be used as those experienced and expected by the CFO.

Table 8-1 shows some misuse of financial terms that appear in the literature. Terms such as return on intelligence (or information), abbreviated as ROI, do nothing but confuse the CFO, who is thinking that ROI is the actual return on investment described earlier. Sometimes return on expectations (ROE), return on anticipation (ROA), or return on client expectations (ROCE) are used, confusing the CFO, who is thinking return on equity, return on assets, and return on capital employed, respectively. Use of these terms in the

Table 8-1
Misuse of Financial Terms

Term	Misuse	CFO definition
ROI	Return of information or return of intelligence	Return on investment
ROE	Return on expectation	Return on equity
ROA	Return on anticipation	Return on assets
ROCE	Return on client expectation	Return on capital employed
ROP	Return on people	??
ROR	Return on resources	??
ROT	Return on training	??
ROW	Return on web	??

calculation of a payback of a leadership development program will do nothing but confuse and perhaps lose the support of the finance and accounting staff. Other terms, such as return on people, return on resources, return on training, and return on web, are often used with almost no consistent financial calculations. The bottom line: do not confuse the CFO. Consider this individual to be an ally and use the same terminology, processes, and concepts when applying financial returns for programs.

ROI Objectives: The Ultimate Challenge

When reviewing the specific ROI calculation and formula, it is helpful to position the ROI calculation in the context of all data. The ROI calculation is only one measure generated with the leadership development scorecard. Seven types of data are developed, five of which are the five levels of evaluation. Data in each level of evaluation are driven by a specific objective, as described earlier. In terms of ROI, specific objectives are often set, creating the expectations of an acceptable ROI calculation.

Table 8-2 shows the payoff of a leadership development program as results at the different levels are clearly linked to the specific objectives of the program. As objectives are established, data are collected to indicate the extent to which that particular objective was met. This is the ideal framework that clearly shows the powerful connection between objectives and measurement and evaluation data. Table 8-2 also shows the chain of impact as reaction leads to learning, which leads to application, which leads to business impact and to ROI. The intangible data shown in the business impact category are items that are purposely not converted to monetary value. Some of those could have been anticipated in the project before it was implemented. Others may not have been anticipated, but were described as a benefit from those involved in the program. In this particular example, there was an expectation of 25 percent for ROI (ROI objective). This organization uses 25 percent as a standard for all of their ROI projects and the actual result of 105% clearly exceeds the expectation.

ROI Targets

Specific expectations for ROI should be developed before an evaluation study is undertaken. While there are no generally accepted standards, four strategies have been used to establish a minimum

Table 8-2
The Chain of Impact Drives ROI

Level	Objectives	Results
1 Reaction/ satisfaction	■ Obtain a positive reaction on the program ■ At least 75% of participants provide action plans	■ Overall rating of 4.11 out of a possible 5 ■ 93% provided list of action items
2 Learning	■ Knowledge of policy/knowledge of inappropriate leadership behavior ■ Effective leadership skills	■ Posttest scores average 84; pre test scores average 51 (improvement 65%) ■ Participants demonstrated they could use skills successfully
3 Application/ implementation	■ Conduct meeting with employees ■ Administer policy ■ Apply skills ■ Complete action items	■ 95% complete—meeting records ■ 83% complete—self report ■ 4.2% out of 5 on survey ■ 72% completed—self report
4 Business impact	■ Reduce the number of complaints ■ Reduce turnover ■ Reduce absenteeism	■ Complaints reduced from 55 to 35 ■ Turnover reduced from 24.2 to 19.9% ■ Absenteeism reduced from 8.2% to 5.1% ■ Increased job satisfaction ■ Increased teamwork ■ Reduced stress
5 ROI	■ Obtain at least a 25% ROI	ROI = 105%

expected requirement, or hurdle rate, for ROI in a leadership development program. The first approach is to set the ROI using the same values used to invest in capital expenditures, such as equipment, facilities, and new companies. For North America, western Europe, and most of the Asian Pacific area, including Australia and New Zealand, the cost of capital is quite low and this internal hurdle rate for ROI is usually in the 15 to 20 percent range. Thus, using this strategy, organizations would set the expected ROI the same as the value expected from other investments.

A second strategy is to use an ROI minimum that represents a higher standard than the value required for other investments. This target value is above the percentage required for other types of investments. The rationale: the ROI process for leadership development is still relatively new and often involves subjective input, including estimations. Because of that, a higher standard is required or suggested. For most areas in North America, western Europe, and the Asia Pacific area, this value is usually set at 25 percent.

A third strategy is to set the ROI value at a break-even point. A 0 percent ROI represents break-even. This is equivalent to a cost benefit ratio of 1. The rationale for this approach is an eagerness to recapture the cost of leadership development only. This is the ROI objective for many public sector organizations. If the funds expended for programs can be captured, there is still value and benefit from the program through the intangible measures, which are not converted to monetary values and the behavior change that is evident in the application and implementation data. Thus, some organizations will use a break-even, under the philosophy that they are not attempting to make a profit from leadership development.

Finally, a fourth, and sometimes recommended, strategy is to let the client or program sponsor set the minimum acceptable ROI value. In this scenario, the individual who initiates, approves, sponsors, or supports the program establishes the acceptable ROI. Almost every program has a major sponsor and that person may be willing to offer the acceptable value. This links the expectations or financial return directly to the expectations of the individual sponsoring the program.

ROI Can Be Very Large

As the examples have demonstrated, the actual ROI value can be quite large—far exceeding what might be expected from other types of investments in plant, equipment, and companies. It is not unusual for programs involved in leadership, team building, management development, and supervisor training, to generate ROIs in the 100 to 700 percent range. This does not mean that all ROI studies are positive—many are negative. However, the impact of leadership development can be quite impressive. It is helpful to remember what constitutes the ROI value. Consider, for example, the investment in one week of training for a team leader. If the leader's behavior changes as he or she works directly with the team, a chain of impact can produce a measurable change in performance from the team.

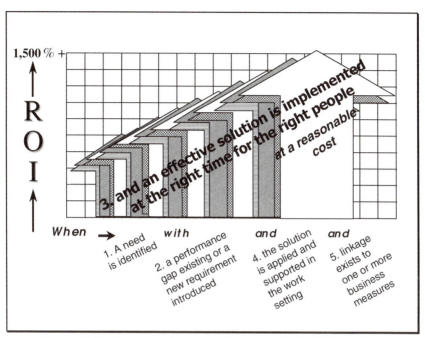

Figure 8-1. Factors that contribute to high ROI values.

This measure now represents the team's measure. That behavior change, translated into a measurement improvement for the entire year, can be quite significant. When the monetary value of the team's improvement is considered for an entire year and compared to the relatively small amount of investment in one team leader, it is easy to see why this number can be quite large.

More specifically, as Figure 8-1 shows, some very important factors contribute to high ROI values. The impact can be quite large when a specific need has been identified and a performance gap exists; a new requirement is introduced and the solution is implemented at the right time for the right people at a reasonable cost; the solution is applied and supported in the work setting; and there is a linkage to one or more business measures. When these conditions are met, high ROI values can be recognized.

It is important to understand that a very high ROI value can be developed that does not necessarily relate directly to the health of the rest of the organization. For example, a high-impact ROI can be generated in an organization that is losing money (or in bankruptcy) because the impact is restricted to those individuals involved in the leadership development program and the monetary value of their improvement is connected to that program. At the same time, there can be some disastrous programs generating a very negative ROI in a company that is very profitable. This is a microlevel activity that evaluates the success of a particular program within a particular time frame.

What Happens When the ROI Is Negative?

Perhaps one of the greatest fears of using ROI is the possibility of having a negative ROI. This is a fear that concerns not only the program sponsor or owner, but also those who are involved in the design, development, and delivery of the program. Few individuals want to be involved in a process that exposes a failure. They are concerned that the failure may reflect unfavorably on them. On the positive side, a negative ROI study provides the best opportunity for learning. The ROI methodology reveals problems and barriers. As data are collected through the chain of impact, the reasons for failure become clear. Data on barriers and enablers to the transfer of training captured at Level 3 (Application) usually reveal why the program did not work. While a negative ROI study is the ultimate learning situation, no one wants to invite the opportunity to his or her back door. The preference would be to learn from others. Sometimes the damage created by a negative ROI is the sense of expectations that are not managed properly up front and the fear of consequences of the negative ROI.

The following steps can help minimize or avoid this dilemma:

1. Raise the question about the feasibility of the impact study: Is it appropriate to use the ROI methodology for this particular program? Sometimes, a program, by its very nature, may appear to be a failure, at least in terms of ROI.
2. Make sure there is a clear understanding of the consequences of a negative ROI. This issue should be addressed early and often. ROI methodology is a process improvement tool and not a performance evaluation tool. The individuals involved should not necessarily be penalized or have their performance evaluated unfavorably because of the negative ROI.
3. Look for warning signs early in the process—they are usually everywhere. Level 1 data can often send strong signals that an evaluation may result in a negative ROI. Signals of a negative ROI study may be if the participants react negatively, see no

relevance in the program to their jobs, perceive the content to be inappropriate, consider the information outdated, offer no intent to use the material, or refuse to recommend the program to anyone else.

4. Manage expectations. It is best to lower expectations around ROI. Anticipating a high ROI and communicating that to the client or other stakeholders may create a false expectation that will not materialize. Keep the expectations low and the delivery performance high.

5. Using negative data, reposition the story. Instead of communicating that great results have been achieved with this very effective program, the story now becomes, "We have some great information that tells how to change the program to obtain better results." This is more than a play on words—it underscores the importance of learning what went wrong and what can be done in the future.

6. Use the information to drive change. Sometimes the negative ROI can be transformed into a positive ROI with some minor alterations of the program. Implementation issues may need to be addressed in terms of support and use of knowledge and skills in the workplace. In other situations, a complete redesign of the program may be necessary. In a few isolated cases, discontinuing the program may be the only option. Whatever the option, use data to drive action so that the overall value of conducting the study has been realized.

These strategies can help minimize the unfavorable, and sometimes disastrous, perceptions of a negative ROI.

ROI Is Not for Every Program

The ROI methodology should not be applied to every program. It takes time and resources to create a valid and credible ROI study. ROI is appropriate for those programs that

- have a long life cycle. At some point in the life of the program, this level of accountability should be applied to the program.
- are very important to the organization in meeting its operating goals. These programs are designed to add value. ROI may be helpful to show that value.
- are closely linked to the organization's strategic initiatives. Anything this important needs a high level of accountability.

- are very expensive to implement. An expensive program, expending large amounts of company resources, should be subjected to this level of accountability.
- are highly visible and sometimes controversial. These programs often require this level of accountability to satisfy the critics.
- have a large target audience. If a program is designed for all employees, it may be a candidate for ROI.
- command the interest of a top executive group. If top executives are interested in knowing the impact, the ROI methodology should be applied.

These are only guidelines and should be considered in the context of the organization. Other criteria may also be appropriate. These criteria can be used in a scheme to sort out those programs most appropriate for this level of accountability.

It is also helpful to consider the programs where the ROI methodology is not appropriate. ROI is seldom appropriate for programs that

- are very short in duration, such as two-hour briefings. It is difficult to change behavior in such a short time frame.
- are legislated or required by regulation. It would be difficult to change anything as a result of this evaluation.
- are required by senior management. It may be that these programs will continue regardless of the findings.
- serve as operator and technical training. It may be more appropriate to measure only at Levels 1, 2, and 3 to ensure that participants know how to do the job and are doing it properly.

This is not meant to imply that the ROI methodology cannot be implemented for these types of programs. However, when considering the limited resources for measurement and evaluation, careful use of these resources and time will result in evaluating more strategic types of programs. It is also helpful to think about the programs that are appropriate for the first one or two ROI studies. Initially, the use of this process will be met with some anxiety and tentativeness. The programs initially undertaken should not only meet the aforementioned requirements, but should also meet other requirements. These programs should:

1. Be as simple as possible. Reserve the complex programs for later.

2. Be a known commodity. This helps ensure that the first study is not negative.

3. Be void of hidden agendas and political sensitivity. The first study should not necessarily be wrapped up in the organization politics.

Cautions when Using ROI

Because of the sensitivity of the ROI process, caution is needed when developing, calculating, and communicating the return on investment. The implementation of the ROI process is a very important issue and a goal of many leadership development departments. In addition to the guiding principles, a few issues should be addressed to keep the process from going astray. The following cautions are offered when using ROI.

Take a conservative approach when developing both benefits and costs. Conservatism in ROI analysis builds accuracy and credibility. What matters most is how the target audience perceives the value of data. A conservative approach is always recommended for both the numerator of the ROI formula (benefits) and the denominator (program costs). The conservative approach is the basis for the guiding principles.

Use caution when comparing the ROI in leadership development with other financial returns. There are many ways to calculate the return on funds invested or assets employed. The ROI is just one of them. Although the calculation for ROI in leadership development uses the same basic formula as in other investment evaluations, it may not be fully understood by the target group. Its calculation method and its meaning should be clearly communicated. More importantly, it should be an item accepted by management as an appropriate measure for leadership development program evaluation.

Involve management in developing the return. Management ultimately makes the decision if an ROI value is acceptable. To the extent possible, management should be involved in setting the parameters for calculations and establishing targets by which programs are considered acceptable within the organization.

Fully disclose the assumptions and methodology. When discussing the ROI methodology and communicating data, it is very important to fully disclose the process, steps, and assumptions used in the process. Strengths should be clearly communicated as well as weaknesses and shortcomings.

Approach sensitive and controversial issues with caution. Occasionally, sensitive and controversial issues will be generated when discussing an ROI value. It is best to avoid debates over what is measurable and what is not measurable unless there is clear evidence of the issue in question. Also, some programs are so fundamental to the survival of the organization that any attempt to measure it is unnecessary. For example, a program designed to improve customer service in a customer-focused company may escape the scrutiny of an ROI evaluation, on the assumption that if the program is well designed, it will improve customer service.

Teach others the methods for calculating the return. Each time an ROI is calculated, the leadership development manager should use this opportunity to educate other managers and colleagues in the organization. Even if it is not in their area of responsibility, these individuals will be able to see the value of this approach to leadership development evaluation. Also, when possible, each project should serve as a case study to educate the leadership development staff on specific techniques and methods.

Recognize that not everyone will buy into ROI. Not every audience member will understand, appreciate, or accept the ROI calculation. For a variety of reasons, one or more individuals may not agree with the values. These individuals may be highly emotional about the concept of showing accountability for leadership development. Attempts to persuade them may be beyond the scope of the task at hand.

Do not boast about a high return. It is not unusual to generate what appears to be a very high return on investment for a leadership development program. A leadership development manager who boasts about a high rate of return will be open to potential criticism from others unless there are indisputable facts on which the calculation is based.

Choose the place for debates. The time to debate the ROI methodology is not *during* a presentation (unless it can not be avoided). There are constructive times to debate the ROI process: in a special forum, among the leadership development staff, in an educational session, in professional literature, on panel discussions, or even during the development of an ROI impact study. The time and place for debate should be carefully selected so as not to detract from the quality and quantity of information presented.

Do not try to use ROI on every program. As discussed earlier, some programs are difficult to quantify, and an ROI calculation may not be feasible. Other methods of presenting benefits may be more appropriate. Also, specific criteria should be established that select programs for ROI analysis, as briefly described.

FINAL THOUGHTS

After the program benefits are collected and converted to monetary values and the program costs are developed in a fully loaded profile, the ROI calculation for the leadership scorecard becomes a very easy step. It is just a matter of plugging the values into the appropriate formula. This chapter presented two basic approaches for calculating the return—the ROI formula and the cost/benefit ratio. Each has its own advantages and disadvantages. Several examples were presented along with key issues that must be addressed in ROI calculations. Cautions surrounding the ROI capped off the chapter.

The use of a leadership scorecard that includes ROI data represents a tremendous paradigm shift as an organization attempts to bring more accountability and results to the entire leadership development process, from needs assessment to the development of an impact study. The leadership scorecard brings a results-based focus to learning issues. This process is client focused, requiring much contact, communication, dialogue, and agreement with the client group.

CASE STUDY—PART G
INTERNATIONAL CAR RENTAL

Analysis

The benefit/cost ratio is calculated as follows:

$$\text{BCR} = \frac{\text{Total benefits}}{\text{Total costs}} = \frac{\$329,201}{\$160,754} = 2.05$$

The return on investment is calculated as follows:

$$\text{ROI}(\%) = \frac{\text{Net total benefits}}{\text{Total costs}} \times 100$$

$$= \frac{\$329,201 - \$160,754}{\$160,754} \times 100 = 105\%$$

Credibility

Data were perceived to be very credible by both the L&D staff and the senior management group. Credibility rests on eight major issues and, collectively, these issues made a convincing case for the program.

1. The information for the analysis is provided directly from the new managers. The managers have no reason not to be straightforward and unbiased in their input.
2. Data are anonymous, as no one has had to provide his or her name. This helps remove the opportunity for potential bias.
3. The data collection process is conservative, with the assumption that an unresponsive individual has realized no improvement. This concept—no data, no improvement—is ultra conservative in the data collection.
4. The L&D staff did not assign complete credit to this program. The participants isolated a portion of data that should be credited directly to this program.
5. Data were adjusted for the potential error of the estimate. Estimates are used to isolate the effects of the program on the individual data.
6. Only the first year of benefits is used in the analysis. Most of the improvement should result in second- and third-year benefits.
7. The costs of the program are fully loaded. All direct and indirect costs are included, including the time away from work for the participants and managers.
8. Data are a balanced profile of success. Very favorable reaction, learning, and application data were presented along with business impact, ROI, and intangibles.

DISCUSSION QUESTIONS

1. Are the BCR and ROI numbers lower or higher than you expected? Comment.
2. What are the potential intangible benefits from this program?

REFERENCES

Anthony, R.N., and Reece, J.S. *Accounting: Text and Case.*, 7th ed. Homewood, IL: Irwin, 1983.

Bernthal, P., and Byham, B. "Evaluation of Techniques for an Empowered Workforce," *In Action: Measuring Return on Investment*, Vol. 2. J.J. Phillips (Ed.). Alexandria, VA: American Society for Training and Development, 1997, pp. 73–88.

Devaney, M. "Measuring ROI of Computer Training in a Small to Medium-Sized Enterprise," *In Action: Measuring Return on Investment*, Vol. 3. J.J. Phillips (Ed.). Alexandria, VA: American Society for Training and Development, 2001, pp. 185–196.

Horngren, C.T. *Cost Accounting*, 5th ed. Englewood Cliffs, NJ: Prentice-Hall, 1982.

Phillips, P.P. (Ed.). *In Action: Measuring Return on Investment*, Vol. 3. Alexandria, VA: American Society for Training and Development, 2001.

CHAPTER 9

Identifying the Intangible Benefits

The intangible benefits are the seventh type of measure to include in the leadership development scorecard. The other six measures were covered in previous chapters. Chapter 3 focused on measuring indicators, satisfaction and learning, Chapter 4 focused on measuring application and business impact, and Chapter 8 focused on the return on investment. Intangible measures are the benefits (or detriments) linked directly to the leadership development program, which cannot or should not be converted to monetary values. These measures are often monitored after the leadership development program has been conducted and, although not converted to monetary values, they are still very important in the evaluation process. While the range of intangible measures is almost limitless, this chapter describes a few common measures, listed in Table 9-1, often linked with leadership development.

KEY ISSUES

Importance

Not all measures are in the tangible category. By design, some measures are captured and reported as intangible measures. Although they may not be perceived as valuable as the measures converted to monetary values, intangible measures are critical to the overall success of the organization (Oxman, 2002). In some programs, such as interpersonal skills training, team development, leadership, communications training, and management development, the intangible benefits can be more important than the tangible measures. Consequently, these measures should be monitored and reported as part of the overall evaluation. In practice, every project or program, regardless of its nature, scope, and content, will have

Table 9-1
Typical Intangible Variables Linked with Leadership Development

• Attitude survey data	• Image
• Organizational commitment	• Customer satisfaction survey data
• Climate survey data	• Customer complaints
• Employee complaints	• Customer retention
• Grievances	• Customer response time
• Discrimination complaints	• Teamwork
• Stress reduction	• Cooperation
• Employee turnover	• Conflict
• Employee absenteeism	• Decisiveness
• Employee tardiness	• Communication
• Employee transfers	• Innovation and creativity
	• Competencies

intangible measures associated with it (Fitz-enz, 2001). The challenge is to identify and report them efficiently.

Perhaps the first step to understanding an intangible is to clearly define the difference between tangible and intangible assets in a business organization. As presented in Table 9-2, tangible assets are required for business operations and are readily visible, rigorously quantified, and are represented as a line item on a balance sheet (Saint-Onge, 2000). The intangible assets are key to competitive advantage in the knowledge era and are invisible, difficult to quantify, and not tracked through traditional accounting practices. With this distinction, it is easier to understand why intangible measures are difficult to convert to monetary values.

Another distinction between tangible and intangible is the concept of hard data vs soft data. This concept, discussed earlier, is perhaps more familiar to leadership development practitioners. Table 9-3 shows the difference between hard and soft data, used earlier in this book. The most significant part of the definition is the difficulty in converting data to monetary value. It is from this point that the definition of intangible data is derived. Intangible measures are defined as measures that are purposely not converted to monetary values.

Using this simple definition avoids confusion of whether a data item should be classified as hard data or soft data. It is considered soft data if a credible, economically feasible process is unavailable for conversion.

Table 9-2
Comparison of Tangible and Intangible Assets

Tangible assets Required for business operations	Intangible assets Key to competitive advantage in the knowledge area
• Readily visible	• Invisible
• Rigorously quantified	• Difficult to quantify
• Part of the balance sheet	• Not tracked through accounting practices
• Investment produces known returns	• Assessment based on assumptions
• Can be duplicated easily	• Cannot be bought or imitated
• Depreciates with use	• Appreciates with purposeful use
• Has finite application	• Multiapplication without reducing value
• Best managed with "scarcity" mentality	• Best managed with "abundance" mentality
• Best leveraged through control	• Best leveraged through alignment
• Can be accumulated	• Dynamic: short shelf life when not in use

Table 9-3
Comparison of Hard Data and Soft Data

Characteristics of data	
Hard data	Soft data
• Objectively based	• Subjectively based in many cases
• Easy to measure and quantify	• Difficult to measure and quantify, directly
• Relatively easy to assign monetary values	• Difficult to assign monetary values
• Common measures of organizational performance	• Less credible as a performance measure
• Very credible with management	• Usually behaviorally oriented

Identification of Measures

Intangible measures can be identified from different sources representing different time frames, as illustrated in Figure 9-1. First, they can be uncovered early in the process, during the needs assessment. Once identified, intangible data are planned for collection as part of the overall data collection strategy. For example, a team leader training program has several hard data measures linked to the program. An intangible measure, such as employee satisfaction, is identified and monitored with no plans to convert it to a monetary value. Thus, from the beginning, this measure is destined to be a nonmonetary benefit reported along with the ROI results as a part of the leadership scorecard.

A second time an intangible benefit is identified is during discussions with clients or sponsors about the impact of leadership development. Clients can usually identify intangible measures that are expected to be influenced by the program. For example, a leadership development program in a large multinational company was conducted, and an ROI analysis was planned. During the ROI planning session, program developers, instructors, a sample of participants' managers, and a senior executive identified potential intangible measures that were perceived to be influenced by the program. These measures are included on the ROI analysis planning document.

A third time an intangible measure is identified is during a follow-up evaluation. Although the measure was not expected or anticipated in the initial program design, the measure surfaces on a questionnaire, in an interview, or during a focus group. Questions are often asked about other improvements linked to the leadership development program. Several intangible measures are usually provided and there are no planned attempts to place a value on the actual measure.

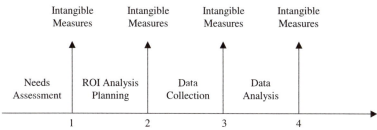

Figure 9-1. Identification of intangible measures: timing and source.

For example, in a leadership development program, participants were asked specifically what had improved in their work as a result of the program. The participants provided several intangible measures, which managers perceived to be linked to the program.

The fourth time an intangible measure is identified is during an attempt to convert data to monetary values. If the process loses credibility, the measure should be reported as an intangible benefit. For example, in a leadership development program, organizational commitment is identified early in the process as one of the measures of leadership development success. A conversion of data to monetary values was attempted. However, the process of assigning a value to data lost credibility; therefore, organizational commitment was reported as an intangible benefit.

Is It Measurable?

Sometimes debate will erupt over whether a particular item perceived as intangible (soft) can actually be measured. In reality, anything that can influence the outcome of the leadership development program can be measured. (The measure may have to be a perception of the issue taken from a particular stakeholder involved in the process, but it is still a measure.) The ROI methodology rests on the assumption that anything can be measured. In the mind of the sponsor or senior executive, if an intangible (soft) item cannot be measured, why bother? The state of that situation or issue will never be known. Thus, on a practical basis, any intangible can be measured—some, precisely; others not precisely. For example, tracking customer complaints is a measure that can be captured and categorized precisely. Every complaint received is recorded and the types of complaints are placed in categories. However, to place a value on having less complaints may cause the data item to be intangible if there is not a credible, economically feasible way to convert it to monetary value.

Can It Be Converted?

Chapter 6 focused on different ways to convert data to monetary values. The philosophy taken is that any data item can be converted to monetary value (i.e., there is no measure that can be presented to which a monetary value cannot be assigned). The key issue is credibility. Is it a believable value? Is the process to convert it to monetary value credible? Does it cost too much to convert it? Is that

Table 9-4
The Four-Part Test for Converting Intangibles to Monetary Values

Tangible vs intangible

1. Does an acceptable, standard monetary value exist for the measure? If yes, use it; if not, go to the next step.
2. Is there a method that *can* be used to convert the measure to money? If not, list it as an intangible; if yes, go to the next step.
3. Can the conversion be accomplished with minimum resources? If not, list it as an intangible; if yes, go to the next step.
4. Can the conversion process be described to an executive audience *and* secure their buy-in in two minutes? If yes, use it in the ROI calculation; if not, list it as an intangible.

value stable over time? These are critical issues that will be explored mentally by senior executives when they examine the conversion of data to monetary value. For tangible data conversion, the issue is of little concern. Tangible data items are converted easily, such as increased output, reduction in rejects, and time savings. However, the soft measures (stress, complaints, and attitudes) often lose credibility in the process. Table 9-4 shows a four-part test for converting intangibles to monetary values. The ultimate test is #4. If the converted value cannot be communicated to the management group and secure their buy-in in two minutes, data should be listed as intangible. This is a practical test that protects the credibility of the impact study and also allows for consistency from one study to another. It would be unreliable if one evaluator converted a particular data item to monetary value whereas another evaluator did not. This is an important part of building the standards necessary for the ROI methodology.

Intangible Measures vs Intellectual Capital

With the attention given to the concept of intellectual capital in recent years, and the value of intangible assets in organizations, it is helpful to distinguish between the intangible measures from a leadership development program and those that might appear in a variety of measures in intellectual capital. Figure 9-2 shows the categories of intangible benefits and their relationship to intellectual capital. Intellectual capital typically involves customer capital, human capital, and structural capital (Saint-Onge, 2000). Most of the leadership

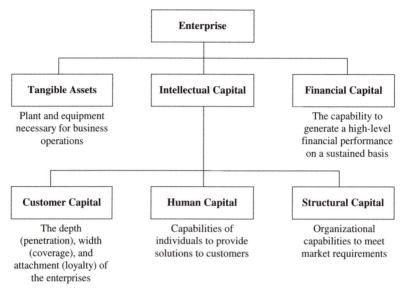

Figure 9-2. Categories and relationship of intellectual capital.

TABLE 9-5
Common Human Capital Measures

Human capital measures	
• Innovation	• Learning
• Job satisfaction	• Competencies
• Organizational commitment	• Educational level
• Turnover	• HR investment
• Tenure	• Leadership
• Experience	• Productivity

development programs are driving measures in the human capital area, which includes the capability of individuals to provide solutions to customers. More specifically, Table 9-5 offers the common human capital measures tracked by organizations as part of their human capital monitoring processes (Phillips, 2002). Many of these measures are driven by the leadership development programs and are often considered intangible. Some of these are described in this chapter.

Analysis

For most intangible data, no specific analysis is planned. Previous attempts to convert intangible data to monetary units resulted in aborting the process, thus no further data analysis was conducted. In some cases, there may be attempts to isolate the effects of leadership development using one or more of the methods outlined in Chapter 5. This step is necessary when there is a need to know the specific amount of change in the intangible measure that is linked to the program. In many cases, however, intangible data reflect evidence of improvement. Neither the precise amount of the improvement nor the amount of improvement related directly to leadership development is needed. Because the value of these data is not placed in the ROI calculation, intangible measures are not normally used to justify additional leadership development. Consequently, a detailed analysis is not justified. Intangible benefits are viewed as supporting evidence of the programs success and are presented as qualitative data.

TYPICAL INTANGIBLE MEASURES

Most of the remainder of the chapter focuses on typical intangible measures. These measures are often presented as intangibles in leadership scorecards. For each individual measure, there may be exceptions where organizations *can* convert data to monetary value. Three notable exceptions are offered. Retention (employee turnover) is now converted to monetary value in most cases and is presented as a tangible. Reliable ways are available to arrive at the value for absenteeism without exhausting resources. Also, recent developments in the measurement of customer satisfaction include ways to convert these critical measures to monetary value. These three, plus others, are described in more detail in this section.

Job Satisfaction

Employee satisfaction is perhaps one of the most important intangible measures. Some leadership development programs are designed to improve job satisfaction. Attitude surveys are conducted to measure the extent to which employees are satisfied with the organization, their jobs, their supervisor, co-workers, and a host of other job-related factors. Attitude survey data are usually linked to leadership development results when specific issues on the survey are related to leadership development. For example, in a diversity training program conducted for all employees at a television station, the annual attitude survey contained five questions tied directly to perceptions and attitudes influenced by the program.

While job satisfaction has always been an important issue in employee relations, in recent years it has taken on new importance because of the key relationships of job satisfaction to other measures. A classical relationship with job satisfaction is in the area of employee recruitment and retention. Firms with excellent job satisfaction ratings are often attractive to potential employees. It becomes a subtle but important recruiting tool. "Employers of Choice" and "Best Places to Work," for example, often have high levels of job satisfaction ratings, which attract employees. There is also a relationship between job satisfaction and employee turnover. This relationship has taken on a new meaning as turnover and retention have become critical issues in the last decade and are projected to continue to be critical in the future. Today these relationships are often easily developed as many of the human resource information systems have modules to calculate the correlation between the turnover rates and the job satisfaction scores for the various job groups, divisions, departments, etc.

Job satisfaction has taken on new meanings in connection with customer service. Hundreds of applied research projects are beginning to show a very high correlation between job satisfaction scores and customer satisfaction scores. Intuitively, this seems obvious— a more satisfied employee is likely to provide more productive, friendly, and appropriate customer service. Likewise, a disgruntled employee will provide poor service. These links, often referred to as a service-profit-chain, create a promising way to identify important relationship between attitudes and profits in an organization.

Even with these developments, most organizations do not or cannot place credible values on job satisfaction data. The trend is definitely in that direction, but until that occurs, job satisfaction is usually listed as an intangible benefit in most impact studies.

Organizational Commitment

In recent years, organizational commitment (OC) measures have complemented or replaced job satisfaction measures. OC measures go beyond employee satisfaction and include the extent to which the employees identify with organizational goals, mission, philosophy, value, policies, and practices. The concept of involvement and becoming a part of the organization is the key issue. OC is a measure that correlates more closely with productivity and other performance improvement measures, whereas job satisfaction does not always correlate with improvements in productivity. As OC scores improve (taken on a standard index), there should be corresponding improvement in productivity. The OC is often measured the same way as attitude surveys, using a five- or seven-point scale taken directly from employees or groups of employees.

Organizational commitment is rarely converted to monetary value. Although some relationships have been developed to link it to more tangible data, this research is still in the developing stage. For most studies, organizational commitment would be listed as an intangible.

Climate Survey Data

Some organizations conduct climate surveys, which reflect work climate changes such as communication, openness, trust, and quality of feedback. Closely related to organizational commitment, climate surveys are more general and often focus on a range of workplace issues and environmental enablers and inhibitors. Climate surveys conducted before and after a leadership development program may reflect the extent to which the program has changed these intangible measures.

Employee Complaints

Some organizations record and report specific employees' complaints. These feedback mechanisms are usually highly visible with catchy names such as "Speak Out," "Talk Back," or "Hey, Mike" (in an organization where the CEO's first name is Mike). A reduction of employee complaints is sometimes directly related to leadership development. Consequently, the level of complaints is used as a measure of the program's success and is usually reported as an intangible measure. Because of the difficulty in converting complaints to monetary values, this measure is almost always listed as an intangible benefit.

Grievances

In both union and nonunion organizations, grievances often reflect the level of dissatisfaction or disenchantment with a variety of factors in their organization. Sometimes, leadership development programs are designed to reduce the number of grievances when they are considered excessive. An improvement in the grievance level may reflect the success of the program. The impact of grievances can be significant—affecting a variety of cost categories. While this measure may be converted to a monetary value, it may be reported as an intangible measure.

Discrimination Complaints

Employee dissatisfaction shows up in different types of discrimination complaints, ranging from informal complaints to external charges and even litigation against the organization. Leadership development programs, such as a sexual harassment prevention workshop, may be designed to prevent complaints or to reduce the current level of complaint activity. This measure can be devastating in organizations. However, the success of the program, in terms of complaint reduction, is sometimes not converted to monetary values because of the various assumptions and estimations involved in the process. When this is the case, these measures are reported as intangible program benefits.

Stress Reduction

Leadership development programs, such as time management, personal productivity, or conflict resolution, can reduce work-related stress by preparing participants to identify and confront stress factors, improve job performance, accomplish more in a workday, and relieve tension and anxiety. The subsequent reduction in stress may be directly linked to the program. Although excessive stress may be directly linked to other, easy to convert data, such as productivity, absenteeism, and medical claims, it is usually listed as an intangible.

Employee Retention

When job satisfaction deteriorates to the point where employees withdraw from work or the organization, either permanently or temporarily, the results can be disastrous. Perhaps the most critical employee withdrawal variable is employee turnover (or employee retention). An extremely costly variable, turnover, can have devastating consequences on organizations when it is excessive. Few measures have attracted so much attention as employee turnover. Fueled, in part, by low unemployment rates in North America and industrialized countries, retention has become a strategic issue. The survival of some firms depends on low turnover rates for critical job groups. Not only is turnover compared to historical rates, but it is often compared to best practice firms.

The good news is that many firms have made important strides in maintaining low turnover even in high turnover industries such as retail, hotel, and restaurant. Turnover is defined as the number of employees leaving in a month divided by the average number of employees in the month. This is a standard turnover rate that includes all individuals leaving. A more appropriate measure would be to include only turnover considered to be avoidable, usually referring to employees who leave voluntarily or those whose departure could have been prevented. For example, if an employee is terminated for poor performance in the first six months of employment, something went wrong that could have been prevented. Avoidable turnover is an important issue.

Many leadership development programs are designed to reduce employee turnover in work units. In many situations, turnover is actually converted to monetary values, using one of the methods described in Chapter 6. However, because of the multitude of costs and assumptions involved in developing the value, some organizations prefer not to convert turnover to a monetary value. In this case, turnover is reported as an intangible benefit, reflecting the success of the leadership development program.

Employee Absenteeism

Absenteeism is another disruptive and costly variable. Many leadership development programs are designed to reduce absenteeism; the amount of absenteeism reduction related to training can usually be pinpointed. Although the cost of absenteeism can be developed, the variety of costs—direct and indirect—necessary for a fully loaded cost impact make the process difficult. Consequently, the conversion process is not credible enough for some audiences and absenteeism changes are reported as intangible benefits.

Employee Tardiness

Some organizations actually monitor tardiness, especially in highly focused work and tightly contained work environments, such as call centers. Tardiness is an irritating work habit problem that can cause inefficiencies and delays. Electronic and computerized time reporting is used to pinpoint the problem area. Tardiness is very difficult to convert to a monetary value because of the many aspects of the impact of the unacceptable work habit. Consequently, when tardiness is presented as an improvement from a leadership development program, it is usually listed as an intangible benefit.

Employee Transfers

Another way for employees to withdraw is to request a transfer to another section, department, or division of the organization. Requests for transfers often reflect dissatisfaction with a variety of issues, including management, policies, and practices in the organization. Transfers are essentially internal turnover. Leadership development programs are sometimes designed to reduce or remove these unpleasant environmental influences. In these situations, requests for transfers are monitored and reported as an intangible benefit of leadership development. Although it is possible to place a value on this internal turnover, usually no attempt is made to assign monetary values to transfers.

Innovation and Creativity

For technology companies and other progressive organizations, innovation is a critical issue. A variety of innovation and creativity programs are implemented to make improvement in this critical area. Innovation is both easy and difficult to measure. It is easy to measure outcomes in areas such as copyright, patents, inventions, and employee suggestions. It is more difficult to measure the creative spirit of employees. Perhaps the most obvious measure is tracking the patents and trademarks that are not only used internally but are licensed for others to use through a patent and license exchange website.

An employee suggestion system, a longtime measure of the innovative and creative processes of an organization, still flourishes today in many firms. Employees are rewarded for their suggestions if they are approved and implemented. Tracking the suggestion rates and comparing them with other organizations are important benchmarking items for innovation and creative capability. Other measures, such as the number of new projects, products, processes, and strategies, can be monitored and measured in some way. Subjectivity often enters the measurement process with these issues. Some organizations will actually measure the creative capability of employees using inventories and instruments. Comparing actual scores of groups of employees over time reflects the degree to which employees are improving innovativeness and creativity in the workplace. Having consistent and comparable measures is still a challenge. Because of the difficulty of converting data to monetary values, these measures are usually listed as intangibles.

Competencies

Organizations are interested in developing key competencies in particular areas such as the core mission, key product lines, and important processes. Core competencies are often identified and implemented in critical job groups. Competencies are measured with self-assessments from the individual employee as well as assessments from the supervisor. In some cases, other inputs may be important or necessary to measure. That approach goes beyond just learning new skills, processes, or knowledge to using a combination of skills, knowledge, and behavior on the job to develop an acceptable level of competence to meet competitive challenges.

Customer Satisfaction

Because of the importance of building and improving customer service, a variety of measures are often monitored and reported as a payoff of training. One of the most important measures is survey data showing the degree to which customers are pleased with the products and services. These survey values, reported as absolute data or as an index, represent important data from which to compare the success of a customer service training program.

As described earlier, customer satisfaction data are achieving a lot of interest and their value is often connected with linkages to other measures, such as revenue growth, market share, and profits. Several models are available to show what happens when customers are dissatisfied, along with the economic impact of those decisions. In the health care area, researchers are showing linkages between patient satisfaction and customer retention. Still others are showing relationships among customer satisfaction, innovation, product development, and other tangible measures. Techniques are available to convert survey data to monetary values, but in most situations, the conversion is rarely attempted. Consequently, customer satisfaction improvements at the present time are usually reported as intangible benefits.

Customer Complaints

Most organizations monitor customer complaints. Each complaint is recorded along with the disposition and the time required to resolve the complaint, as well as specific costs associated with the complaint resolution. The total cost and impact of a complaint have three components: the time it takes to resolve the complaint, the cost of making restitution to the customer, and the ultimate cost of ill-will generated by the dissatisfaction (lost future business). Because of the difficulty of assigning an accurate monetary value to a customer complaint, the measure usually becomes a very important intangible benefit.

Customer Loyalty

Customer retention is a critical measure that is sometimes linked to sales, marketing, and customer service training and performance improvement programs. Long-term, efficient, and productive customer relationships are important to the success of an organization. While the importance of customer retention is understood, it is not always converted to a monetary value. Specific models have been developed to show the value of a customer and how to keep customers over a period of time. For example, the average tenure of a customer can translate directly into a bottom-line savings.

Tied very closely with customer loyalty is the rate at which customers leave the organization. The churn rate is a critical measure that can be costly, not only in lost business (profits from lost customers), but in the cost necessary to generate a new customer. Because of the difficulty of converting directly to a specific monetary value, customer loyalty is listed as an intangible benefit.

Customer Response Time

Providing prompt customer service is a critical issue in most organizations. Consequently, the time it takes to respond to specific customer service requests or problems is recorded and monitored. Thus, customer response time becomes an important intangible benefit.

Other Customer Responses

A variety of other types of customer responses can be tracked, such as creativity with customer response, responsiveness to cost and pricing issues, and other important issues customers may specify or require. Monitoring these variables can provide more evidence of the training program's results when the program influences particular variables. Because of the difficulty of assigning values to the items, they are usually reported as intangible measures.

Teamwork

A variety of measures are often monitored to reflect how well teams are working. Although the output of teams and the quality of their work are often measured as hard data and converted to monetary values, other interpersonal measures may be monitored and reported separately. Sometimes organizations survey team members before and after training to determine if the level of teamwork has increased. Using a variable scale, team members provide a perception of improvement. The monetary value of increased teamwork is rarely developed and, consequently, it is reported as an intangible benefit.

Cooperation

The success of a team often depends on the cooperative spirit of team members. Some instruments measure the level of cooperation before and after training using a perception scale. Because of the difficulty of converting this measure to a monetary value, it is almost always reported as an intangible benefit.

Conflict

In team environments, the level of conflict is sometimes measured. A reduction in conflict may reflect the success of leadership development. Although conflict reduction can be measured by perception or numbers of conflicts, the monetary value is an illusive figure. Consequently, in most situations, a monetary value is not placed on conflict reduction and it is reported as an intangible benefit.

Decisiveness

Teams make decisions, and the timing of the decision-making process often becomes an issue. Consequently, decisiveness is sometimes measured in terms of the speed at which decisions are made. Some leadership development programs are expected to influence this process. Survey measures may reflect the perception of the team or, in some cases, may monitor how quickly decisions are made. Although reductions in the timing of decisions can be converted to monetary values, improvements are usually reported as intangible benefits.

Communication

A variety of communication instruments reflect the quality and quantity of communication within a team. Improvement in communications effectiveness, or perceptions of effectiveness, driven by a leadership development program is not usually converted to monetary values and is reported as an intangible benefit.

FINAL THOUGHTS

A variety of available intangible benefits reflect the success of a leadership development program and intangible benefits should be included in the leadership development scorecard. Although they may not be perceived as valuable as specific monetary measures, they are an important part of an overall evaluation. Intangible measures should be identified, explored, examined, monitored, and analyzed for changes when they are linked to the program. Collectively, they add a unique dimension to the overall program results, as most, if not all, programs have intangible measures associated with them. While some of the most common intangible measures were covered in this chapter, the coverage was not meant to be complete. The number of intangible measures is almost unlimited.

CASE STUDY—PART H
INTERNATIONAL CAR RENTAL

ROI Analysis

The values presented in this study were higher than the L&D team and management expected. In discussions held with the executives at ICR prior to program implementation the L&D team and the executives agreed that for the program to be considered successful, a 20 percent ROI would need to be achieved. The 105 percent ROI that was achieved, along with the additional intangible benefits, was perceived to be an excellent result. In addition the process was credible with an acceptable level of accuracy.

Intangible Benefits

Data collected from the postprogram questionnaire (Figure 5-4), questions 23 and 24, revealed that the leadership challenge resulted in several intangible benefits. The intangible benefits were:

- Increased participant job satisfaction
- Increased employee job satisfaction
- Improved communication
- Improved teamwork

The Leadership Scorecard

The L&D team collected and compiled follow-up evaluation data from the leadership challenge based on their initial planning and

Leadership Scorecard				
Program Title: **The Leadership Challenge**				
Target Audience: **36 first-level managers**				
Duration: **8 days total (2 programs, 4 days each, were conducted)**				
Business Objectives: **Drive improvements in at least two business measures**				
Results				
Satisfaction	**Learning**	**Application**	**Tangible Benefits**	**Intangible Benefits**
(1-5 scale)	(1-5 scale)	(1-5 scale)		
Level 1	**Level 2**	**Level 3**	**Levels 4 & 5**	Increased participant job satisfaction
4.5 relevancy 4.7 importance to job success	4.2 ability to apply skills	4.6 extent applied 4.1 level of effectiveness in applying skills	$329,201 total benefits BCR: 2.05:1 ROI: 105%	Increased employee job satisfaction Improved communication Improved teamwork
Technique to Isolate Effects of Program: **Participant estimations**				
Technique to Convert Data to Monetary Value: **Participant estimations and internal experts**				
Fully-loaded Program Costs: **$160,754**				
Barriers to Application of Skills: **Lack of support from colleagues and peers, lack of support tools**				
Recommendations: **Provide additional support tools to participants, communicate competency model to all employees to increase knowledge and support of first-level manager training, communicate program results to executive team, program participants and other employees, continue to offer The Leadership Challenge to all first-level managers**				

Figure 9-3. Leadership scorecard for the leadership challenge.

leadership scorecard format. The resulting data were placed in the leadership scorecard to track and communicate the results. Figure 9-3 shows the results of the L&D leadership scorecard for the two leadership challenge programs that were evaluated.

DISCUSSION QUESTIONS

1. What should the strategy be for communicating these data?
2. How can leadership scorecard results be used to generate additional funding for leadership development, measurement, and evaluation?
3. How should management support for leadership development and the leadership scorecard be enhanced?

REFERENCES

Chang, R.Y., and Morgan, M.W. *Performance Scorecards: Measuring the Right Things in the Real World*. San Francisco, CA: Jossey-Bass, 2000.

Denzin, M.K., and Lincoln, Y.S. (Eds.). *Handbook of Qualitative Research*. Thousand Oaks, CA: Sage Publications, 1994.

Fitz-enz, J. *The ROI of Human Capital: Measuring the Economic Value of Employee Performance*. New York: American Management Association, 2001.

Fitz-enz, J., and Davison, B. *How to Measure Human Resources Managemen.*, 3rd ed. New York: McGraw-Hill, 2002.

Gummesson, E. *Qualitative Methods and Management Research* (revised ed.). Thousand Oaks, CA: Sage Publications, 1991.

Oxman, J.A. "The Hidden Leverage of Human Capital," *MIT Sloan Management Review*, Summer 2002.

Phillips, P.P. (Ed.). *In Action: Measuring Intellectual Capital*. Alexandria, VA: American Society for Training and Development, 2002.

Saint-Onge, H. "Shaping Human Resource Management within the Knowledge-Driven Enterprise." *Leading Knowledge Management and Learning*, D. Bonner (Ed.). Alexandria, VA: American Society for Training and Development, 2002.

PART III

Leadership Scorecard Implementation Considerations

Communicating Results and Overcoming Resistance

With data in hand, what next? Should the data be used to modify the program, change the process, show the contribution, justify new programs, gain additional support, or build goodwill? How should the data be presented? Who should present the data? Where should the data be communicated? These and other questions are examined in this chapter. Communicating results is as important as achieving them. Effective communication can also help in overcoming any resistance to the process that might be encountered. With the implementation of any new process or change there may be resistance. This chapter provides suggestions on how to overcome resistance to implementing a leadership scorecard.

THE IMPORTANCE OF COMMUNICATION

Communicating results is a critical issue. While it is essential to communicate results to interested stakeholders after the project is completed, it is also important to communicate throughout the leadership development program as well. This ensures that information is flowing so adjustments can be made and all stakeholders are aware of the success and issues surrounding the program. There are at least five key reasons for being concerned about communicating results.

Measurement and Evaluation Mean Nothing without Communication

Measuring success and collecting evaluation data mean nothing unless the findings are communicated promptly to the appropriate audiences so that they will be aware of what is occurring and can take action if necessary. Communication allows a full loop to be made from the program results to necessary actions based on those results.

Communication Is Necessary to Make Improvements

Because information is collected at different points during the process, the communication or feedback to the various groups that will take action is the only way adjustments can be made. Thus, the quality and timeliness of communication become critical issues for making necessary adjustments or improvements. Even after the project is completed, communication is necessary to make sure the target audience fully understands the results achieved and how the results could be enhanced either in future projects or in the current project, if it is still operational. Communication is the key to making these important adjustments at all phases of the program.

Communication Is Necessary for Explaining Contributions

The contribution of the leadership development program explained with seven types of measures is a confusing issue, at best. The different target audiences will need a thorough explanation of the results. A communication strategy, including techniques, media, and the overall process, will determine the extent to which they understand the contribution. Communicating results, particularly with business impact and ROI, can quickly become confusing for even the most sophisticated target audiences. Communication must be planned and implemented with the goal of making sure the audiences understand the full contribution.

Communication Is a Sensitive Issue

Communication is one of those important issues that can cause major problems. Because the results of a program can be closely linked to the performance of others and the political issues in an organization, communication can upset some individuals while pleasing others. If certain individuals do not receive the information or it is delivered inconsistently from one group to another, problems can surface quickly. Not only is it an understanding issue, it is also a fairness, quality, and political correctness issue to make sure communication is constructed properly and delivered effectively to all key individuals who need the information.

A Variety of Target Audiences Need Different Information

Because there are so many potential target audiences for receiving communication on the success of a program, it is important for the communication to be tailored directly to their needs. A varied audience will command varied needs. Planning and effort are necessary to make sure the audience receives all of the information it needs, in the proper format, and at the proper time. A single report for all audiences may not be appropriate. The scope, size, media, and even the actual information of different types and different levels will vary significantly from one group to another, making the target audience the key to determining the appropriate communication process.

Collectively, these reasons make communication a critical issue, although it is often overlooked or underestimated in leadership development projects. This chapter builds on this important issue and shows a variety of techniques for accomplishing all types of communication for various target audiences.

PRINCIPLES OF COMMUNICATING RESULTS

The skills required to communicate results effectively are almost as delicate and sophisticated as those needed to obtain results. The style is as important as the substance. Regardless of the message, audience, or medium, a few general principles apply and are explored next.

Timeliness

Usually, results should be communicated as soon as they are known. From a practical standpoint, it may be best to delay the communication until a convenient time, such as the publication of the next newsletter or the next general management meeting. Timing issues must be addressed. Is the audience ready for the results in light of other things that may have happened? Is it expecting results? When is the best time for having the maximum effect on the audience? Are there circumstances that dictate a change in the timing of the communication?

Target Audiences

Communication will be more effective if it is designed for a particular group. The message should be specifically tailored to the interests, needs, and expectations of the target audience.

The results described in this chapter reflect outcomes at all levels, including the seven types of data developed in this book. Some of the data are developed earlier in the project and are communicated during the project. Other data are collected after implementation and are communicated in a follow-up study. Thus, the results, in their broadest sense, may involve early feedback in qualitative terms to ROI values in varying quantitative terms.

Media Selection

For particular groups, some media may be more effective than others. Face-to-face meetings may be better than special bulletins. A memo distributed exclusively to top management may be more effective than the company newsletter. The proper method of communication can help improve the effectiveness of the process.

Communication Bias

It is important to separate fact from fiction and accurate statements from opinions. Various audiences may accept communication from the leadership development staff with skepticism, anticipating biased opinions. Boastful statements sometimes turn off recipients, and most of the content is lost. Observable, believable facts carry far more weight than extreme or sensational claims. Although such claims may get audience attention, they often detract from the importance of the results.

Consistent Communication

The timing and content of the communication should be consistent with past practices. A special communication at an unusual time during the training program may provoke suspicion. Also, if a particular group, such as top management, regularly receives communication on outcomes, it should continue receiving communication, even if the results are not positive. If some results are omitted, it might leave the impression that only positive results are reported.

Testimonials

The more effective test comes from individuals the audience respects. Opinions are strongly influenced by others, particularly those who are respected and trusted. Testimonials about results, when solicited from individuals respected by others in the organization, can influence the effectiveness of the message. This respect may be related to leadership ability, position, special skills, or knowledge. A testimonial from an individual who commands little respect and is regarded as a substandard performer can have a negative impact on the message.

Audience Perceptions

The audience's opinion of the leadership development staff and function will influence the communication strategy. Opinions are difficult to change, and a negative opinion of the leadership development group may not change with the mere presentation of facts. However, the presentation of facts alone may strengthen the opinions held by those who already agree with the results. It helps reinforce their position and provides a defense in discussions with others. A leadership development group with a high level of credibility and respect may have a relatively easy time communicating results. Low credibility can create problems when trying to be persuasive. The reputation of the leadership development group is an important consideration in developing the overall strategy.

These general principles are important to the overall success of the communication effort. They should serve as a checklist for the leadership development team when disseminating program results.

ANALYZING COMMUNICATION NEEDS

Because there are many reasons for communicating results, a list should be tailored to the situation and project. The specific reasons depend on the project, the setting, and the unique needs of the sponsor. The most common reasons are:

- To secure approval for the project and allocate resources of time and money. The initial communication presents a proposal, projected ROI, or other data that are intended to secure the project approval. This communication may not have very much data but rather anticipates what is to come.
- To gain support for the project and its objectives. It is important to have support from a variety of groups. This communication is intended to build the necessary support to make the project work successfully.

- To secure agreement on the issues, solutions, and resources. As the program begins, it is important for all those directly involved to have some agreement and understanding of the important elements and requirements surrounding the program.
- To build credibility for the leadership development group, its techniques, and the finished products. It is important early in the process to make sure that those involved understand the approach and reputation of the leadership development staff and, based on the approach taken, the commitments made by all parties.
- To reinforce the processes. It is important for key managers to support the program and reinforce the various processes used in design, development, and delivery. This communication is designed to enhance those processes.
- To drive action for improvement in the project. This early communication is designed as a process improvement tool to affect changes and improvements as the needs are uncovered and various individuals make suggestions.
- To prepare participants for the program. It is necessary for those involved most directly in the program, the participants, to be prepared for learning, application, and responsibilities that will be required of them as they bring success to the project.
- To enhance results throughout the project and the quality of future feedback. This communication is designed to show the status of the project and to influence decisions, seek support, or communicate events and expectations to the key stakeholders. In addition, it will enhance both the quality and the quantity of information as stakeholders see the feedback cycle in action.
- To show the complete results of the leadership development program. This is perhaps the most important communication, where all of the results involving all seven types of measures are communicated to the appropriate individuals so that they have a full understanding of the success or shortcomings of the project.
- To underscore the importance of measuring results. Some individuals need to understand the importance of measurement and evaluation and see the need for having important data on different measures.
- To explain techniques used to measure results. The program sponsor and support staff need to understand the techniques used in measuring results. In some cases, these techniques may be transferred internally to use with other projects. In short,

these individuals need to understand the soundness and theoretical framework of the process used.

- To stimulate desire in participants to be involved in the program. Ideally, participants want to be involved in the program. This communication is designed to pique their interest in the program and inform them of its importance.
- To stimulate interest in the leadership development function. From a leadership development perspective, some communications are designed to create interest in all of the products and services based on the results obtained by the current programs.
- To demonstrate accountability for expenditures. It is important for a broad group to understand the need for accountability and the approach of the leadership development staff. This ensures accountability for expenditures on the project.
- To market future projects. From a leadership development perspective, it is important to build a database of successful projects to use in convincing others that the training and performance improvement can add value.

Although this list is comprehensive, there may be other reasons for communicating results. The situation context should be considered when developing others.

Planning the Communication

Any successful activity must be planned carefully for it to produce the maximum results. This is a critical part of communicating the results of major programs. The actual planning of the communications is important to ensure that each audience receives the proper information at the right time and that appropriate actions are taken.

Communication Policy Issues

In examining the overall leadership development process, policy issues need to be developed around the communication of results. These range from providing feedback during a project to communicating the ROI from an impact study. Seven different areas will need some attention as the policies are developed:

1. What will actually be communicated? It is important to detail the types of information communicated throughout the project—not only the seven types of data from the leadership

scorecard, but the overall progress with leadership development may be a topic of communications as well.

2. When will the data be communicated? With communications,
   timing is critical. If adjustments in the program need to made,
   the information should be communicated quickly so that swift
   actions can be taken.

3. How will the information be communicated? This shows the
   preferences toward particular types of communication media.
   For example, some organizations prefer to have written documents sent out as reports, others prefer face-to-face meetings,
   and still others want electronic communications utilized as
   much as possible.

4. The location for communication. Some prefer that the communication take place close to the sponsor; others prefer the
   leadership development offices. The location can be an important issue in terms of convenience and perception.

5. Who will communicate the information? Will the leadership
   development staff, an independent consultant, or an individual
   involved from the sponsor's office communicate the information? The person communicating must have credibility so that
   the information is believable.

6. The target audience. Identify specific target audiences that
   should always receive information and others that will receive
   information when appropriate.

7. The specific actions that are required or desired. When information is presented, in some cases no action is needed; in
   others, changes are desired and sometimes even required. Collectively, these seven issues frame the policy around communication as a whole.

Table 10-1 shows the communication plan for a leadership development program. Five different communication pieces were developed for different audiences all including the leadership scorecard.
The complete report was an ROI impact study, a 75-page report that
served as the historical document for the project. It went to the
sponsor, the leadership development staff, and the particular
manager of each of the teams involved in the studies. An executive
summary, a much smaller document, went to some of the higher-
level executives. A general interest overview and summary without
the ROI calculation went to the participants. A general-interest
article was developed for company publications, and a brochure was
developed to show the success of the program. That brochure was

Table 10-1
Communication Plan for Program Results

Communication document	Communication target(s)	Distribution method
Complete report with appendices (75 pages), including leadership scorecard	• Program sponsor • Leadership development staff • Intact team manager	Distribute and discuss in a special meeting
Executive summary (8 pages) including leadership scorecard	• Senior management in business units • Senior corporate management	Distribute and discuss in routine meeting
General interest overview and summary without the actual ROI calculation (10 pages)	• Participants	Mail with letter
General interest article (1 page)	• All employees	Publish in company publication
Brochure highlighting program, objectives, and specific results	• Team leaders with an interest in the program • Prospective sponsors	Include with other marketing materials

used in marketing the same process internally to other teams and served as additional marketing material for the leadership development staff. This detailed plan may be part of the overall plan for the assignment but may be fine-tuned during the actual process.

Selecting the Audience for Communications

The potential target audiences to receive information on results are varied in terms of job levels and responsibilities. Determining which groups will receive a particular communication piece deserves careful thought, as problems can arise when a particular group receives inappropriate information or when another is omitted altogether. A sound basis for proper audience selection is to analyze the reason for communication, as discussed in an earlier section. Table 10-2 shows common target audiences and the basis for selecting the audience.

While Table 10-2 shows the most common target audiences, there can be others in a particular organization. For instance, management or employees could be subdivided into different departments, divi-

Table 10-2
Common Target Audiences

Reason for communication	Primary target audiences
To secure approval for the project	Sponsor, top executives
To gain support for the project	Immediate managers, team leaders
To secure agreement with the issues	Participants, team leaders
To build credibility for leadership development	Top executives
To enhance reinforcement of the processes	Immediate managers
To drive action for improvement	Sponsor, leadership staff
To prepare participants for the project	Team leaders
To enhance results and quality of future feedback	Participants
To show the complete results of the project	Sponsor
To underscore the importance of measuring results	Sponsor, leadership staff
To explain techniques used to measure results	Sponsor, support staff
To create desire for a participant to be involved	Team leaders
To stimulate interest in the leadership development staff	Top executives
To demonstrate accountability for expenditures	All employees
To market future projects	Prospective sponsors

sions, or even subsidiaries of the organization. The number of audiences can be large in a complex organization. At a minimum, four target audiences are always recommended: a senior management group, the participants' immediate manager or team leader, the participants, and the leadership development staff.

Developing the Information: The Formal Evaluation Report

The type of formal evaluation report depends on the extent of detailed information presented to the various target audiences. Brief summaries of results with appropriate charts may be sufficient for some communication efforts. In other situations, particularly with significant programs requiring extensive funding, the amount of detail in the evaluation report is more crucial. A complete and comprehensive impact study report may be necessary. This report can then be used as the basis of information for specific audiences and various media. The report may contain the following sections.

Executive Summary

The executive summary is a brief overview of the entire report explaining the basis for the evaluation and the significant conclusions and recommendations. It is designed for individuals who are too busy to read a detailed report. It is usually written last but appears first in the report for easy access and may include the leadership scorecard as a one-page summary.

Background Information

The background information provides a general description of the project. If applicable, the needs assessment that led to the implementation of the project is summarized. The program is fully described, including the events that led to the intervention. Other specific items necessary to provide a full description of the project are included. The extent of detailed information depends on the amount of information the audience needs.

Objectives

The objectives for both the impact study and the actual leadership development program are outlined. Sometimes they are the same, but they may be different. The report details the particular objectives of the study itself so that the reader clearly understands the rationale for the study and how the data will be used. In addition, specific objectives of the leadership development program are detailed, as these are the objectives from which the different types or levels of data will be collected.

Evaluation Strategy/Methodology

The evaluation strategy outlines all of the components that make up the total evaluation process. Several components of the results-based model and the ROI methodology presented in this book are discussed in this section of the report. The specific purposes of evaluation are outlined, and the evaluation design and methodology are explained. The instruments used in data collection are also described and presented as exhibits. Any unusual issues in the evaluation design are discussed. Finally, other useful information related to the design, timing, and execution of the evaluation is included.

Data Collection and Analysis

This section explains the methods used to collect data as outlined in earlier chapters. Data collected are usually presented in the report in summary form. Next, the methods used to analyze data are presented with interpretations.

Reaction and Satisfaction

This section details data collected from key stakeholders, particularly the participants involved in the process, to measure reactions to the program and levels of satisfaction with various issues and parts of the process. Other input from the sponsor or managers may be included to show the levels of satisfaction.

Learning

This section shows a brief summary of the formal and informal methods for measuring learning. It explains how participants have learned new processes, skills, tasks, procedures, and practices.

Application and Implementation

This section shows how the project was actually implemented and the success with the application of new skills and knowledge. Implementation issues are addressed, including any major success and/or lack of success.

Business Impact

This section shows the actual business impact measures representing the business needs that initially drove the project. This shows the extent to which performance has changed during the implementation of the program.

Program Costs

Program costs are presented in this section. A summary of the costs by category is included. For example, analysis, development, implementation, and evaluation costs are recommended categories for cost presentation. The assumptions made in developing and classifying costs are discussed in this section of the report.

Return on Investment

This section actually shows the ROI calculation along with the benefits/cost ratio. It compares the value to what was expected and provides an interpretation of the actual calculation.

Intangible Measures

This section shows the various intangible measures directly linked to the training program. Intangibles are those measures not converted to monetary values or included in the actual ROI calculation.

Barriers and Enablers

The various problems and obstacles affecting the success of the project are detailed and presented as barriers to implementation. Also, those factors or influences that had a positive effect on the project are included as enablers. Together, they provide tremendous insight into what can hinder or enhance projects in the future.

Conclusions and Recommendations

This section presents conclusions based on all of the results. If appropriate, brief explanations are presented on how each conclusion was reached. A list of recommendations or changes in the program, if appropriate, is provided with brief explanations for each recommendation. It is important that the conclusions and recommendations are consistent with one another and with the findings described in the previous section.

These components make up the major parts of a complete evaluation report.

Developing the Report

Table 10-3 shows the table of contents from a formal evaluation report for an ROI evaluation.

While this report is an effective, professional way to present evaluation data, several cautions need to be followed. Because this document reports the success of a group of employees, complete credit for the success must go to the participants and their immediate leaders. Their performance generated the success. Another important caution is to avoid boasting about results. Although the ROI methodology may be accurate and credible, it still may have some subjective issues. Huge claims of success can quickly turn off an audience and interfere with the delivery of the desired message.

A final caution concerns the structure of the report. The methodology should be clearly explained, along with assumptions made in the analysis. The reader should readily see how the values were developed and how the specific steps were followed to make the process more conservative, credible, and accurate. Detailed statistical analyses should be placed in the appendix.

COMMUNICATING THE INFORMATION

Perhaps the greatest challenge of communication is the actual delivery of the message. This can be accomplished in a variety of ways and settings based on the target audience and the media selected for the message. Presenting the leadership scorecard and evaluation results to senior management may be one of the most challenging tasks. Guidelines are provided that can help make this process successful.

Perhaps one of the most challenging and stressful company communications is presenting the results of a leadership development program to the senior management team, which also serves as the sponsor on a project. The challenge is convincing this highly skeptical and critical group that outstanding results have been achieved (assuming they have), in a very reasonable time frame, addressing the salient points, and making sure the managers understand the process. Two particular issues can create challenges. First, if the results are very impressive, it may be difficult to make the managers believe the data. On the other extreme, if data are negative, it will be a challenge to make sure managers do not overreact to the negative results and look for someone to blame. The following guidelines can help make sure that this process is planned and executed properly:

Table 10-3
Format of an Impact Study Report

- Executive summary
  - Leadership Scorecard
- General information
  - Background
  - Objectives of study
- Methodology for impact study — *Builds credibility for the process*
  - Levels of evaluation
  - ROI process
  - Collecting data
  - Isolating the effects of training
  - Converting data to monetary values
  - Assumptions
- Data analysis issues
- Program costs
- Results: Indicators
  - Response profile
  - Success with objectives
- Results: Reaction and satisfaction — *The results with six measures: Levels 1, 2, 3, 4, 5, and intangibles*
  - Data sources
  - Data summary
  - Key issues
- Results: Learning
  - Data sources
  - Data summary
  - Key issues
- Results: Application and implementation
  - Data sources
  - Data summary
  - Key issues
- Results: Business impact
  - General comments
  - Linkage with business measures
  - Key issues
- Results: ROI and its meaning
- Results: Intangible measures
- Barriers and enablers
  - Barriers
  - Enablers
- Conclusions and recommendations
  - Conclusions
  - Recommendations

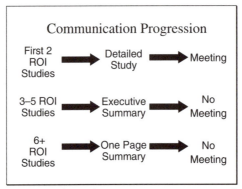

Figure 10-1. Streamline the communication with executives.

- Plan a face-to-face meeting with senior team members for the first one or two major impact studies, as detailed in Figure 10-1. If they are unfamiliar with the leadership scorecard, a face-to-face meeting is necessary to make sure that they understand the process. The good news is that they will probably attend the meeting because they have not seen ROI data developed for a leadership development program. The bad news is that it takes a lot of time, usually an hour for this presentation.
- After a group has had a face-to-face meeting with a couple of presentations, an executive summary may suffice for the next three to nine studies. At this point they understand the process, so a shortened version may be appropriate.
- After the target audience is familiar with the process the leadership scorecard may be the only document that needs to be provided.
- When making the initial presentation, distribution of the results should be saved until the end of the session. This will allow enough time to present the process and obtain reaction to it before the target audience sees the actual ROI number.
- Present the process step by step, showing how data were collected, when they were collected, who provided the data, how the data were isolated from other influences, and how they were converted to monetary values. The various assumptions, adjustments, and conservative approaches are presented along with the total cost of the program. The costs are fully loaded so that the target audience will begin to buy into the process of developing the actual ROI.

- When data are actually presented, the results are presented step by step, starting with indicators, moving through Level 1 to Level 5, ending with the intangibles. This allows the audience to see the chain of impact with reaction and satisfaction, learning, application and implementation, business impact, and ROI. After some discussion on the meaning of the ROI, the intangible measures are presented. Allocate time to each level, as appropriate, for the audience. This helps overcome the potentially negative reactions to a very positive or negative ROI.
- Show the consequences of additional accuracy if it is an issue. The trade-off for more accuracy and validity often means more expense. Address this issue whenever necessary, agreeing to add more data if required.
- Collect concerns, reactions, and issues for the process and make adjustments accordingly for the next presentation.

Collectively, these steps will help prepare for and present one of the most critical meetings in the leadership scorecard process.

ANALYZING REACTIONS TO COMMUNICATION

The best indicator of how effectively the results of a leadership development program have been communicated is the level of commitment and support from the management group. The allocation of requested resources and strong commitment from top management are tangible evidence of management's perception of the results. In addition to this macrolevel reaction, there are a few techniques the leadership development staff can use to measure the effectiveness of their communication efforts.

Whenever results are communicated, the reaction of the target audiences can be monitored. These reactions may include nonverbal gestures, oral remarks, written comments, or indirect actions that reveal how the communication was received. Usually, when results are presented in a meeting, the presenter will have some indication of how the results were received by the group. The interest and attitudes of the audience can usually be evaluated quickly.

During the presentation, questions may be asked or, in some cases, the information is challenged. In addition, a tabulation of these challenges and questions can be useful in evaluating the type of information to include in future communications. Positive comments about the results are desired and, when they are made—formally or informally—they should also be noted and tabulated.

Leadership development staff meetings are an excellent arena for discussing the reaction to communicating results. Comments can come from many sources depending on the particular target audiences. Input from different members of the staff can be summarized to help judge the overall effectiveness.

The purpose of analyzing reactions is to make adjustments in the communication process—if adjustments are necessary. Although the reactions may involve intuitive assessments, a more sophisticated analysis will provide more accurate information to make these adjustments. The net result should be a more effective communication process.

OVERCOMING RESISTANCE TO A LEADERSHIP MEASUREMENT

With any new process or change, there is resistance. Resistance shows up in many ways—negative comments, inappropriate actions, or dysfunctional behaviors. Table 10-4 shows some comments that reflect open resistance to the measuring the impact of leadership development. Each represents an issue that must be resolved or addressed in some way. A few of the comments are based on realistic barriers, whereas others are based on myths that must be dis-

Table 10-4
Typical Objections to a Leadership Scorecard

Open resistance
1. It costs too much.
2. It takes too much time.
3. Who is asking for this?
4. It is not in my job duties.
5. I did not have input on this.
6. I do not understand this.
7. What happens when the results are negative?
8. How can we be consistent with this?
9. The ROI process is too subjective.
10. Our managers will not support this.
11. ROI is focused too narrowly.
12. This is not practical.

pelled. Sometimes, resistance to evaluation reflects underlying concerns. The individuals involved may have fear of losing control and others may feel that they are vulnerable to actions that may be taken if their programs are not successful. Still others may be concerned about any process that requires additional learning and actions.

Resistance can appear in all major audiences addressed in this book. It can appear in the leadership development staff as they resist implementing a leadership scorecard and openly make comments similar to those listed in Table 10-4. Heavy persuasion and evidence of tangible benefits may be needed to convince those individuals that this is a process that should be implemented because it is in their best interest. Another major audience, the sponsor, will also experience resistance. Although most sponsors would want to see the results of a leadership development project, they may have concerns about the quality and accuracy of data. Also, they may be concerned about the time commitments and the costs of the evaluation.

The managers of participants in programs may develop resistance. They may have concerns about the information they are asked to provide and about whether their performance is being judged along with the evaluation of the participants. In reality, they may express the same fears listed in Table 10-4.

The challenge is to implement the process in organizations methodically and consistently so that it becomes a routine and standard process built into leadership development programs. Implementation is a plan for overcoming resistance.

PLANNING THE IMPLEMENTATION

Few initiatives will be effective without proper planning and the leadership scorecard is no exception. Planning is synonymous with success. Several strategies are identified to help with overcoming resistance.

Identifying a Champion

As a first step in the process, one or more individuals should be designated as the internal leader for the leadership scorecard. As in most change efforts, someone must take the responsibility for ensuring that the process is implemented successfully. This leader serves as a champion for evaluation and is usually the one who understands the process best and sees the vast potential for the contribution of the process. More important, this leader is willing to show and teach others.

Table 10-5
Various Roles of the Measurement Leader

Technical expert	Cheerleader
Consultant	Communicator
Problem solver	Process monitor
Initiator	Planner
Designer	Analyst
Developer	Interpreter
Coordinator	Teacher

Developing the Measurement Leader

In preparation for this assignment, individuals usually obtain special training to build specific skills and knowledge in the evaluation process. The role of the implementation leader is very broad and serves a variety of specialized duties. The leader can take on many roles, as shown in Table 10-5.

It is a difficult and challenging assignment that will need special training and skill building. In the past there have been only a few programs available that help build these skills. Now there are many available and some are quite comprehensive. For example, a program has been developed by Jack Phillips to certify the individuals who are assuming a leadership role in the implementation of ROI. The process involves pre-work and preparation prior to attending a one-week workshop. The comprehensive workshop is designed to build 10 essential skills, listed in Table 10-6, needed to apply and implement the ROI process. For more information on certification, contact Jack Phillips (phillipsroi@aol.com).

Preparing the Leadership Development Staff

One group that will often resist ROI methodology is the leadership development staff who must design, develop, deliver, and coordinate leadership development solutions. These staff members often see evaluation as an unnecessary intrusion into their responsibilities, absorbing precious time, and stifling their freedom to be creative.

On each key issue or major decision, the leadership development staff should be involved in the process. As evaluation guidelines are developed, staff input is absolutely essential. It is difficult for the staff

Table 10-6
Ten Skill Sets for Certification

Skill areas for certification

- Planning for ROI calculations
- Collecting evaluation data
- Isolating the effects of training
- Converting data to monetary values
- Monitoring program costs
- Analyzing data, including calculating the ROI
- Presenting evaluation data
- Implementing the ROI process
- Providing internal consulting on ROI
- Teaching others the ROI process

to be critical of something they helped design, develop, and plan. Using meetings, brainstorming sessions, and task forces, the leadership development staff should be involved in every phase of developing the framework and supporting documents for the leadership scorecard.

One reason the leadership development staff may resist the evaluation process is that the effectiveness of their programs will be fully exposed, placing their reputation on the line. They may have a fear of failure. To overcome this, the leadership scorecard should clearly be positioned as a tool for process improvement and not as a tool to evaluate leadership development staff performance, at least during its early years of implementation. Leadership development staff members will not be interested in developing a tool that will be used to expose their shortcomings and failures.

Assigning Responsibilities

Determining the specific responsibilities is a critical issue because there can be confusion when individuals are unclear about their specific assignments in the leadership scorecard process. Responsibilities apply to two broad groups. The first is the measurement and evaluation responsibility for the entire leadership development staff. It is important for all of those involved in designing, developing, delivering, coordinating, and supporting programs to have some responsibility for measurement and evaluation. These responsibilities include providing input on the design of instruments, planning a specific evaluation, collecting data, and interpreting the results.

Tapping into a Network

Because the ROI methodology is new to many individuals, it is helpful to have a peer group experiencing similar issues and frustrations. Tapping into an international network (already developed), joining or creating a local network, or building an internal network are all possible ways to utilize the resources, ideas, and support of others.

ASTD ROI Network. In 1996, the ROI network was created to exchange information among graduates of the certification workshop. During certification the participants bond and freely exchange information with each other. The ROI network is an attempt to provide a permanent vehicle of information and support.

The ROI Network is a professional organization, which claims about 500 members. It is now affiliated with ASTD and is poised for growth. The network operates through a variety of committees and communicates with members through newsletters, websites, listservs, and annual meetings. The ROI network represents an opportunity to build a community of practice around the ROI methodology. To learn more about the ASTD ROI network, visit www.ASTD.org.

COST-SAVINGS APPROACHES

One of the most significant barriers to the implementation of the leadership development scorecard is the potential time and cost involved in implementing the process. Sometimes, the perception of excessive time and cost is only a myth; at other times it is a reality. The leadership development scorecard can be implemented for about 3 to 5 percent of the leadership development budget. However, this is still a significant expense and represents additional time requirements. The cost-savings approaches outlined have commanded much attention recently and represent an important part of the implementation strategy (Phillips and Burkett, 2001).

Take shortcuts at lower levels. When resources are a primary concern and shortcuts need to be taken, it is best to take them at lower levels in the evaluation scheme. This is a resource allocation issue. For example, if a Level 4 evaluation is conducted, Levels 1–3 do not have to be as comprehensive. This requires the evaluator to place most of the emphasis on the highest level of the evaluation.

Fund measurement and evaluation with savings from the ROI methodology. Almost every ROI study will generate data from which to make improvements. Results at different levels often show how the program can be altered to make it more effective and efficient. Sometimes, data suggest that the program can be modified, adjusted, or completely redesigned. All of those actions can result in cost savings. In a few cases, the program may have to be eliminated because it is not adding the value and adjustments will not necessarily improve it (i.e., it was not needed). In this case, a tremendous cost savings is realized as the program is eliminated. A logical argument can be made to shift a portion of these savings to fund additional measurement and evaluation. Some organizations gradually migrate to the 5 percent of the budget target for expenditures for measurement and evaluation by utilizing the savings generated from the use of the ROI methodology. This provides a disciplined and conservative approach to additional funding.

Plan early and thoroughly. One of the most critical, cost-saving steps to evaluation is to develop program objectives and plan early for the evaluation. Evaluations often succeed because of proper planning. The best way to conserve time and resources is to know what must be done at what time. This prevents unnecessary analysis, data collection after the appropriate time, and the task of having to reconstruct events and issues because they were not planned in advance.

Integrate evaluation into leadership development. To the extent possible, evaluation should be built into the leadership development program. Data collection tools should be considered part of the program. If possible, these tools should be positioned as application tools and not necessarily as evaluation tools. This removes the stigma of providing data to an evaluator, but instead enables the participant or others to capture data to clearly understand the success of the program on the job. Part of this issue is to build in expectations for stakeholders to provide the appropriate data.

Share the responsibilities. Defining specific responsibilities for all the stakeholders involved in leadership development is critical to the successful streamlining of the evaluation process. Many individuals should play an active role in measurement and evaluation. These include performance consultants, designers, developers, facilitators, participants, participants' managers, and internal subject matter experts. These individuals can share much of the load that had previously been part of the evaluator's responsibility. This not only has a value of saving time, but also enriches the success of the process by having the active involvement of all stakeholders.

Involve participants in the process. One of the most effective cost-savings approaches is to have participants conduct major steps of the process. Participants are the primary source for understanding the degree to which learning is applied and has driven success on the job. The responsibilities for the participants should be expanded from the traditional requirement of involvement in learning processes and application of new skills. Now they must be asked to show the impact of those new skills and provide data as a routine part of the process. Consequently, the role of the participant has expanded from learning and application to measuring the impact and communicating information.

Use shortcut methods. Almost every step of the ROI model contains shortcut methods—a particular method that represents a shortcut, but has proven to be an effective process. For example, in data collection, the simple questionnaire is a shortcut method that can be used to generate powerful and convincing data, if it is administered properly. This inexpensive time-savings data collection process can be used in many evaluations. Other shortcut methods are available in the isolation and conversion of data steps.

Use sampling. Not all programs should require a comprehensive evaluation, nor should all participants necessarily be evaluated in a planned follow-up scenario. Thus, sampling can be used in two ways. First, only a few programs are selected for Level 3, 4, and 5 evaluations. Those programs should be selected based on the criteria described early in the chapter. In addition, when a particular program is evaluated, in most cases, only a sample of participants should be evaluated. This keeps costs and time to a minimum.

Use estimates. Estimates are a very important part of the process. They are also the least expensive way to arrive at an issue. Whether isolating the effects of leadership development or converting data to monetary value, estimates can be a routine and credible part of the process. The important point is to make sure that the estimate is as credible as possible and that the process used to collect the estimate follows systematic, logical, and consistent steps.

Use internal resources. An organization does not necessarily have to employ consultants to develop impact studies and address other measurement and evaluation issues. Internal capability can be developed, eliminating the need to depend on consultants. There are many opportunities to build skills and become certified in implementing the process. This approach is perhaps one of the most significant time savers. The difference in using internal resources vs external consultants can save as much as 50 percent of the costs of a specific project.

Streamline reporting processing. When management understands the evaluation process, a streamlined approach to communication may be more appropriate and less time-consuming. The leadership scorecard is a high-level summary of the impact of the program, covering the results at various levels.

Use web-based software. Because this process is sequential and methodical, it is ideal for software application. Comprehensive software has been developed to process data at Levels 1 through 5. Additional information on available software and how it can be used can be obtained directly from Jack Phillips (phillipsroi@aol.com).

Build on the work of others. There is no time to reinvent the wheel. One of the most important cost-savings approaches is to learn from others and build on their work.

These shortcuts are important to weave throughout the implementation of a leadership scorecard to ensure that evaluation does not drain budgets and resources unnecessarily. Other shortcuts can be developed, but a word of caution is in order: shortcuts often compromise the process. When a comprehensive, valid, and reliable study is needed, it will be time-consuming and expensive—there is no way around it. The good news is that many shortcuts can be taken to supply data necessary for the audience and manage the process in an efficient way.

FINAL THOUGHTS

Communicating results is a crucial step in the overall leadership scorecard process. If this step is not taken seriously, the full impact of the results will not be realized. The chapter began with general principles for communicating program results. A communications model was presented, which can serve as a guide for any significant communication effort. The various target audiences were discussed and, because of its importance, emphasis was placed on the executive group. A suggested format for a detailed evaluation report was also provided. When implementing a leadership scorecard it is critical to incorporate ways to overcome resistance to the evaluation process. This chapter presented several suggestions for how to overcome resistance along with several cost-savings approaches.

CASE STUDY—PART I
INTERNATIONAL CAR RENTAL

Communication Strategy

To communicate appropriately with the target audiences outlined in the ROI analysis plan, three specific documents were produced and all included the one-page leadership scorecard. The first report was a detailed impact study showing the approach, assumptions, methodology, and results using all data categories. In addition, barriers and enablers were included in the study, along with conclusions and recommendations. The second report was an eight-page executive summary of the key points, including a one-page overview of the methodology. The third report was a brief, five-page summary of the process and results. These documents were presented to the different groups according to the following schedule:

Audience	Document
Participants	Brief summary
Managers of participants	Brief summary
Senior executives	Complete study, executive summary
L&D staff	Complete study
Learning and development council	Complete study, executive summary
Prospective participants	Brief summary

Because this was the first leadership scorecard implemented in this organization, face-to-face meetings were conducted with the executives. The purpose was to ensure that executives understood the methodology, the conservative assumptions, and each level of data. The barriers, enablers, conclusions, and recommendations were an important part of the meeting. In the future, after two or three studies have been conducted, this group will receive only the leadership scorecard with the summary of key data items. A similar meeting was conducted with the learning and development council. The council members are advisors to the L&D department who are usually middle- and upper-level executives and managers. Finally, a face-to-face meeting was held with the learning and development staff where the complete impact study was described and used as a learning tool.

DISCUSSION QUESTIONS

1. Could an ROI forecast be developed on a preprogram basis? Please explain.
2. Is a forecast with reaction data possible? Please explain.
3. Would an ROI forecast with Level 2 or 3 data be possible? Please explain.

REFERENCES

Block, P. *Flawless Consulting.* 2nd ed. San Francisco, CA: Jossey-Bass/Pfeiffer, 2000.

Phillips, J.J. *The Consultant's Scorecard: Tracking Results and Bottom-Line Impact of Consulting Projects.* New York: McGraw-Hill, 2000.

Phillips, P.P., and Burket, H. "Managing Evaluation Shortcuts," *Info-line.* Alexandria, VA: American Society for Training and Development, November 2001.

The Program Evaluation Standards: How to Assess Evaluations of Educational Programs. 2nd ed. Thousand Oaks, CA: Sage Publications, 1994.

Rae, L. *Using Evaluation in Training and Development.* London, England: Kogan Page, 1999.

Torres, R.T., Preskill, H.S., and Pionte, M.E. *Evaluation Strategies for Communicating and Reporting: Enhancing Learning in Organizations.* Thousand Oaks, CA: Sage Publications, 1996.

CHAPTER 11

Forecasting an ROI

The traditional and recommended approach for developing an ROI for leadership development has been described in previous chapters of this book. In the approach, ROI calculations are based on business impact data obtained after the program has been implemented. Business performance measures (Level 4 data) are easily converted to a monetary value, which is necessary for an ROI calculation. Sometimes these measures are not available, and it is usually assumed that an ROI calculation is out of the question. When measuring leadership development it is important to note that ROI calculations are possible at a variety of time frames using a variety of data. Preprogram ROI forecasts are possible, as well as forecasts with reaction data (Level 1), learning data (Level 2), and application data (Level 3). Part of the implementation plan for a leadership scorecard may be to include ROI forecasts as part of the evaluation process.

WHY FORECAST AN ROI?

Although the most accurate way to assess and develop an ROI calculation is based on postprogram data, sometimes it is important to know the forecast before the final results are tabulated. Forecasting an ROI during the project or, in some cases, even before the program is pursued is an important issue. Critical reasons drive the need for a forecasted ROI.

Reduce Uncertainty

Reducing uncertainty in a proposed program is sometimes critical. In a perfect world, the client or sponsor of a new program would like to know the expected payoff before any action is taken. Realistically, knowing the exact payoff may be impossible and, from a practical standpoint, may not be feasible to obtain. However, there is still the desire to take the uncertainty out of the equation and act on the best data available, sometimes pushing the project to a forecasted ROI before any resources are expended. Some managers will simply not budge without a preproject forecast; they need some measure of expected success before allocating any resources to the project.

New Programs Are Too Expensive to Pursue without Supportive Data

In some cases even a pilot program is not practical until some analysis has been conducted to examine the potential ROI. For example, if the program involves a significant amount of work in design, development, and delivery, a client may not want to expend the resources, even for a pilot, unless there is some assurance of a positive ROI. Although there may be trade-offs with a lower-profile and lower-cost pilot, the preprogram ROI, nevertheless, becomes an important issue, prompting some sponsors to stand firm until an ROI forecast is produced.

Compare with Postdata

Whenever there is a plan to collect data on the success of the leadership development program, impact, and ROI, it is helpful to compare actual results to preprogram expectations. In an ideal world, a forecasted ROI should have a defined relationship with the actual ROI, or they should be very similar. One important reason for forecasting ROI is to see how well the forecast holds up under the scrutiny of postprogram analysis.

Save Costs

There are several cost-saving issues that prompt the use of ROI forecasting. First, developing the forecast itself is often a very inexpensive process because it involves estimations and many different assumptions. Second, if the forecast becomes a reliable predictor of the postprogram analysis, the forecasted ROI might substitute for the actual ROI, at least with some adjustments. This could save money on the postprogram analysis. Finally, the forecasted ROI data might be used for comparisons in other areas, at least as a beginning point for other types of programs. Thus, there may be the potential to transfer the forecasted ROI to other specific programs.

Comply with Policy

More organizations are developing policy statements requiring a forecasted ROI before major projects are undertaken. For example, in one organization, any project exceeding $300,000 must have a forecasted ROI before it can be approved. In the United States, federal government units are required to show a preprogram cost/benefit analysis (ROI) for selecting new programs. In one country, an organization can receive partial payments for a training project if the ROI forecast is positive and likely to enhance the organization. This formal policy and legal structure is becoming a more frequent reason for developing the ROI forecast.

Collectively, these five reasons are causing more organizations to examine ROI forecasts so that the client or sponsor will have some estimate of the expected payoff.

THE TRADE-OFFS OF FORECASTING

An ROI can be developed at different times using different levels of data. Unfortunately, the ease, convenience, and low cost involved in capturing a forecasted ROI create trade-offs in accuracy and credibility. As shown in Figure 11-1 and as follows, there are five distinct time intervals during the implementation of a program when the ROI can actually be developed. The relationship with credibility, accuracy, cost, and difficulty is also shown in Figure 11-1.

1. A preprogram forecast can be developed using estimates of the impact of the leadership development program. This approach lacks credibility and accuracy, but it also the least expensive and least difficult ROI to calculate. There is value in developing the ROI on a preprogram basis. This is discussed in the next section.
2. Reaction and satisfaction data can be extended to develop an anticipated impact, including the ROI. In this case, participants actually anticipate the chain of impact as a program is applied, implemented, and influences specific business measures. While the accuracy and credibility are greater than the preprogram forecast, this approach still lacks the credibility and accuracy desired in most situations.
3. Learning data in some programs can be used to forecast the actual ROI. This approach is applicable only when formal testing shows a relationship between acquiring certain skills or

ROI with:	Data Collection Timing (Relative to Program Implementation)	Credibility	Accuracy	Cost to Develop	Difficulty
1. Pre-Program Data	Before Program	Not Very Credible	Not Very Accurate	Inexpensive	Not Difficult
2. Reaction and Satisfaction Data	During Program				
3. Learning Data	During Program				
4. Application and Implementation	After Program				
5. Business Impact Data	After Program	Very Credible	Very Accurate	Expensive	Very Difficult

Figure 11-1. ROI at different times and levels.

knowledge and subsequent business performance. When this correlation is available (it is usually developed to validate the test), test data can be used to forecast subsequent performance. The performance can then be converted to monetary impact and the ROI can be developed. This has less potential as an evaluation tool due to the lack of situations in which a predictive validation can be developed.

4. In some situations, when frequency of skills and actual use of skills are critical, the application and implementation of those skills or knowledge can be converted to a value using employee compensation as a basis. This is particularly helpful in situations where competencies are being developed and values are placed on improving competencies, even if there is no immediate increase in pay.

5. Finally, the ROI can be developed from business impact data converted directly to monetary values and compared to the cost of the program. This postprogram evaluation is the basis for the other ROI calculations in this book and has been the principal approach used in previous chapters. It is the preferred approach, but because of the pressures outlined earlier, it is critical to examine ROI calculations at other times and with data other than Level 4.

This chapter discusses in detail preprogram evaluation and ROI calculations based on reactions. To a lesser degree, ROI calculations developed from learning and application data are discussed.

PREPROGRAM ROI FORECASTING

Perhaps one of the most useful steps in convincing a sponsor that a leadership development expense is appropriate is to forecast the ROI for the project. The process is very similar to the postprogram analysis except that the extent of the impact must be estimated along with the forecasted cost.

Basic Model

Figure 11-2 shows the basic model for capturing necessary data for a preprogram forecast. This model is a modification of the postprogram ROI model except that data are projected instead of being collected during different time frames. In place of data collection is an estimation of the change in impact data expected to be influenced

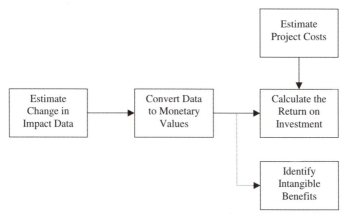

Figure 11-2. Preprogram ROI forecast model.

by the leadership development program. Isolating the effects of the leadership development program becomes a nonissue, as the estimation is focused on the leadership development program only, not considering other factors that may come into play.

The method used to covert data to monetary values is the same as in postprogram ROI because the data items examined in a pre- and postprogram analysis should be the same. Estimating the program's cost should be an easy step, as costs can be anticipated easily based on previous projects using reasonable assumptions about the current project. The anticipated intangibles are merely speculation in forecasting but can be reliable indicators of which measures may be influenced in addition to those included in the ROI calculation. The formula used to calculate the ROI is the same as in the postprogram analysis. The amount of monetary value from the data conversion is included as the numerator, whereas the estimated cost of the leadership development program is inserted as the denominator. The projected cost/benefit analysis can be developed along with the actual ROI. The steps to actually develop the process are detailed next.

Steps to Develop the ROI

The detailed steps to develop the preprogram ROI forecast are presented in a simplified form.

1. Develop the Level 3 and 4 objectives with as many specifics as possible. Ideally, these should be developed from the initial

needs analysis and assessment. They detail what will change in the work setting and identify which measures will be influenced. If these are not known, the entire forecasting process is in jeopardy. There must be some assessment of which measures will change as a result of the training, and someone must be able to provide the extent to which the measures will change.

2. Estimate or forecast the monthly improvement in the business impact data. This is considered to be the amount of change directly related to the intervention and is denoted by ΔP.

3. Convert the business impact data to monetary values using one or more of the methods described previously. These are the same techniques using the same processes as a postprogram analysis; V denotes this value.

4. Develop the estimated annual impact for each measure. In essence, this is the first-year improvement from the leadership development program showing the value for the change in the business impact measures related directly to the leadership development program. In formula form this is $\Delta I = \Delta P \times V \times 12$.

5. Factor additional years into the analysis if a program will have a significant useful life beyond the first year. When this is the case, these values may be factored to reflect a diminished benefit in subsequent years. The sponsor or owner of the program should provide some indication as to the amount of the reduction and the values developed for years two, three, etc. However, it is helpful to be conservative by using the smallest numbers possible.

6. Estimate the fully loaded cost of the program. Using all of the cost categories contained in Chapter 6, the fully loaded cost will be estimated and projected for the program. This is denoted as C. Again, all direct and indirect costs should be included in the calculation.

7. Calculate the forecasted ROI using the total projected benefits and the estimated cost in the standard ROI formula:

$$\mathrm{ROI}(\%) = \frac{\Delta I - C}{C} \times 100$$

8. Use sensitivity analysis to develop several potential ROI values with different levels of improvement (ΔP). When more than one measure is changing, that analysis would perhaps be

performed using a spreadsheet showing different possible scenarios for output and the subsequent ROI.

9. Identify potential intangible benefits by getting input from those most knowledgeable of the situation. These are only anticipated and are based on assumptions from previous experience with this type of program implementation.

10. Communicate the ROI projection and anticipated intangibles with much care and caution. The target audience must clearly understand that this is based on several assumptions (clearly defined) and that the values are the best possible estimates. However, there is still room for error.

These 10 steps enable an individual to forecast the ROI. The most difficult part of the process is the initial estimate of performance improvement. Several sources of data are available for this purpose, as described next.

Forecasting/Estimating Performance Improvement

Several sources of input are available when attempting to estimate the actual performance improvement that will be influenced by the leadership development program. The following important considerations should be explored.

1. Experience in the organization with previous leadership development programs or similar programs can help form the basis of the estimate. Adapting that breadth of experience can be an important factor, as comparisons are rarely, if ever, exact.

2. Data sources may have experience with similar programs in other organizations or in other situations. Here, the experience of the designers, developers, and implementers involved in the program will be helpful, as they reflect on their experiences with other organizations.

3. The input of external experts who have worked in the field or addressed similar programs in other organizations can be extremely valuable. These may be consultants, suppliers, designers, or others who have earned a reputation as knowledgeable about this type of process in this type of situation.

4. Estimates can be obtained directly from a subject matter expert (SME) in the organization. This is an individual who is very familiar with the internal processes being altered, modified, or improved by the leadership development program. Internal

SMEs are very knowledgeable and sometimes the most favored source for obtaining conservative estimates.

5. Estimates can be obtained directly from the program sponsor. This is the individual who is ultimately making the purchasing decision and is providing data or input on the anticipated change in a measure linked to the leadership development program. This influential position makes him or her a very credible source.

6. Individuals who are involved directly in the leadership development program, often labeled participants, are sometimes in a position to know how much of a measure can be changed or improved with a particular type of program. These individuals understand the processes, procedures, and performance measurements being influenced. Their close proximity to the situation makes them highly credible and often the most accurate sources for estimating the amount of change.

Collectively, these sources provide an appropriate array of possibilities to help estimate the value of an improvement. This is the weakest link in the ROI forecasting process and deserves the most attention. It is important that the target audience understands where the estimates came from, as well as who provided them. Even more important, the target audience must view the source as credible. Otherwise, the forecasted ROI will have no credibility.

FORECASTING WITH A PILOT PROGRAM

Although the steps just listed provide a process for estimating the ROI when a pilot program is not conducted, the more favorable approach is to develop a small-scale pilot project and develop the ROI based on postprogram data. This scenario involves the following five steps.

1. As in the previous process, develop Level 3 and 4 objectives.
2. Initiate the program on a very small-scale sample as a pilot program, without all the bells and whistles. This keeps the cost extremely low without sacrificing the fundamentals of the project.
3. Fully implement the program with one or more of the typical groups of individuals who can benefit from the program.
4. Develop the ROI using the ROI model for postprogram analysis. This is the ROI process used in the previous chapters.

5. Finally, decide whether to implement the program throughout the organization based on results of the pilot program.

Postprogram evaluation of a pilot program provides much more accurate information by which to base decisions regarding full implementation of the program. Using this scenario, data can be developed using all seven types of measures outlined in this book.

FORECASTING ROI WITH REACTION DATA

When reaction data include planned applications of leadership development, these important data can ultimately be used in forecasting ROI. In detailing how participants plan to use what they have learned and the results that they expect to achieve, more valuable evaluation information can be developed. The questions presented in Figure 11-3 illustrate how data are collected with an end-of-program questionnaire for a supervisory training program. Participants are asked to state specifically how they plan to use the program material and the results they expect to achieve. They are asked to convert their

---

Planned Improvements

•As a result of this program, what specific actions will you attempt as you apply what you have learned?

1. _____
2. _____
3. _____

•Please indicate what specific measures, outcomes, or projects will change as a result of your actions.

1. _____
2. _____
3. _____

•As a result of the anticipated changes in the above, please estimate (in monetary values) the benefits to your organization over a period of one year.

_____

•What is the basis of this estimate?

_____
_____

•What confidence, expressed as a percentage, can you put in your estimate? (0% = No Confidence; 100% = Certainty) _____%

Figure 11-3. Important questions to ask on feedback questionnaires.

accomplishments to an annual monetary value and show the basis for developing the values. Participants can moderate their responses with a confidence estimate to make data more credible while allowing participants to reflect their uncertainty with the process.

When tabulating data, the confidence level is multiplied by the annual monetary value, which yields a conservative estimate for use in the data analysis. For example, if a participant estimated that the monetary impact of the program will be $10,000, but is only 50 percent confident, a $5000 value is used in the calculations.

To develop a summary of the expected benefits, several steps are taken. First, any data that are incomplete, unusable, extreme, or unrealistic are discarded.

Next, an adjustment is made for the confidence estimate as described previously. Individual data items are then totaled. Finally, as an optional exercise, the total value is adjusted again by a factor that reflects the subjectivity of the process and the possibility that participants will not achieve the results they anticipate. In many training programs, the participants are very enthusiastic about what they have learned and may be overly optimistic about expected accomplishments. This figure adjusts for this overestimation and can be developed with input from management or established by the training and development staff. In one organization, the benefits are multiplied by 50 percent to develop an even more conservative number to use in the ROI equation. Finally, the ROI is developed using the net program benefits divided by the program costs. This value, in essence, becomes the expected return on investment, after the two adjustments for accuracy and subjectivity.

A word of caution is in order when using Level 1 ROI data. These calculations are highly subjective and do not reflect the extent to which participants actually apply what they have learned to achieve results. A variety of influences in the work environment can enhance or inhibit the participants' attainment of performance goals. Having high expectations at the end of the program is no guarantee that those expectations will be met. Disappointments are documented regularly in programs throughout the world and are reported in research findings (Kaufman, 2002).

While this process is subjective and possibly unreliable, it does have some usefulness. First, if evaluation must stop at this level, this approach provides more insight into the value of the program than data from typical reaction questionnaires. Managers will usually find these data more useful than a report stating, "40 percent of participants rated the program above average." Unfortunately, a high percentage of evaluations stop at this first level of evaluation (Van Buren, 2002). The majority of leadership development programs do not enjoy rigorous evaluations at Levels 3 and 4. Reporting Level 1 ROI data is a more useful indication of the potential impact of the program than the alternative of reporting attitudes and feelings about the program and facilitator.

Second, ROI forecast data can form a basis for comparison of different presentations of the same program. If one program forecasts an ROI of 300 percent, whereas another projects 30 percent, it appears that one program may be more effective than the other. The participants in the first program have more confidence in the planned application of the program material.

Third, collecting this type of data brings increased attention to program outcomes. Participants leave the program with an understanding that specific behavior change is expected, which produces results for the organization. This issue becomes very clear to participants as they anticipate results and convert them to monetary values. Even if this projected improvement is ignored, the exercise is productive because of the important message sent to participants. It helps change mind-sets about the value, impact, and importance of leadership development.

Fourth, if a follow-up is planned to pinpoint postprogram results, data collected in the Level 1 evaluation can be very helpful for comparison. This end of program data collection helps participants plan the implementation of what they have learned. For example, in a relationship management training program for Wachovia Bank, the results after training are compared to the forecasted results (Wallace, 2001). Figure 11-4 shows the results of training, the participant's projections at the end of training, and the results attributed to the training. As Figure 11-4 illustrates, the forecasts are lower than the results attributed to training. This comparison begins to build credibility in a forecasting method and, in this case, revealed that forecasting was actually more conservative than the actual results.

The use of Level 1 ROI is increasing, as more organizations base a larger part of ROI calculations on Level 1 data. Although it may be very subjective, it does add value, particularly when it is included as part of a comprehensive evaluation system.

FORECASTING ROI WITH LEARNING DATA

Testing for changes in skills and knowledge in leadership development programs is a technique sometimes used for learning evalu-

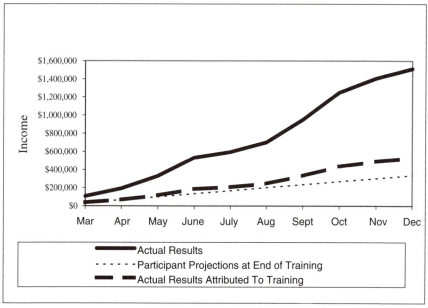

Figure 11-4. Results of training.

ation (Level 2). In many situations, participants are required to demonstrate their knowledge or skills at the end of the program, and their performance is expressed as a numerical value. When this type of test is developed and utilized, it must be reliable and valid. A reliable test is one that is stable over time with consistent results.

A valid test is one that measures what it purports to measure. Because a test should reflect the content of the leadership development program, successful mastery of program content should be related to improved job performance. Consequently, there should be a relationship between test scores and subsequent on-the-job performance. Figure 11-5 illustrates a perfect correlation between test scores and job performance. This relationship, expressed as a correlation coefficient, is a measure of validity of the test.

This testing situation provides an excellent opportunity for an ROI calculation with Level 2 data using test results. When there is a statistically significant relationship between test scores and on-the-job performance, and the performance can be converted to monetary units, then it is possible to use test scores to estimate the ROI from the program using the following steps:

- Ensure that the program content reflects desired on-the-job performance.

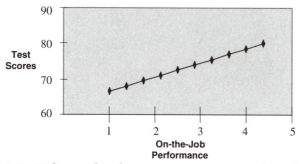

Figure 11-5. Relationship between test scores and performance.

- Develop an end-of-program test that reflects program content.
- Establish a statistical relationship between test data and output performance for participants.
- Predict performance levels of each participant with given test scores.
- Convert performance data to monetary value.
- Compare total predicted value of program with program costs.

As with the previous ROI estimate with end-of-program questionnaires, some cautions are in order. This is a forecast of the ROI and not the actual value. Although participants acquired the skills and knowledge from the program, there is no guarantee that they will apply the techniques and processes successfully and that the results will be achieved. This process assumes that the current group of participants has the same relationship to output performance as previous groups. It ignores a variety of environmental influences, which can alter the situation entirely. Finally, the process requires calculating the initial correlation coefficient that may be difficult to develop for most tests.

Although this approach develops an estimate, based on historical relationships, it can be useful in a comprehensive evaluation strategy and has several advantages. First, if postprogram evaluations (Level 4) are not planned, this process will yield more information about the projected value of the program than what would be obtained from the raw test scores. This process represents an expected return on investment based on the historical relationships involved. Second, by developing individual ROI measurements and communicating them to participants, the process has reinforcement potential. It communicates to participants that increased sales and market share are expected through the applications of what was learned in the program. Third, this process can have considerable credibility with management and can preclude expensive follow-ups and postprogram monitoring. If these relationships are statistically sound, the estimate should have credibility with the target group.

FORECASTING ROI WITH SKILLS AND COMPETENCIES

In almost every leadership development program, participants are expected to change their on-the-job behaviors by applying the program materials. On-the-job applications are very critical to program success. Although the use of skills on the job is no guarantee that results will follow, it is an underlying assumption for most programs that if the knowledge and skills are applied, then results will follow. Some of the most prestigious training organizations, such as Motorola University, base their ultimate evaluation on this assumption. A few organizations attempt to take this process a step further and measure the value of on-the-job behavior change and calculate the ROI. In these situations, estimates are taken from individual participants, their supervisors, the management group, or experts in the field. This is a forecast of the impact based on the change in behavior on the job immediately after the program. The following steps are used to develop the ROI:

1. Develop competencies for the target job.
2. Indicate percentage of job success that is covered in the leadership development program.
3. Determine monetary value of competencies using salaries and employee benefits of participants.
4. Compute the worth of pre- and postprogram skill levels.
5. Subtract postprogram values from preprogram values.
6. Compare the total added benefits with the program costs.

This analysis attempts to place a value on the improvement of an individual. The concept ignores the consequence of this improvement, but examines the behavior change and factors the monetary value relative to the salary of the individual. This is referred to as a Level 3 ROI forecast because it takes the change in behavior and converts it to monetary value using salaries of participants as a base.

Perhaps an example will illustrate one technique to measure the value of on-the-job applications. The U.S. Government redesigned its five-day leadership development program for newly appointed supervisors (Broad, 1994). The program focused on eight competencies:

1. role and responsibilities of the supervisor;
2. communications;
3. planning, assigning, controlling, and evaluating work;
4. ethics;
5. leadership and motivation;
6. analyzing performance problems;
7. customer service; and
8. managing diversity

The immediate managers of the new supervisors indicated that these eight competencies accounted for 81 percent of first-level supervisors' jobs. For the target group being evaluated, the average annual salary plus benefits for the newly appointed supervisors was $42,202. Thus, multiplying this figure by the amount of job success accounted for by the competencies (81 percent) yielded a dollar value of $34,184 per participant. If a person were performing successfully in these eight competencies for one year, the value to the agency would be $34,184. Of course, this assumes that employees are paid an amount equal to their contribution, when they are fully competent.

Using a scale of 0–9, managers rated the skills for each of the competencies before the program was conducted. The average level of skills required to be successful in the job was rated at 6.44. The skill ratings prior to the program were 4.96, which represented 77 percent of the 6.44 (i.e., participants were performing at 77 percent of the level to be successful in the competencies). After the program, the skill rating was 5.59, representing 87 percent of the level to be successful.

Monetary values were assigned based on the participants' salaries. Performance at the required level of success was worth $34,184 (at the 6.44 rating). At a 77 percent proficiency level, the new supervisors were performing at a contribution value of $26,322 (77 percent of $34,184). After training, this value had reached 87 percent, representing a contribution value of $29,740 (87 percent of $34,184). The difference in these values ($3418) represents the gain per participant attributable to training. The program cost was $1368 per participant. Thus, the ROI is:

$$\text{ROI} = \frac{\$3418 - \$1368}{\$1368} = \frac{2050}{1368} \times 100 = 150 \text{ percent}$$

As with other estimates, a word of caution is in order. These results are subjective because the rating systems used are subjective and may not necessarily reflect an accurate assessment of the value of the program. This is a Level 3 ROI forecast. Because leadership development is usually implemented to help the organization achieve its objectives, some managers insist on tangible changes in business impact data, such as output, quality, cost, and time. For them, a Level 3 ROI forecast is not always an acceptable substitute for business impact (Level 4) data.

Although this process is subjective, it has several useful advantages. First, if there are no plans to track the actual impact of the program in terms of specific measurable business impact (Level 4), this approach represents a credible substitute. In many programs, particularly skill-building and competency programs for supervisors, it may be difficult to identify tangible changes on the job. Therefore, alternative approaches to determine the worth of a program are needed. Second, this has been developed in the literature as utility analysis. Third, this approach results in data that are usually credible with the management group if they understand how it is developed and the assumptions behind it. An important point is that data on the changes in competence level came from the managers who have rated their supervisors. In this specific project, the numbers were large enough to make the process statistically significant. Fourth, this technique can be used to forecast a value before a program is implemented. Essentially, this becomes a pre-program-forecasting tool.

FORECASTING GUIDELINES

With the four different time frames for forecasting outlined in this chapter, a few guidelines may help drive the forecasting possibilities within an organization. These guidelines are based on experience in forecasting a variety of processes along with leadership development (Bowers, 1997).

1. If you must forecast, forecast frequently. Forecasting is a process that is both an art and a science and it needs to be pursued regularly to build comfort, experience, and history with the process. Also, those who use the data need to see forecasting frequently to further integrate it as part of the evaluation mix.

2. Consider forecasting an essential part of the evaluation mix. This chapter began with a listing of reasons why forecasting is

essential. The concept is growing in use and is being demanded by many organizations. It can be a very effective and useful tool when used properly and in conjunction with other types of evaluation data. Some organizations have targets for the use of forecasting (e.g., if a project exceeds a certain cost, it will always require a preprogram forecast). Others will target a certain number of programs for a forecast based on reaction data and use that data in the manner described here. Others will have some low-level targets for forecasting at Levels 2 and 3. The important point is to plan for the forecast and let it be a part of the evaluation mix, working it regularly.

3. Forecast different types of data. Although most of this chapter focuses on how to develop a forecasted ROI using the standard ROI formula, it is helpful to forecast the value of other data. A usable, helpful forecast will include predictions around reaction and satisfaction, the extent of learning, and the extent of application and implementation. These types of data are very important in anticipating movements and shifts, based on the planned program. It is not only helpful in developing the overall forecast, but important in understanding the total anticipated impact of the project.

4. Secure input from those who know the process best. As forecasts are developed, it is essential to secure input from individuals who understand the dynamics of the workplace and the measures being influenced by the project. Sometimes the participants in the leadership development program or the immediate managers are best. In other situations, it is the variety of analysts who are aware of the major influences in the workplace and the dynamics of those changes. The important point is to go to the experts. This will increase not only the accuracy of the forecast, but also the credibility of the final results.

5. Long-term forecasts will usually be inaccurate. Forecasting works much better in a short time frame. For most short-term scenarios, it is possible to have a better grasp of the influences that might drive the measure. On a long-term basis, a variety of new influences, unforeseen now, could enter the process and drastically change the impact measures. If a long-term forecast is needed, it should be updated regularly to become a continuously improving process.

6. Expect forecasts to be biased. Forecasts will consist of data coming from those who have an interest in the issue. Some will want the forecast to be optimistic; others will have a pes-

simistic view. Almost all input is biased in one way or another. Every attempt should be made to minimize the bias, adjust for the bias, or adjust for the uncertainty in the process. Still, the audience should recognize that it is a biased prediction.

7. Serious forecasting is hard work. The value of forecasting often depends on the amount of effort put into the process. High-stakes programs need to have a serious approach, collecting all possible data, examining different scenarios, and making the best prediction available. It is in these situations that mathematical tools can be most valuable.

8. Review the success of forecasting routinely. As forecasts are made, it is imperative to revisit the forecast with actual post-program data to check the success of the forecast. This can aid in the continuous improvement of the processes. Sources could prove to be more credible or less credible, specific inputs may be more biased or less biased, and certain analyses may be more appropriate than others. It is important to constantly improve the ideal methods and approaches for forecasting within the organization.

9. Assumptions are the most serious error in forecasting. Of all the variables that can enter into the process, the one possessing the greatest opportunity for error is assumptions made by the individual providing the forecast. It is important for the assumptions to be clearly understood and communicated. When there are multiple inputs, each forecaster should use the same set of assumptions, if possible.

10. Utility is the most important characteristic of forecasting. The most important use of forecasting is the information and input for the decision maker. Forecasting is a tool for those attempting to make a decision about leadership development programs. It is not a process that is trying to maximize the output or minimize any particular variable. It is not a process that is attempting to dramatically change the way in which the program is implemented. It is a process to provide data for decisions—that is the greatest utility of forecasting.

FINAL THOUGHTS

This chapter illustrated that ROI forecasts can be developed at different time frames. Although most practitioners and researchers use application and impact data for ROI calculations, there are situations when Level 3 and Level 4 data are not available or evaluations at those levels are not attempted or planned. ROI forecasts, developed before the program is implemented, can be very useful and helpful to management and the leadership development staff, while at the same time focusing attention on the potential economic impact of leadership development. Forecasts are also possible with reaction and learning data. Be aware that using ROI forecasts may provide a false sense of accuracy. As would be expected, ROI forecasts on a preprogram basis are the lowest in credibility and accuracy, but have the advantage of being inexpensive and relatively easy to conduct. However, ROI forecasts using Level 3 data are highest in credibility and accuracy, but are more expensive and difficult to develop.

Although ROI calculations with impact data (Level 4) are preferred, ROI forecasts at other times are an important part of a comprehensive and systematic evaluation process and should be considered when implementing a leadership scorecard. This usually means that targets for evaluation should be established.

CASE STUDY—PART J
INTERNATIONAL CAR RENTAL

Level 1 ROI Forecast

Although it was not attempted in this case, it is possible and perhaps instructive to develop a Level 1 ROI forecast. With this process, a series of potential impact questions could be asked where participants anticipate potential changes and estimate the particular impact of changes for each of the two business measures. Estimates could be provided on other measures that may be driven by the program. First-year values could be developed, along with a confidence percentage obtained from participants reflecting their level of certainty with the process. Data could be adjusted with this confidence level to provide a forecast of the benefit and the calculation of the ROI. Although this ROI value is subjective and often inflated, this analysis would provide some insight into the relationship between the projections at the end of the program and the actual performance four months later. Also, it may actually enhance the results because participants who make projections of performance may be motivated to meet those projections.

Level 2 and 3 ROI Forecasts

At ICR, it was impossible to capture data for a Level 2 ROI forecast. For this forecast to be possible, a validated instrument must be developed to measure the performance of first-level managers in the program and have it correlated with subsequent on-the-job performance. This was not feasible in this situation.

A Level 3 ROI forecast was not considered because of the concern over the subjective assessments that must be made using Level 3 data. Also, the client was very bottom-line oriented and preferred to discuss performance in terms of Level 4 business measures. While management recognized that skills must be acquired and behavior must be changed, they were less interested in discussing the extent to which changes have occurred and the value of the change. Thus, a Level 3 ROI forecast would have provided little value for the client.

REFERENCES

Bishop, P. "Thinking Like a Futurist," *The Futurist*, June–July 1998, p. 42.

Bowers, D.A. *Forecasting for Control and Profit*. Menlo Park, CA: Crisp Publications, 1997.

Broad, M. "Built-in Evaluation," *In Action: Measuring Return on Investment*, Vol. 1, J.J. Phillips (Ed.). Alexandria, VA: American Society for Training and Development, 1994, pp. 55–70.

Dixon, N.M. "The Relationship between Trainee Responses on Participant Reaction Forms and Post-test Scores," *Human Resource Development Quarterly*, 1(2), pp. 129–137.

Kaufman, R. "Resolving the (Often-Deserved) Attacks on Training," *Performance Improvement*, Vol. 41, No. 6, 2002.

Van Buren, M. *ASTD Report*. Alexandria, VA: American Society for Training and Development, 2002.

Wallace, D. "Partnering to Achieve Measurable Business Results in the New Economy," *In Action: Measuring Return on Investment*, Vol. 3, J.J. Phillips (Ed.). Alexandria, VA: American Society for Training and Development, 2001, pp. 81–104.

PART IV

Leadership Scorecard Case Studies

CHAPTER 12

Developing Leaders at Imperial National Bank*

By Patricia Pulliam Phillips, Ph.D.

This case shows the monetary impact of a leadership development program and underscores the complexity of measuring the impact of leadership development using an action learning process. More importantly, this case shows how changes in program design can significantly increase the actual return on investment.

BACKGROUND

As with many large global organizations in a competitive industry, Imperial National Bank (INB)—a large, multiservice bank operating in 14 states—recognized that it needed effective leaders. As a result, a comprehensive leadership development program was developed. The program followed a learning-while-earning model, whereby high-potential leaders worked together on selected high-priority business issues with access to just-in-time coaching, advice from senior executives, and a faculty of subject matter experts. The program structure combined class time and project work.

A process called action reflection learning (ARL) was the principal vehicle utilized in the leadership development program to assist in learning new approaches to behavioral change and perceptions. The process helped participants associate learning with making

---

*This case study was published previously in Jack J. Phillips, Ron D. Stone, and Patricia Pulliam Phillips, *The Human Resources Scorecard: Measuring the Return on Investment*. Boston: Butterworth-Heinemann, 2001, pp. 449–476.

things happen in real time. ARL confronted participants with challenges and risks, had them search for information, and had them complete tasks that were outside their regular scope of activities. In essence, ARL took advantage of the fact that when learning is linked to action on real issues, in which there are real consequences and risks, adults are more motivated to learn.

Three critical success factors were identified that needed to be fully operational and executed for the program to achieve the desired success:

- A significant amount of time needed to be invested by the management committee, clients, and participants.
- Real projects that were enterprise-wide and strategic needed to be developed.
- Influential participants needed to be selected based on performance and future potential. These factors capture the most important issues surrounding this program.

Initiation of the Leadership Development Program

Around the globe, there is a need for more accountability and evaluation in leadership development. In accordance with this need, the director of INB's training function initiated an evaluation of the leadership program. Performance Resources Organization (PRO), a leading international consulting firm that focuses on measuring the return on investment in training and development programs, was called in as an external consultant to direct the evaluation. PRO was not involved in the design, development, or delivery of this program, thus ensuring an independent evaluation.

The leadership program was deemed an ideal candidate for ROI evaluation for several reasons:

- The program was INB's first attempt to integrate traditional leadership development with on-the-job, real-life projects designed to add significant value to the organization.
- The program targeted a critical audience at INB—future leaders.
- The vision for the program had been developed and refined at the highest levels of the organization.
- On a per participant basis, the program was perhaps the most expensive program undertaken at INB. It was also the most visible.

- The program was designed to focus on important projects that represented real-life situations and involved key operational and strategic issues.

Several issues apparent at the beginning of the study, however, had the potential to influence the ability to develop a specific return on investment (ROI):

- Initially, the program was not designed to deliver a measurable business impact. Consequently, key performance measures were not linked to the program, and specific objectives were not developed to improve measurable performance.
- Although the projects were included to add value to INB, the nature of some of the projects made this task difficult. Also, the requirements for developing the projects did not include a process for capturing monetary value.
- Data collection systems had not been developed and refined to link with the leadership development program. Performance data were scattered throughout the company and, in some cases, were not readily available.
- The intangible benefits from this program were expected to be significant and long term, providing nonmonetary values that might exceed the monetary benefits.

Even with the presence of the aforementioned difficulties, there was a desire to measure ROI utilizing the most credible processes. Through the implementation of a comprehensive data collection and analysis process spanning a time period of September to June, this evaluation took place using the ROI process described throughout this book.

Data Collection Plan

An effective evaluation must be planned carefully with appropriate timing established and responsibilities defined. Table 12-1 shows the data collection plan for this evaluation. The data collection plan was initially developed and approved by the support team with additional adjustments made during the program to ensure that appropriate input was obtained from all individuals. Although the amount of data collected might be considered excessive and the multiple methods might provide duplication and overlap, this was considered a necessity because of the importance of the program, the cost of

Table 12-1
Data Collection Plan

Level	Broad program objective(s)	Data collection method	Timing of data collection	Responsibilities for Data Collection
I. Reaction, satisfaction	• Favorable reaction from participants, teams, and observers • Suggestions for improvement	• Questionnaire from participants 1 • Follow-up questionnaire from participants 2 • Interviews with participants 5 • Observation • Interviews with sponsors 3 • Follow-up questionnaire from manager 4	• End of each session and end of program • 60–90 days after end of program • 60–90 days after end of program • Daily • 60–90 days after end of program • 60–90 days after end of program	◆ PRO • PRO·PRO • Manager • PRO ◆ PRO
II. Learning	• Enhance knowledge and skills in 14 areas	• Observation • Questionnaire from participants 1 • Values technology instrument • Executive success profile • Follow-up questionnaire from participants 2	• Daily • End of each session and end of program • During Program • During Program • 60–90 days after end of program	◆ Manager • PRO ◆ Facilitators • Facilitators • PRO

Level	Measures	Data Collection Method	Timing	Responsibility
III. Application	• Use of skills and knowledge • Frequency of skill use • Interaction with management and policy committee	• Observation • Follow-up questionnaire from participants 2 • Follow-up questionnaire from manager 4 • Interviews with participants 5 • Interviews with sponsors	• During program • 60–90 days after end of program • 60–90 days after end of program • 60–90 days after end of program • 60–90 days after end of program	◆ Managers • PRO • PRO ◆ ·PRO • PRO
IV. Business impact	• Benefits from research, recommendations made by project teams, and resulting savings and/or earnings • Improvement in business impact measures as each participant applies skills in business unit • Enhanced quality of executive talent pool	• Financial performance indicators from project presentations • Interviews with participants 5 • Follow-up questionnaire from participants 2 • Follow-up questionnaire from manager 4 • HR records	• 60–90 days after end of program • 60–90 days after end of program • 60–90 days after end of program • 60–90 days after end of program • 3 years after end of program	◆ Program Director ◆ PRO·PRO • PRO • PRO

1 Same questionnaire
2 Same questionnaire
3 Same interview
4 Same questionnaire
5 Same interview

the program in both time and money, and the target audience involved.

Timing of Data Collection

The timing of collection was very critical. End-of-program questionnaires were collected at the end of each session and at the end of the program. Reaction data were also collected from a variety of individuals at the program's completion. Learning data were collected during the session and during on-the-job observations.

The most critical timing issue to address was data collection for application and impact. Although a leadership development program is designed to have a long-term impact, the specific improvements from programs are difficult to capture if assessed years after the program is completed. Although the connection may exist, it is difficult for the participants and participants' managers to make the connection between a training program and specific improvement. In addition, for longer periods of time, additional variables will influence business measures, thus complicating the cause and effect relationship between training and improvement.

The timing of data collection was complicated because senior management wanted the evaluation completed before making a decision about the implementation of future programs. Ideally, application and impact data should be captured within six months to one year after a program is completed. Following this schedule would push the data collection and completion of the evaluation beyond the requested time frame desired to make decisions about a second program.

The spacing of the sessions further complicated the timing of the study. The first session was held in September and the last in February. The time needed to apply skills learned in the first session would place the evaluation in the spring. For the last session, the follow-up would normally be in the fall. Thus, a period of 60–90 days from the last session was selected to allow enough time for application.

End-of-Program Feedback

An essential part of any evaluation is the typical feedback obtained at the end of a training program. A modified version of the standard questionnaire used by the training department captured feedback at the end of each session. This feedback was tabulated and provided to the external consultants, as well as the training support team. Adjustments were made routinely using these feedback data.

Observation

An important part of evaluation was provided by the research component of the program. An expert in action reflection learning research provided observation throughout the program. Although most of the observation occurred during sessions and captured actual learning, some observation took place in work settings as part of an executive shadow program. The results of these observations were provided as feedback to program faculty, the training support team, and program participants. Although results of this research are included in this case as part of the total assessment and evaluation, it is important to note that this research was not designed to serve as program assessment and evaluation.

Questionnaire from Participants

One of the most important data collection methods was the detailed follow-up questionnaire completed by participants in the time frame of 60–90 days from the end of the last session. During the third session, participants were briefed about the plans for the questionnaire, and the general topics were discussed. Participants were also reminded about the questionnaire at the last session, and a final reminder was sent approximately one month after the last session. This reminder came directly from the training director, encouraging them to take appropriate notes of details that could be reported in the questionnaires. As of mid-June, the participant response rate was 73 percent, representing 16 of the 22 participants. In addition, questionnaire responses were very thorough and served as a valuable data source. The questionnaire focused on application and impact data (Levels 3 and 4).

Interviews with Participants

To supplement input from questionnaires, interviews were conducted with each participant. Lasting approximately 1 to 1.5 hours, each interview explored individual application and impact topics. Additional probing was used to uncover business impact applications and to gain further insight into skill applications, barriers, concerns, and important issues surrounding the success of the program.

These interviews were conducted within 60 to 90 days after the last session.

Questionnaires for Managers

To gain the perspective of participants' managers, a questionnaire was sent directly to them within the time frame of 60 to 90 days from the end of the program. The managers of participants were involved early in the process when participants were selected. They often had to make adjustments in the business units while participants attended sessions and worked on the project. Manager input was considered important, as their support was necessary for success. As of mid-June, 46 percent of managers had returned the questionnaire.

Interviews with Sponsors

Because senior managers' involvement in this program was significant, their interest was high and, consequently, their influence was critical to its success. Interviews with these project sponsors provided a wealth of candid input about the success of the program, as well as concerns from the unique perspective of these key executives.

Questionnaires from the Support Team

To provide additional input from other members critical to the success of the program, a customized questionnaire was distributed to the external consultants and the training support team. Their input focused on reaction to the program, assessment of success, and suggestions for improvement.

Performance Monitoring

Capturing specific data from business impact applications and project evaluation required collecting data from the business records of the organization. This was a factor only in those areas in which impact was identified or on which the projects had a direct influence.

Project Review

To capture the potential value of the projects, the status of the projects was explored with each project owner to determine the extent of implementation and the prospects for future implementations. In some cases, the project review went a step further by placing an actual value on the projects.

Summary

Collectively, these data collection methods yielded a tremendous amount of data, far exceeding expectations. The different perspectives and types of data ensured a thorough assessment of the program and provided a backdrop for insightful recommendations for making improvements.

REACTION AND LEARNING

Table 12-2 shows how data were integrated for analysis and reporting along the four levels of evaluation, as well as the cost of the program. End-of-session feedback obtained in each session provided input about the reaction to the program, as well as relevant learning that took place.

Reaction

Data collected throughout the first leadership development program indicated both high and low points during the program. The participant overall mean score indicated a decline in the value of the sessions. Also, as the participants progressed through the program, a number of issues arose. These issues centered on the (1) progress of project team work, (2) lack of time, (3) external presenters/content (2 of 4), and (4) team dynamics.

The components that contributed the most to the participant learning using a five-point scale were (1) project work (4.6), (2) cross-functional team work (4.6), and (3) being involved in strategic issues at INB (4.5). Components that contributed the least were external resources (2.8) and feedback instruments (3.4). Therefore, the areas that were sources of frustration during the program were also the areas that contributed the most to the learning—project work and team dynamics.

Learning

Learning was examined in significant detail as part of the research component for the program. The major findings from the research program are contained in Table 12-3.

Table 12-2
Data Integration

	Level 1 Reaction to program	Level 2 Learning: Skills, knowledge, changes in perceptions	Level 3 Application implementation and use on the job	Level 4 Impact in business unit	Costs
End of session Feedback	X	X			
Research		X	X		
Interviews with participants	X	X	X	X	X
Question- naires from participants	X	X	X	X	
Question- naires from managers of participants	X		X	X	
Interviews with sponsors	X				
Questionnaires for faculty/ support team	X				
Company records				X	X
		♄ Barriers/concerns ♅		♄ ROI ♅	

APPLICATION

Applications of Skills, Knowledge, and Behavior

Although the leadership development program was not designed to develop a number of skills to produce immediate on-the-job results, specific areas were addressed that had immediate application potential. The questionnaire response from participants showed significant changes in behavior in several important skill areas. Not surprisingly, "reflection and dialogue" showed the most significant change, followed closely by "thinking strategically" and "communicating effectively." This mirrored, to a certain extent, the results obtained from participant interviews and manager questionnaires.

Table 12-3
Major Findings from Research Project: Measures of Learning

Learning
- Learning was "managed" by the participants through the use of several "filters."
- Learning was impacted by the existing culture of the organization.
- Executive learning included cognitive reframing, as well as information transfer and skill development.

Team skill development
- Development was affected by executive role and position.
- Skill development was affected by cultural norms and values.
- Skill development was affected by project focus.
- Development was affected by interaction with learning coaches.

Projects
- Projects were affected by team and individual sponsorship.
- Projects were affected by program schedule and design.
- Projects were affected by interaction among teams and by interaction as a whole group.

"Using market research and data analysis" showed the least change, principally because it was not developed much in the program, although it was part of the original plan. Surprisingly, "planning personal development" did not show the extent of the transfer to the job as anticipated. Ironically, the manager questionnaire input provided a more positive assessment of behavior change, particularly with "applying power and influence" and "managing small work groups."

Action Reflection Learning Approach

The action reflection learning approach (ARL) was at the core of the learning process in the sessions. Although the reaction for most of the elements of ARL was positive, there was concern about the overall success of some of the initiatives. Questionnaire responses from participants revealed that the most successful elements of ARL were the abilities to "engage in cross-functional work teams" and "learn from your own experience." The least successful appeared to be "associate learning with making things happen in real time."

BUSINESS IMPACT

Linkage with Key Measures

To achieve results, participants needed to realize a connection or linkage between the application of acquired knowledge and skills and changes in key business measures. According to input from participants and other groups, the strongest linkage occurred with employee satisfaction and customer satisfaction. Building effective leadership skills often improves employee satisfaction while improving the relationship with customers. In addition, the projects contributed significantly to this connection. The weakest linkage with key business measures and this program appeared to be with productivity, revenue generation, profits, cost control, and customer response time. These were some of INB's most important business measures. This assessment was to be expected, unless the program had had mechanisms to provide a connection to these key business variables.

Specific Impact from Individual Projects

Although the team projects were expected to add significant value to INB, it was anticipated that individual participants would undertake specific improvements in their work settings. Participants were asked to identify these improvements, where possible. Usually when this type of improvement data is desired from a leadership development program, individual business action plans are developed to guide the application of the new skills and report the results. This process of capturing values from individual plans is much more difficult when the action plans have not been developed, as was the case with the leadership development program. Because the team projects were developed for the program, the program designers were not interested in requiring action plans for individual application. Consequently, there was no formal planning for the use of individual skills and no mechanism in place for capturing specific improvements.

In the follow-up questionnaire, participants were asked to explore business results with a series of impact questions, which provided an opportunity to offer details about specific impact. As anticipated, only a small number of participants were able to place values on the questionnaire. Four participants provided values. Two are reported in Table 12-4, which identifies the specific impact derived from the program.

In an effort to capture additional input about business impact, the same series of questions were asked of the participants during one-on-one interviews whenever there was an opportunity to explore business results. This questioning yielded 11 more instances in which value may be linked to the program. These projects, without monetary values, are listed in Table 12-5.

Collectively, these values do not appear very reliable at this stage. However, this attempt to find specific individual project results related to the program is essential to the evaluation. At the outset, it was concluded that this would be a difficult exercise and that it would be unlikely to generate a tremendous amount of specific and reliable data. Although several individual projects were identified, the values were not used in the ROI calculation.

Turnover Prevention/Reduction

Perhaps an unexpected benefit linked to the leadership development program was staff turnover prevention. The program caused several of the participants to examine their careers and gain a renewed respect for INB. Suddenly they realized that the company valued them as executives, was interested in their careers, and, more importantly, was interested in developing critical skills for additional responsibilities. In essence, this program strengthened the bond between the employee and the company, increasing loyalty and commitment. For example, four individuals indicated that this program prevented or probably prevented them from leaving the company within the next couple of years.

Project Results

Team projects were an integral part of the program from the design and delivery perspective and turned out to be the most significant and meaningful part of the process from the participant viewpoint. Without exception, the reaction to the projects was extremely favorable. Participants saw them as extremely frustrating and stressful but very rewarding. Eighty percent of the participants considered the project successful or very successful. There was, however, some debate and concern about the purpose of the projects. All stakeholders felt that the projects served as excellent learning activities and that even if the recommendations were never implemented, they learned much about themselves, their team, the bank, and the particular topic as a result of the project development

Table 12-4
Impact of Individual Projects from Questionnaires

Description of project	Monetary impact	Basis/time frame	Contribution factor	Confidence of values	Comments
1. This project involves the delivery strategy for the customer centric enterprise. Combining both business and technology strategies, the project involves a combination of: • Identification, profiling, and delivery of the customer to the most appropriate and cost-effective resource. • Enhancement of the customer–employee interaction through effective real time delivery of meaningful customer intelligence to the specialists.	$3,625,000 annually	The utilization of call by call Intelligent Network Routing will provide load balancing and optimization across the entire organization. The industry estimates 10 to 15% efficiency in the areas of staffing resources and telecommunications expenses. A conservative estimate of 5% for INB would provide the following annual benefit based on current assumptions: • Agent efficiency based on 2000 agents @ $30K annual salary with a 5% gain would provide a benefit of $3,000,000 annually. • Telecommunication costs based on	25%	75%	This is an extensive project, which was initiated directly from the program. However, due to other factors and influences that may have brought this project forward in the future, only 25% of the improvement is credited to the program. A more detailed document, including a proposal that was presented to the executive group, is available.

• Collection measurement and reporting on the customer experience and behaviors.		100,000,000 minutes annually at 7.5¢ per minute with a 5% gain would provide a benefit of $375,000 annually. The use of shared equipment at the network level and the repositioning of equipment to provide efficiencies is estimated at a 5% gain on a $5,000,000 annual capital budget resulting in a benefit of $250,000 annually.			
2. This project involves designed strategic development and implementation planning to turn INB into a more customer centric organization.	$20,000,000	When the customer centric organization is implemented successfully, a 10% impact on customer loyalty, at a minimum, should be realized. A one-point improvement on any of the loyalty measures is estimated to deliver 30¢ per month, per customer. This produces a $20,000,000 improvement.	N/A	The program moved this project ahead by one year. Thus one year of results can be attributed to this program.	This is only one element of the customer centric implementation but affects all of the bank. This is being driven by an individual who participated in the program and the estimates are based only on one element of the project within the scope of that individual.

Table 12-5
Individual Projects from Interviews

Type of contribution	Brief description of improvement
1. Department initiative	One participant used the communication skills and action-reflection learning skills in an off-site meeting to plan improvements for the department. In this meeting, 14 initiatives were generated from the group using skills taken directly from the leadership development program. This participant estimated that typically in this type of meeting, only 5 initiatives would have surfaced. However, using a different approach with new skills, 14 initiatives surfaced. Thus, 9 initiatives can be credited with the leadership development program.
2. New product development	Two participants are teaming to develop a project for small business. This is a web-based product and the value is generated because the bank will actually provide the service instead of another contractor. Without the leadership development program connection and collaboration, an external resource would have been used instead of the bank.
3. New customers	One participant has obtained a new customer in the United States as a result of the networking from the leadership development program. The new customer is providing a direct benefit to the bank.
4. Partnership	One participant is building a partnership to share resources, referrals, and technology as well as assets with another important and often competing part of the organization.
5. Tool application	One participant has used the strategic planning process on a particular project for which he/she is responsible. This improved process is adding direct benefits.

and presentation. However, almost all participants indicated that the projects represented real issues that needed to be resolved and were concerned that they be implemented.

An important part of the leadership development program design was to use the processes and principles of action reflection learning as participants developed their projects and identified recommendations. Participants gave mixed responses about using ARL as an important and successful part of project success. Some felt ARL was not important to project success.

Program Costs

A fully loaded cost profile was used in this study. Table 12-6 shows the listing of cost elements considered in this analysis.

All costs for the program were absorbed by the training department with the exception of some project-related costs incurred by

Table 12-6
Leadership Development Program Costs

Program costs	
Design/development	
External consultants	$525,330
Training department	28,785
Management committee	26,542
Delivery	
Conference facilities (hotel)	$142,554
Consultants/external	$812,110
Training department salaries and benefits (for direct work with the program)	$15,283
Training department travel expenses	$37,500
Management committee (time)	$75,470
Project costs ($25,000 × 4)	$100,000
Participant salaries and benefits (class sessions) (average daily salary × benefits factor × number of program days)	$84,564
Participant salaries and benefits (project work)	$117,353
Travel and lodging for participants	$100,938
Cost of materials (handouts, purchased materials)	$6,872
Research and evaluation	
Research	$110,750
Evaluation	$125,875
Total costs	$2,309,926

the team members. Fees charged by the consultants and hotels are actual. The rest of the costs are aggregated estimates (i.e., salary and benefits were calculated by number of participants × average salary × benefit factor × number of hours).

Although there is often some debate as to whether participant salaries and benefits should be included in the cost of the program, in reality the participants were not replaced while they attended this program; therefore, the company did not experience a replacement cost. However, employees are compensated for being on the job every day, and they are expected to make a contribution roughly equal to their compensation. If they are removed from the job for a week, or four weeks in the case of the leadership development program, then the company has lost their contribution for that period of time. To be fully loaded with costs and also be conservative, this value was estimated and included in the overall cost profile.

The issue of prorating costs was an important consideration. In this case, it was reasonably certain that a second session would be conducted. The design and development expenses of $580,657 could therefore be prorated over two sessions. Consequently, in the actual ROI calculation, half of this number was used to arrive at the total value. This left a total program cost of $2,019,598 to include in the analysis. On a participant basis this was $91,800, or $22,950 for each week of formal sessions. Although this was expensive, it was still close to a rough benchmark of weekly costs of several senior executive leadership programs, including one at Nortel.

ROI ANALYSIS

When developing the ROI, two important issues had to be addressed: (1) isolating the effects of the program and (2) converting data to monetary values. The role of the participants was extremely critical because the participants provided data on actual improvements, isolated the effects of the program on the improvements, and, in some cases, converted data to actual monetary values. Although there are many other approaches to isolate the effects of the program and a variety of techniques to convert data to monetary values, several issues prevented the use of a majority of other approaches and techniques:

- The timing of the decision to measure the ROI eliminated some of the possibilities. The decision to measure the impact was

made after the program had begun and it was too late to influence the design and to use more objective approaches to isolating the effects of the program.
- The nature of leadership development eliminated many other
  techniques. The application and ultimate impact is an individual process and the improvements must come from the participants themselves—who may all influence different performance
  improvement measures. This situation makes it difficult to link
  the program to any finite set of performance measures.
- The vast number of business units represented and the nature
  of their issues, challenges, and performance measures made the
  process difficult to link to any small number of applications.

Challenges in Developing ROI for the Leadership Development Program

Several challenges were encountered as the return on investment
was developed for the program:

- There was a lack of data tied to specific improvements from
  each individual. Part of this was caused by a lack of design
  initiatives around the requirement and the focus on achieving
  results.
- There was concern about the nature and scope of the projects
  and the implementability of their recommendations. A different
  type of project with specific guidelines for capturing value
  would have made the ROI values of projects much easier to
  capture.
- The timing issue hampered the ROI analysis. The need to have
  the evaluation study completed soon after the last session of the
  program so that a decision could be made to proceed or adjust
  the program led to an earlier than desired analysis of the actual
  impact.
- The nature of this program, in terms of its soft skills and the
  focus on learning without the implications of the impact of what
  was being learned, made the program more difficult to evaluate
  at this level.

Collectively, these problems represented critical challenges that
had to be overcome to a certain extent to develop values. The result
was a less than optimum value.

ROI Calculations

The ROI calculations had several components, as illustrated in Figure 12-1. For the first component, project value, two approaches were considered. The first was to develop the value of a project based on the equivalent value as if a consulting firm had developed the project. This resulted in a value of $2,050,000 and was the most credible way of placing a value on the projects at such an early time frame. The second approach was to place a value on a project at the actual value of an implementation. This value is difficult to develop, but it is estimated to be in the hundreds of millions of dollars. The first approach was used to calculate a project value.

The second component involved the value of the individual projects undertaken by the participants, collected anonymously using questionnaires and confidentialty in interviews. It was too early to develop a precise value at the time of evaluation. Thus individual project values, estimated to be in the millions, were not used in the ROI analysis. Finally, the last component was the prevention of turnover. The program conclusively prevented several turnover statistics. Although the exact number will never be known, it was conservative to forecast that four could be attributed to this program, yielding a value of $1,225,566.

The conservative ROI calculation is as follows:

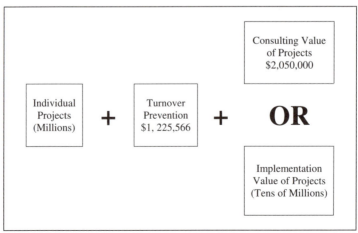

Figure 12-1. Business impact categories.

$$\text{ROI} = \frac{\text{Net benefits}}{\text{Program costs}} = \frac{(\$2,050,000 + \$1,225,566) - \$2,019,598}{\$2,019,598}$$

$$= 62\%$$

If the other blocks in Figure 12-1 had been included, the value would have been much larger.

Up-Front Emphasis: A Key to ROI Success

The application of the ROI process model is much more effective when programs are designed to have a specific business impact on the organization. Unfortunately for INB's leadership development program, the decision to calculate an ROI was made after the program was implemented. The original objectives of the programs did not reflect a bottom-line contribution. Consequently, the process of calculating the ROI became a much more difficult issue.

INTANGIBLE BENEFITS

Perhaps the most important results of the leadership development program were the intangible benefits, both short and long term. By definition, these benefits were not converted to monetary value for use in the ROI calculation. They were not measured precisely and are subjective but still important. Most leadership development programs have been evaluated through perceived or actual intangible benefits. The main intangible benefits reported were as follows:

- Without exception, each participant considered networking a positive and important outcome. The individuals developed close relationships and, more importantly, came to understand each other's perspectives, viewpoints, issues, concerns, and problems.
- Participants now take a more enterprise view of their jobs, their decisions, and the challenges facing INB. They have a much greater appreciation for the other functions and their relationship to the whole.
- Participants are reducing, and sometimes removing, silos that have developed within INB. Participants now see each other as contributors who have the bank's interest at the forefront.
- Participants reported that their decision-making capability was enhanced greatly through this program. They are using many

of the communication techniques to build the proper rapport with the staff so that they will have free-flowing ideas and input into the decision-making process.

- A surprising intangible benefit was increased loyalty to INB as a result of participation in the leadership program. Participation in this program left many participants with the desire and determination to remain with INB and continue to make a contribution.
- Through the project teams and other team-related exercises, including those involving the larger group of 22, the participants gained a much greater appreciation for the advantages of teamwork and team building. Many of them are using teams to a greater extent in their own work, and they are encouraging teams to be used in other aspects of the bank.
- Some rated this program as a significant personal development experience.
- One of the important objectives of this program was the development of an executive talent pool of capable leaders who would be available for future key positions. Some participants think the program did not help build the talent pool, whereas others feel they are more capable to take on increased responsibility. Two things are certain: Participants understand the enterprise view and are better prepared for a potential promotion, and they know the areas that need improvement to continue to sharpen their skills and enhance their ability for future promotions.

RESULTS

The major objectives of the program were met, although they were not completely successful. Participants rated the most success with the objectives that related to participants taking an enterprise view and acting on synergies within the INB business areas. The least success was achieved with the objective characterized as "participants are prepared to assume senior leadership roles that become vacant or are created based on market needs."

Two major goals were established for the program, and the program was less than successful in meeting these goals. There was more success with the goal to increase the capability of leaders to be high-performing, cross-functional executives. Less success was realized with helping INB become more competitive by tackling and resolving major organizational projects.

There was general agreement about the achievement level for the critical success factors. Less success was attained on the first factor ("a significant amount of time must be invested by the management committee, clients, and participants") because participants did not perceive that, on the whole, the executive and management committee invested significant time in the program. The most success was realized with the second factor, "real projects must be developed that are enterprise-wide and strategic." The success achieved in the third factor, "influential participants must be selected based on performance and future potential," however, was mixed. The selection of the participants was an issue of much concern and debate. It was generally assumed that the participants were high potential executives with the ability to move into key senior management positions. In reality, most participants think this did not occur. The selection criteria were not followed consistently across both major operational units or within those units.

There was general agreement about the success of major outcomes both from the organizational perspective and from the individual perspective. There were mixed results in terms of the outcomes of enhancing the quality of executive talent and on the outcome of research and recommendations for solutions to key strategic issues. There was general agreement that success was realized with management committee interaction with high potential leaders. Generally, the individuals felt that the outcomes related directly to them faired much better. There was consistent agreement that they were exposed to a broader range of INB businesses and to establishing networks across business lines. There was less agreement relative to building skills in systems and strategic thinking, communication, and building high-performance teams. There were varied results identified for reaching accelerated personal and leadership development.

Frequently, a program is only as successful as the support provided to ensure that it functions efficiently, effectively, and achieves its desired goals. The overall support was rated quite good, with some specific issues raising concerns. Learning coaches were rated as effective, as was executive support. In the interviews, most indicated that executive support improved during the program and was at its peak toward the end during the presentations. There was a perception of a "wait and see" attitude. The mentor role was misunderstood and not appreciated and most felt it was not very effective. The clients generally received good remarks, although the results were mixed for certain individuals. The clients were often referred to as sponsors and met with the individual teams to help develop the projects. The faculty received good ratings; the subject-matter experts, however, did not receive favorable ratings. Although some were outstanding, others were considered extremely ineffective. The support provided by the program director was rated as somewhat effective.

There was expectation that the program would be one of the most significant personal development experiences encountered by the participants. However, most participants disagreed, and only 27 percent rated the experience as very effective. In the interviews, almost every participant indicated that he or she had previously experienced a more effective leadership and personal development program. Overall, the success versus the plans was mixed, with several areas requiring adjustments in the future.

DISCUSSION QUESTIONS

1. Why are the intangible benefits perhaps the most important results of the leadership program?
2. How might the background of this organization have affected the program?
3. If you had been in charge of this program, would you have done anything differently?
4. Create the leadership scorecard for this leadership development program.

THE AUTHOR

Dr. Patricia Pulliam Phillips is president and CEO of ROI Institute, Inc., the leading source of ROI competency building, implementation support, networking, and research. She is also chairman of The Chelsea Group, Inc., an international consulting organization supporting organizations and their efforts to build accountability into their training, human resources, and performance improvement programs. She helps organizations implement the ROI methodology in countries around the world, including South Africa, Singapore, Japan, New Zealand, Australia, Italy, Turkey, France, Germany, Canada, and the United States.

Phillips' academic accomplishments include a Ph.D. in international development and a master of arts degree in public and private management. She is certified in ROI evaluation and has been awarded the designation of Certified Performance Technologist. She has authored a number of publications on the subject of accountability and ROI. Her most recent publications include *The Bottomline on ROI*, Center for Effective Performance (2002), which won the 2003 ISPI Award of Excellence; the ASTD *In Action* casebooks, *Measuring Return on Investment*, Vol. 3 (2001), *Measuring ROI in the Public Sector* (2002), and *Retaining Your Best Employees* (2002); the ASTD *Infoline* Series including *Planning and Using Evaluation Data* (2003), *Mastering ROI* (1998), *Managing Evaluation Shortcuts* (2001), and *The Human Resources Scorecard: Measuring Return on Investment*, Butterworth-Heinemann (2001). She is published in a variety of journals, serves as adjunct faculty teaching training evaluation, and speaks on the subject at conferences including ASTD's International Conference and Exposition and the ISPI International Conference. Phillips can be reached at patti@roiinstitute. net.

Index

Page numbers followed by "f" denote figures; those followed by "t" denote tables

A

Absenteeism, 217
Acquisition costs, 177
Action learning, 14–16
Action plan
  advantages of, 104
  categories of, 99
  data from, 102
  description of, 85, 97
  development of, 98–101
  disadvantages of, 104
  follow-up of, 102
  group presentation of, 102
  items in, 99
  monetary values for
      improvements, 101,
      103
  negative reactions to, 100
  participants in, 101
  return on investment
      calculations, 103
  teaching of, 100
  template for, 98f
  uses of, 100–104
Action reflection learning,
    277–278, 287
Administrative purpose, 11

American Society for Training
    and Development, 36,
    119
Annualized values, 190
Application measurements
  description of, 80
  focus groups for, 91–92
  interviews for. *See* Interviews
  observations for. *See*
      Observation(s)
  shortcuts for, 110
Assessment
  business coaching model, 20
  in leadership development,
      9–10
  needs, 15
Assumptions
  of reflection, 22–23
  in return on investment
      forecasting, 272
Audience
  for communicating results,
      229–230, 235–236,
      236t
  for leadership scorecard, 32
  reactions of, 243
  types of, 236t

Audience bias, 164
Audio recording of
        observations, 94–95

B
Behavior checklist, 94
Behavior codes, 94
Benefits factor, 174–175
Benefits/cost ratio, 47–48,
        189–191, 203
Best-practice organizations,
        21–22
Bias
    audience, 164
    return on investment
            forecasting, 271–272
Blended learning environment,
        21
Board of directors, 4
Bossidy, Larry, 3
Business coaching model, 20
Business games, 73
Business impact measurements
    description of, 80, 118
    focus groups for, 91–92
    interviews for. *See* Interviews
    observations for. *See*
            Observation(s)
    questionnaire for, 81–88
    return on investment
            calculations from, 258
    shortcuts for, 110
Business measures data
            converted to monetary
            values
    adjustments, 166
    case study of, 166–168
    data accuracy and credibility,
            163–166
    employee time for, 153–154
    external experts' input for,
            155–156

hard data, 145–147, 146t
historical costs, 154–155
immediate manager estimates
        used for, 159
internal experts' input,
        155–156
leadership development staff
        estimates for, 161
linking with other measures,
        159–161
output data to contribution,
        149–152, 152f
participant estimates used for,
        158–159
preliminary issues, 145–149
quality costs, 152–153
selection of technique for,
        161–162
soft data, 147t, 147–148
steps involved in, 148–149,
        150f
techniques for, 149
values from external
        databases used for,
        156–158
Business performance
        monitoring
    description of, 95
    measures for, 95–97
Business strategy, 6

C
Case studies
    business measures data
            converted to monetary
            values, 166–168
    communication of results,
            252
    costs, 186–187
    definition of, 73
    executive coaching. *See*
            Executive coaching

forecasting return on
investment, 273–274
Imperial National Bank. *See*
Imperial National
Bank case study
leadership development,
277–301
leadership scorecard, 54–56,
223–224
return on investment,
203–204, 222–223
satisfaction measurements,
76–78
Chain of impact, 118–119, 195f
Checklist
leadership development, 53f
leadership scorecard, 53f
questionnaire use of, 64
Chief financial office, 193
Climate survey data, 215
Coach, 18
Coaching
benefits of, 19
business coaching model used
in, 20
case study of. *See* Executive
coaching case study
challenges associated with, 19
definition of, 18–19
evaluation of, 20–21
goals of, 19–20
return on investment, 21
standard for, 19
Communication of results
audience perceptions effect
on, 231
bias in, 230
case study of, 252
consistency in, 230
description of, 227
formal evaluation report for
components of, 237–240

description of, 236–237
development of, 240, 241f
format of, 241f
importance of, 227–229
improvements made
secondary to, 228
media used for, 230
plan for, 234–235, 235t
policy issues for, 233–235,
235t
principles of, 229–231
reactions to, 243–244
reasons for, 231–233
target audience for, 229–230,
235–236
testimonials for, 230–231
timeliness in, 229
Competencies
measurement of, 219
return on investment
forecasting with,
265–268
in 360-degree feedback, 10
Complaints
customer, 220
discrimination, 216
employee, 215
Computer recording of
observations, 95
Conflict, 221
Contract, performance,
104–106
Contributions
communication necessary for
explaining, 228
output data converted to,
149–152, 152f
Control groups
advantages and disadvantages
of, 122–123
cautions associated with,
121–122

contamination of, 122–123
description of, 121
inappropriate use of, 122
research-oriented view of,
123
selection of, 122
settings for, 121
time considerations, 123
Coordinator salary, 177
Core competencies, 219
Cost(s)
accumulation of, 180–184
acquisition, 177
benefits not communicated
with, 171–172
case study of, 186–187
categories for, 175t, 175–180,
185
classification matrix, 182,
183t
controlling of, 170
delivery, 177–179
description of, 47, 169
design and development,
176–177
direct, 173–174
disclosure of, 171
employee benefits factor,
174–175
estimation of, 184, 185f–186f
evaluation, 179
forecasting of return on
investment and, 255
fully loaded, 171
guidelines for, 172
historical, 154–155
importance of, 169–171
leadership scorecard,
248–251
monitoring of, 170
needs assessment, 175–176
overhead, 179–180

policies regarding, 172
prorated, 173–174, 176
quality-related, 152–153
reasons for collecting, 170
reporting of, 180, 181t
return on investment, 179
sources of, 172–173, 173t
tracking of, 172–175
Cost/benefit ratio, 47–48,
189–191, 203
Creativity, 218–219
Criterion-referenced test, 71
Customer(s)
complaints by, 220
loss of, 220
loyalty of, 220
satisfaction of, 219–220
Customer service, 214, 220

D
Data
action plan, 102
climate survey, 215
credibility of, 109, 163–166,
204
extreme, 110
hard, 145–147, 146t, 165,
207, 208t
indicators. See Indicators
missing, 109
reputation of source of, 164
satisfaction, 69–70, 219
soft, 147t, 147–148, 207,
208t
Data collection
built-in systems for,
108–110
case study of, 279–285
description of, 40–41
disruptions caused by, 107
methods of
accuracy of, 108

for application
measurements,
106–108
for business impact
measurements,
106–108
costs, 107
cultural bias for, 109
description of, 46
focus groups for, 91–92
interviews for. *See*
Interviews
multiple, 108
observations. *See*
Observation(s)
questionnaires for. *See*
Questionnaires
selection of, 106–108
participants' time, 107
plan for, 41–43
Data conversion to monetary
values
adjustments, 166
case study of, 166–168
data accuracy and credibility,
163–166
description of, 148–149
employee time for, 153–154
external experts' input for,
155–156
hard data, 145–147, 146t
historical costs, 154–155
immediate manager estimates
used for, 159
intangible measures identified
during, 210
internal experts' input,
155–156
leadership development staff
estimates for, 161
linking with other measures,
159–161

output data to contribution,
149–152, 152f
participant estimates used for,
158–159
preliminary issues, 145–149
quality costs, 152–153
selection of technique for,
161–162
soft data, 147t, 147–148
steps involved in, 148–149,
150f
techniques for, 149
values from external
databases used for,
156–158
Data summary, 109
Databases, for converting
business measures to
monetary values,
156–158
Decision making
before action learning, 15
team-based, 221–222
Delayed report method, of
observation, 94
Delivery costs, 177–179
Demographics of workforce, 4
Developmental purpose, 11
Direct costs, 173–174
Discrimination complaints,
216

E
Electrical/mechanical
simulation, 73
Employee(s)
absenteeism of, 217
complaints by, 215
retention of, 216–217
suggestions by, 218–219
tardiness of, 217–218
transfer of, 218

Employee benefits factor,
174–175
Employee time converted to
monetary values,
153–154
Employee turnover
definition of, 217
job satisfaction and,
159–160, 214
monetary value conversion
of, 213
organizational effects of,
216–217
reduction of, 217
Enablers, 87
Evaluation costs, 179
Executive summary, 237
Experiences, learning through,
11–14
External databases, for
converting business
measures to monetary
values, 156–158
External expert input, for
converting business
measures to monetary
values, 155–156

F
Facilitator salary, 177
Facility costs, 178
Fallback isolation strategy, 137
"Fatal flaws," 11
Feedback
leadership development by,
9–11
questionnaire, 67–68, 263f
360-degree, 9–11, 95
Focus groups
data collection using, 91–92
leadership development
program effects and

impact isolated using,
128–132
Follow-up evaluation
intangible benefits identified
during, 209
questionnaire, 81–88,
112f–113f
Forecasting of return on
investment
assumptions in, 272
bias in, 271–272
case study of, 273–274
competencies for, 268–270
cost-saving benefits, 255
frequency of, 270
guidelines for, 270–272
learning data for, 265–268
long- vs. short-term, 271
methods for, 127
model for, 258–259, 259f
performance improvement,
261–262
pilot program for, 262–263
for policy compliance, 256
preprogram, 256
reaction data used for,
263–265
reasons for, 254–256
review of, 272
skills for, 268–270
steps involved in, 259–261
time intervals for, 256–258,
257f
trade-offs, 256–258
uncertainty reduced by,
254–255
Formal evaluation report
components of, 237–240
description of, 236–237
development of, 240, 241f
format of, 241f
Formal mentoring, 17–18

G

Grievances, 215–216

H

Hard data, 145–147, 146t, 165, 207, 208t

Historical costs, 154–155

I

Imperial National Bank case study

  application, 286–287

  background, 277–279

  business impact, 288–293

  data collection plan, 279–285

  intangible benefits, 297–298

  leadership development program

    costs of, 293–294

    initiation of, 278–279

    results of, 298–300

  learning, 285

  reaction, 285

  return on investment analysis, 294–297

In-basket, 73

Indicators

  description of, 61–62

  measuring, 61–63

  types of, 62–63

Informal tests, for measuring learning, 73–75

Innovation, 218–219

Intangible benefits and measures

  analysis, 213

  case studies of, 222–224, 297–298, 315–316

  climate survey data, 215

  competencies, 219

  conversion to monetary values, 210–211, 211t

  creativity, 218–219

  customer-related

    complaints, 220

    loyalty, 220

    response time, 220

    satisfaction, 219–220

  definition of, 207

  description of, 48–49, 206, 213–222

  discrimination complaints, 216

  employee-related

    absenteeism, 217

    complaints, 215

    retention, 216–217

    transfer, 218

  follow-up evaluation, 209

  grievances, 215–216

  identification of, 209–210

  importance of, 206–207

  innovation, 218–219

  intellectual capital vs., 211–212, 212f

  job satisfaction, 213–214

  leadership development and, 207t

  measurement of, 210

  organizational commitment, 214–215

  stress reduction, 216

  tangible benefits vs., 207, 208t

  teamwork-related, 221–222

Intellectual capital, 211–212, 212f

Internal expert input, for converting business measures to monetary values, 155–156

Interviews

  description of, 88–89

  disadvantages of, 89

  guidelines for, 90

structured, 90
types of, 90
unstructured, 90
Investment
in leadership development,
6–7, 31
perception of, 87

J
Job assignments, 12–14
Job satisfaction
customer service and, 214
description of, 213–214
employee turnover and,
159–160, 214
Job simulations. *See* Simulations

L
Leaders
competition for, 4
measurement, 246, 246t
self-assessments, 10–11
self-awareness by, 9
strengths of, 10–11
technology effects on, 4
Leadership ability, 7
Leadership development
accelerating of, 5–6
assessment, 9–10
benefits of, 52
business strategy and, 6
case study of, 277–301
challenges of, 5–7
checklist for, 53f
cycle of, 173, 174f
description of, 3–4
economic benefits of, 24–25
factors that affect, 25–26, 26t
funding of, 6–7
influences on, 117
initiatives for, 25–26, 26t
intangible benefits and, 207t

investment in, 6–7, 31, 87
planning of, 7
questionnaires for, 81–88
scorecard. *See* Leadership
scorecard
staff for, 246–247
stakeholder responsibilities,
247–249
summary of, 26–27
systems approach to, 5
Leadership development
accountability
description of, 23
reasons for, 24–25, 27
trends in, 23–24, 27
Leadership development
methods
challenging experiences
action learning, 14–16
description of, 11–12
job assignments, 12–14
feedback, 9–11
formal relationships
mentoring, 16–18
professional coaching,
18–21
reasons for creating, 16
ranking of, 8t
schematic diagram of, 6f
summary of, 26–27
training, 21–22
Leadership development
programs
case study of, 278–279
chain of impact requirement,
118–119
communicating the results of.
See Communication of
results
costs
accumulation of, 180–184
acquisition, 177

benefits not communicated with, 171–172
case study of, 186–187
categories for, 175t, 175–180, 185
classification matrix, 182, 183t
controlling of, 170
delivery, 177–179
description of, 47, 169
design and development, 176–177
direct, 173–174
disclosure of, 171
employee benefits factor, 174–175
estimation of, 184, 185f–186f
evaluation, 179
fully loaded, 171
guidelines for, 172
importance of, 169–171
monitoring of, 170
needs assessment, 175–176
overhead, 179–180
policies regarding, 172
prorated, 173–174, 176
reasons for collecting, 170
reporting of, 180, 181t
return on investment, 179
sources of, 172–173, 173t
tracking of, 172–175
estimates for, 250
evaluation, 249
impact and effects of
calculation of, 139–140
case study of, 141–143
conservative approach to estimating, 140
control groups for. See Control groups
debate regarding, 116–117

description of, 46, 116
forecasting methods, 126–128
management estimation of, 137–139
participant estimation of
advantages and disadvantages of, 136–138
assumptions of, 128
focus groups, 128–132
questionnaires, 132–136
preliminary considerations for, 116–120
steps involved in, 119–120
subordinate input on, 139
techniques for estimating, 117–118, 140–141
trend line analysis for, 124–126
intangible benefits of, 48–49
internal resources used for, 250–251
objectives of, 39–41
participants in, 250
performance and, 116
pilot programs, 176–177
results of. See Communication of results
return on investment calculations, 47–48
Leadership scorecard
application of, 51
balanced, 25
barriers to, 248
benefits of, 26–27, 31–32, 51–52
case study of, 54–56, 223–224
challenges associated with, 51

checklist for, 53f
cost-savings approaches,
    248–251
data collection
    description of, 40–41
    methods of, 46
    plan for, 41–43
definition of, 31
evaluation of
    data collection plan, 41–43
    feasibility, 38–39
    framework for, 34–36,
        35f
    levels of, 38–39
    planning of, 36, 38
    plans for, 41–46
    project plan for, 45–46
    purpose of, 38
    return on investment
        analysis plan for,
        43–45
factors that affect, 165
foundation of, 33–34
implementation of, 50–51
leadership development
        program objectives,
        39–41
maintaining of, 33
operating standards for,
    49–50, 50t
philosophy of, 49–50
planning of
    description of, 245
    leader selected for,
        245–246
    responsibilities assigned,
        247–248
    staff selection, 246–247
pre-work, 32–33
purpose of, 31–32
reasons for creating, 32

reporting, 49
resistance to, 244–245
return on investment
    analysis plan for, 43–45
    application of, 51
    calculation of, 47–49
    data conversion to
        monetary values,
        47–48
    feasibility, 38–39
    implementation effects,
        50–51
    intangible benefits, 48–49
    levels of, 38–39
    planning of, 36, 38
    purpose of, 38
    reporting, 49
    summary of, 54
summary of, 52, 54
target audience for, 32
template for, 49f
Leadership talent, 5
Leadership training, 21–22
Learning
    action, 14–16
    action reflection, 277–278,
        287
    blended environment for, 21
    from job assignments, 13
    from life experiences, 11–14
    measuring. See Learning
        measurements
Learning data for return on
        investment forecasting,
        265–268
Learning measurements
    administrative issues for,
        75–76
    case study of, 76–78
    description of, 70
    facilitator assessments, 75

informal tests, 73–75
self-assessments, 74–75
simulations, 72–73
tests/testing for
   criterion-referenced, 71
   description of, 70–71
   norm-referenced, 71
   performance, 71–72
   types of, 71–72
Learning objectives, 39–40
Life experiences, 11–14
Loan profitability analysis, 151f

M
Management estimation
   conversion of business
      measures to monetary
      values using, 159
   isolating the leadership
      development program
      effects and impact
      using, 137–139
Measurement trends, 24, 27
Measuring
   indicators for, 61–63
   of learning. *See* Learning
      measurements
   of satisfaction. *See*
      Satisfaction
Mentoring, 16–18
Monetary values
   business measures data
      converted to
      adjustments, 166
      case study of, 166–168
      data accuracy and
         credibility, 163–166
      employee time for, 153–154
      external experts' input for,
         155–156
      hard data, 145–147, 146t

historical costs, 154–155
immediate manager
   estimates used for, 159
intangible measure
   identified during, 210
internal experts' input,
   155–156
leadership development
   staff estimates for, 161
linking with other
   measures, 159–161
output data to
   contribution, 149–152,
   152f
participant estimates used
   for, 158–159
preliminary issues,
   145–149
quality costs, 152–153
selection of technique for,
   161–162
soft data, 147t, 147–148
steps involved in, 148–149,
   150f
techniques for, 149
values from external
   databases used for,
   156–158
employee turnover converted
   to, 213
for improvements, 101
intangible benefits converted
   to, 210–211, 211t
leadership scorecard data
   converted to, 47–48
questionnaire for evaluating, 86
Multiple-choice question, 65

N
Needs analysis, 40, 175–176
Needs assessment

costs of, 175–176
description of, 15
Norm-referenced test, 71

O
Observation(s)
audio recording of, 94–95
behavior checklist for, 94
computer recording of, 95
delayed report method of,
94
guidelines for, 92–93
methods of, 93–95
observers for, 93
systematic, 93
video recording of, 94
Open-ended questions, 64
Organization
employee turnover effects on,
216–217
formal mentoring programs,
17–18
Organizational commitment,
214–215
Overhead costs, 179–180

P
Participant estimation
conversion of business
measures to monetary
values, 158–159
isolating effects and impact of
leadership
development programs
using
advantages and
disadvantages of,
136–138
assumptions of, 128
focus groups, 128–132
questionnaires, 132–136
Performance

factors that influence,
119–120
leadership development
program and, 116
variables of, 120
Performance contract, 104–106
Performance improvement
forecasting, 261–262
Performance testing, 71–72
Pilot programs
description of, 176–177
return on investment
forecasting using,
262–263
Preprogram forecast, 256
Professional coaching. *See also*
Executive coaching
case study
benefits of, 19
business coaching model used
in, 20
challenges associated with,
19
definition of, 18–19
evaluation of, 20–21
goals of, 19–20
return on investment, 21
standard for, 19
Project plan, 45–46
Prorated costs, 173–174, 176

Q
Quality
conversion to monetary
values, 152–153
customer satisfaction and,
153
description of, 152
Questionnaires. *See also* Surveys
advantages of, 107
anonymity of, 66
case study of, 111, 112f–113f

content of, 67–69
data collection, 69, 106t
description of, 63
design steps for, 65–67
feedback, 67–68, 263f
follow-up, 112f–113f
leadership development,
    81–88
leadership development
    program effects and
    impact isolated using,
    132–136
questions used in, 64–65,
    132–133
reaction, 69
reading level of, 66
response rate for, 88, 89f
tabulation of, 66, 67f

R
Ranking scale, 65
Reaction and satisfaction
    objectives, 39
Reaction data for return on
    investment forecasting,
    263–265
Reaction questionnaire, 69
Reflection
    assumptions of, 22–23
    description of, 27
    implementation of, 22
    strategies for, 22–23
Resistance, 244–245
Return on anticipation, 193
Return on client expectations,
    193
Return on expectations, 193
Return on investment
    from action learning, 15–16
    action plan, 103
    annualized values, 190
    appropriateness of, 199–201

benefits/cost ratio, 47–48
calculation of
    cost accumulation and, 171
    formula for, 203, 260, 269
    methods, 47–49
case studies of, 203–204,
    222–223, 294–297
cautions when using,
    201–203
chain of impact effects on,
    195f
from coaching, 21
conservative approach, 201
costs, 179, 249
debates about, 202
definition of, 189, 192
description of, 254
education regarding, 202
elements of, 34f
expectations for, 194
financial terms, 193t
forecasting of
    assumptions in, 272
    bias in, 271–272
    case study of, 273–274
    competencies for, 268–270
    cost-saving benefits, 255
    frequency of, 270
    guidelines for, 270–272
    learning data for, 265–268
    long- vs. short-term, 271
    methods for, 127
    model for, 258–259, 259f
    pilot program for, 262–263
    for policy compliance, 256
    preprogram, 256
    reaction data used for,
        263–265
    reasons for, 254–256
    review of, 272
    skills for, 268–270
    steps involved in, 259–261

time intervals for, 256–258, 257f
trade-offs, 256–258
uncertainty reduced by, 254–255
formula, 191–194, 203, 260, 269
indications for, 199–201
interpretation of, 192–201
issues regarding, 201–203
from leadership training, 22
management involvement in, 201
model of
analysis plan, 43–45
application of, 51
evaluation planning, 36, 38
illustration of, 37f
negative, 198–199
objectives, 194
size of, 141, 196–198
strategies for, 194–196
targets, 194–196
values, 196–198
Return on Investment Network, 248
ROI. See Return on investment
Role playing, 73

S
Satisfaction
employee turnover and, 159–160
measuring of. See Satisfaction measurements
quality effects on, 153
Satisfaction measurements
case study of, 76–78
data from, 69–70
description of, 63
questionnaires
anonymity of, 66

content of, 67–69
data collection, 69
description of, 63
design steps for, 65–67
feedback, 67–68
questions used in, 64–65
reaction, 69
reading level of, 66
tabulation of, 66, 67f
shortcut methods for, 70
surveys for, 63, 213
Scorecard. See Leadership scorecard
Self-assessments
leaders, 10–11
learning measurement by, 74–75
Self-awareness, 9
Simulations, 72–73
Soft data, 147t, 147–148, 207, 208t
Staff, for leadership development, 246–247
Stress reduction, 216
Structured interviews, 90
Subject matter expert, 261–262
Surveys. See also Questionnaires
climate, 215
measuring satisfaction using, 63, 213
response rate for, 88, 89f
Systems approach to leadership development, 5

T
Tangible benefits, 207, 208t
Tardiness of employees, 217–218
Target audience
for communicating results, 229–230, 235–236, 236t

for leadership scorecard, 32
reactions of, 243
types of, 236t
Task simulation, 73
Teamwork, 221–222
Technology
  changes in, 4
  knowledge dissemination
    using, 21–22
Testimonials, 230–231
Tests, for measuring learning
  criterion-referenced, 71
  description of, 70–71
  norm-referenced, 71
  performance, 71–72
  types of, 71–72
360-degree feedback
  description of, 9–11
  developmental vs.
    administrative purpose
    of, 11
  learning behavior change
    evaluated by, 95
Time savings, 154

Training
  effectiveness measurements,
    25
  leadership, 21–22
Transfer of employee, 218
Trend line analysis,
    124–126
Trends, 23–24, 27
Two-way question, 65

U
Unstructured interviews, 90

V
Video recording of
    observations, 94

W
Workplace
  changes in, 3–4
  demographic changes in, 4
  diversity in, 4
  factors that affect, 3
  technology changes, 4

About the Authors

As a world-renowned expert on measurement and evaluation, Dr. Jack J. Phillips is chairman of the ROI Institute. Through the Institute, Phillips provides consulting services for Fortune 500 companies and workshops for major conference providers throughout the world. Phillips is also the author or editor of more than 30 books—10 about measurement and evaluation—and more than 100 articles. Books most recently authored by Phillips include *The Human Resources Scorecard: Measuring the Return on Investment,* Butterworth-Heinemann 2001; *A New Vision for Human Resources: Defining the Human Resources Function By Its Results,* Crisp Learning 1998; *Managing Employee Retention,* Butterworth-Heinemann, 2003; *Retaining Your Best Employees,* ASTD 2002; *Return on Investment in Training and Performance Improvement Projects, 2nd Edition* Butterworth-Heinemann 2003; *The Project Management Scorecard,* Butterworth-Heinemann 2002; *How to Measure Train-*

ing Results, McGraw-Hill 2002; *The Consultant's Scorecard,* McGraw-Hill 2000.

His expertise in measurement and evaluation is based on extensive research and more than twenty-seven years of corporate experience in five industries (aerospace, textiles, metals, construction materials, and banking). Phillips has served as training and development manager at two Fortune 500 firms, senior HR officer at two firms, president of a regional federal savings bank, and management professor at a major state university.

Lynn Schmidt is Vice President, Learning & Development, for Charter Communications. She currently has responsibility for all learning & development functions at Charter including OD, management, leadership, HR, sales, technical, customer service and curriculum design and development. She has nineteen years of experience as a human and organization development professional in the fast-paced high technology industry. In her previous position as Director of Nextel Communications' Leadership Institute Lynn had responsibility for succession management, identification, and development of high potential candidates, diversity and mentoring programs, as well as executive development. Lynn has also previously had responsibility for performance consulting, management and employee training curricula, new employee onboarding, distance learning, instructional systems design, competency modeling, and employee satisfaction surveys.

Lynn has extensive experience in the field of measurement and evaluation. She is certified in ROI evaluation and currently serves as the Chairperson of the ASTD ROI Network Advisory Committee.

In 2002 she received the Jack and Patti Phillips ROI Practitioner of the Year Award. Lynn authored a case study for ASTD's In Action series book *Measuring Learning and Performance* on evaluating soft-skills training. She has conducted several ROI/impact studies on programs such as change management, time management, performance management, and diversity awareness. She is an author and editor for the 2003 ASTD In Action series book *Implementing Training Scorecards* and co-author of *The Leadership Scorecard*, to be published in May 2004.

Lynn has presented at several International Quality and Productivity Center conferences, ASTD conferences, and ROI Network conferences on the topic of measurement and evaluation. She has taught both Needs Assessment and Measurement & Evaluation at Georgetown University. She has served as Co-Director of Programs for the Metro DC ASTD chapter and was a member of the 2001 and 2002 ASTD program committee for the annual ASTD international conference. Lynn has B.S. in Business Administration, an MBA, and she is currently pursuing a Ph.D. in Human and Organization Development.